ANGLER
WALKABOUT

In memory of Ron & Nisbet Skilling, the best grandparents a
boy could have hoped for.

New Zealand

Cover images:

Front - NZ South Island brown trout and river stones

Back - Lake Pukaki and Mount Cook

Author image: - NZ South Island brown trout

All images © Julian Wicksteed

NEW ZEALAND

Angler Walkabout Series - Book 7

JULIAN WICKSTEED

ANGLER WALKABOUT Publications

Also by Julian Wicksteed

A CATCH ON AFRICA – In Colour

Containing over 200 images, this book is the complete pictorial account of the first book and journey in Julian Wicksteed's 'Angler Walkabout Series.'

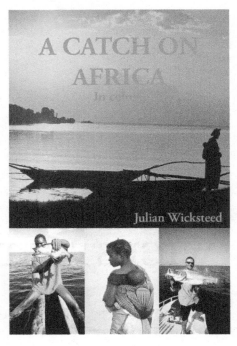

THE ANGLER WALKABOUT SERIES
2004 - 2020

Book 1. A CATCH ON AFRICA

Book 2. ALASKA

Book 3. PATAGONIA

Book 4. TASMANIA

Book 5. WEST AFRICA

Book 6. Best Of 2004 - 2014

Book 7. NEW ZEALAND

ISBN: 978-0-9875904-1-1

DISTRIBUTION:

Available on Amazon for personal orders only, not for wholesale purchase.

For distributors, wholesalers, and retailers, please make contact on info@anglerwalkabout.com for wholesale prices and orders.

New Zealand & Australia:
Nationwide Book Distributors- www.nationwidebooks.co.nz
Booktopia- Booktopia.com.au
Footprint   Books-www.footprint.com.au
Westbooks- www.westbooks.com.au

North America:
Ingram - www.ingramcontent.com
Barnes & Noble - www.barnesandnoble.com

United Kingdom/Europe:
make contact on info@anglerwalkabout.com
Ingram - www.ingramcontent.com
Barnes & Noble - www.barnesandnoble.com

Africa/Asia/South America
make contact on info@anglerwalkabout.com

ANGLER WALKABOUT Publications and Julian Wicksteed believe in the use of recycled papers and that sourced from sustainable regrowth forests.

Access to Julian Wicksteed's photography can be made via the Angler Walkabout website.

About the Author

Photo: © Julian Wicksteed

Born 1976, Bundaberg, Queensland, Australia, Julian Wicksteed completed the majority of his school years in Townsville, Australia. A keen surfer, sailor, angler, traveller, and conservationist, Julian has a science degree in Fisheries Management and Aquaculture and a higher diploma in education.

When not on the road travelling and sailing, he can usually be found writing, surfing, and fishing in southwest Victoria, Australia.

New Zealand South Island Regions

CONTENTS

JULIAN WICKSTEED

Angler Walkabout Series - Book 7

1. NORTH CANTERBURY

1

After a week in Ashburton catching up with my grandparents and aunt on my mother's side, I started my Angler Walkabout of New Zealand's South Island by driving through the rural landscape of Canterbury, towards what is arguably one of New Zealand's most emblematic rivers, the Rakaia. Flowing one hundred and fifty kilometres from the Southern Alps, across the Canterbury Plains where it braids into a vast network of streams before reaching the east coast, a two kilometre road bridge is reuired to traverse these lower reaches. The river really is one of New Zealand's, if not the world's, most majestic waterways.

It was a beautiful day as I drove in my second-hand van that I'd purchased on arrival in Christchurch, the sun was shining, spring flowers were in full bloom, and the snow was still thick on the Southern Alps.

Forming the backbone of New Zealand's South Island, and blessing us with a lot of the island's fishing, the Southern Alps basically run the length of the South Island; a wide alluvial plain stretches to the east and a narrower, far wetter one to the west.

I couldn't wait to lose myself, far upstream on the Rakaia, away from the endless fields of dairy farms and irrigators.

It had been ten years since I had been to New Zealand and, by all reports, the 'Dairy Boom', and subsequent irrigation demand that had befallen New Zealand, had devastated many of the smaller rivers in Canterbury. Not to mention the over nitrification of lakes and rivers due to excessive fertiliser use and excessive excrement runoff and absorption in groundwater. It was all through the news! All through federal politics, and it didn't sound good! What have I arrived to, I found myself wondering, this isn't the New Zealand I grew up knowing and loving, please don' let it be true?

The Rakaia River is generally better known for its salmon fishing, which is also arguably not what it once was. Nevertheless, there are also rainbow and brown trout in the river and being early summer; it was trout that I was hoping to encounter.

At some point along these larger braided rivers of the Canterbury Plains, they all tend to have a deeper stretch of river that flows through rocky gorge country. As the summer sets in, it's towards these deeper and cooler stretches of water that many of the trout move. Maori legend says that a 'taniwa' of the Rakaia River was said to have defended itself against a demon from the north that attempted to occupy its stretch of river. Pronounced tanifa, a taniwa is a mythological Maori being that lives in deep holes and caves in violent stretches of river and exposed ocean. The Rakaia River taniwa is said to have moved huge boulders to hold back the demon, and eventually imprisoned it in what is the Rakaia Gorge.

My intention was to investigate the upper reaches of the Rakaia, where I hoped to find resident trout still taking up residence in the braided headwaters. Not only did I hope to get above the detrimental impact of the intensive dairy farming, I also hoped to get above the jet boats, which tend to congregate around the Rakaia Gorge.

As I left the paved road behind and pulled onto a gravel track matching the colour of the river, I quickly realised that the scenery was worth the trip alone.

The further upstream I drove; hints of turquoise in the grey milky coloured river became more predominant, until the braids of the river took on that spectacular colour alone. In between these beautiful threads of water were vast beds of yellow wild flowers. The purple of thistles and various shades of foxglove helped to colour in between the lines. I know they're all introduced weeds, but whether it's against flood

water or the relentless wind, they do help to hold the soil together, even if just a little bit. They do a lot more than many of the graziers and their livestock do, and besides, they're also pleasing to the eye. I'm a fan!

Being mid-December, I felt there was a fine line between going too far upstream and not far enough. The trout should have well and truly vacated their upstream spawning beds from the previous winter, but the heat of summer was also just around the corner – in theory anyway – you never really do know in New Zealand, sometimes it never shows up at all.

Another thing that had me zeroing in on a specific upstream stretch of the Rakaia was my interest in one of its larger tributaries. Eventually I parked for the night, well within walking distance from the tributary's confluence with the Rakaia, four or five kilometres away, on the other side of the riverbed.

The days were long at that time of year, and with plenty of light ahead of me, I rigged up my six-weight rod and tied a new leader in readiness for the morning. Then, after a simple packet pasta meal, I fell asleep with high hopes of encountering a few trout amongst the flowers.

An endless troupe of stars danced across the sky during the night and by morning, there wasn't a cloud to be seen.

Although the riverbed had branches of water fingering their way in all directions, I knew I stood the best chance of finding a trout if I found water that was reasonably deep, and relatively slow flowing. Another positive attribute would be if I could find water that was flowing slow enough to allow some kind of aquatic weed to grow, an attribute that is often hard to find in the ever-changing, shingle bottomed, braided rivers of New Zealand. As we all know, aquatic weed is the foundation of the food chain beneath the surface; it provides habitat and food to a wide range of organisms that trout prey upon.

Vegetation lining the bank wouldn't hurt either. Insects get blown into the river from terrestrial vegetation and thus provide trout with surface prey. The bankside vegetation can also provide shade and concealment.

Apart from the flowers, the Rakaia riverbed is generally a windswept and dusty affair, but with the naked eye, I could just make out some greenery above steep banks on the other side. It was definitely worth a look and as I made my way down onto the river stones through flowers scenting the air, it was in that direction that I went.

The various braided channels of the river slowed my progress reaching the other side; not only due to the fact that some of the streams were still quite deep and powerful, but also because some of the riffles and chutes and confluence points looked too good not to have a few casts. The beautiful turquoise water was clean, but it was far from clear; who knew what might be concealing itself beneath the silt clouds.

It was for this very reason that I had chosen to fish a black streamer, I hoped it would silhouette well in the turquoise and milky coloured water. I had decided to use a six-weight outfit, but with the wind strengthening rapidly as the day warmed, I reached the opposite side of the riverbed an hour or two later, and found myself wishing I'd chosen an eight-weight – it was blowing a gale!

The entire expanse of the riverbed must have been at least three kilometres at this point and, as I had suspected, it was flowing clear and not too fast. There was a beautiful stream here, and judging by the well-established gorse and lupines, it looked to be a relatively permanent feature of this changeable river.

As I had been doing on my way across the riverbed, I hiked upstream scanning the water of this beautiful stream, eagerly hoping to spot the first trout of my trip. Sadly, I didn't see such a fish. Surely not, I thought to myself. Amidst the root structure of the overhanging vegetation, there had to be a resident fish on the lookout for an easy meal . . . surely . . .

I fished my way back downstream through this idyllic stretch of water, but came up unrewarded. If there was anywhere on the river where fish may have wished to stay out the summer and not head to deeper water in the gorge, this was it; there was structure for cover, and the water was deep enough to stay cool on the hottest summer day. It wasn't just a barren, wind-blown stretch of shingle bank so typical of these glacial rivers; the terrestrial and aquatic plants would have housed more than enough food for a hungry trout hoping to grow large and establish itself as the 'top dog', on what was quite a lengthy stretch of water.

Judging by my lack of success and the seemingly dead water, I began doubting my judgement. In virtual disbelief, I moved on, setting my focus on the large tributary.

It was early afternoon by this stage and the wind had strengthened to a steady thirty knots. Some of the gusts roared off the Alps at an easy forty knots, bullets of wind, relentless; I could see them coming from a mile away, clouds of glacial silt raging down the valley like an uprising. Sucking in my last gulps of air before they hit, I negotiated my steps through squinted eyes, bowing my head to the onslaughts, like a camel in the desert.

"Shit! This is worse than Patagonia!" I mumbled to myself. "At least there were fish to be caught there . . ."

I must say that I was getting a little disillusioned by this stage. I had heard the stories of polluted rivers, illegal netting, and ultimately, fish stocks in decline, but a part of me had refused to believe it, naah' not New Zealand, they wouldn't let that happen would they, surely not? New Zealand was the 'green' country; it was the place all the Europeans and Asians visited from their overpopulated countries and labeled as 'beautiful'; the land of clean air, clean water, and trout that literally lived in the storm water drains.

As young kids, my cousin and brother and I had caught trout on the occasional overnight setline through the gratings in the gutters and cooked the pan-sized brown trout and occasional eel on the barbecue for breakfast. Not good fisheries management behaviour I know, but we didn't overdo it, and besides, that particular stream is barely a trickle these days, you'd be lucky to find a tadpole in it. Yes, New Zealand's frog numbers are also far fewer than they once were. It seemed the days of swimming in the rivers were also long gone, people wouldn't even dip their toe in the Ashburton River due to the agricultural runoff; a river I had grown up swimming in without a second thought. Sadly, things seemed to have changed. What had brought about this change? Money! As simple as that!

More fertiliser, more pasture, more irrigation, larger milking sheds, larger herds, it all spelt SUCCESS! DOLLARS! ACHIEVEMENT! But did it?

With the wind and dust suffocating me there on the riverbed as I reminisced about the wind in Argentinean Patagonia, I pondered the overexploitation of New Zealand and compared it to the plains of southern Argentina. Ironically, I came to the conclusion that the thing saving the isolated southern reaches of Argentina from over development (for now) is its vastness; and to a certain extent, its somewhat dysfunctional government. Both Argentina and Chile's management of their fisheries suffers from a sad state of incompetence, but with the major population density of both Argentina and Chile being so far from the Patagonian region, the lakes and rivers tend to attract more foreign recreational anglers than they do local. That said; they do end up suffering from foreign investors buying up their land; primarily Americans who buy properties bordering on prime fishing water so that they can whack a mollycoddling lodge on it, and then charge exorbitant amounts of money to fish it. Think about that for a moment, a foreigner buys property on your local river and then charges people hundreds, if not thousands of dollars to fish it. In my view, this sanctimonious form of foreign investment is arrogant, obnoxious, selfish, and downright greedy. The only positive that I can see is that it might add 'value' to a fishery, which might otherwise be neglected.

Of course this also opens the legislation issue of riparian rights; who is it that owns the bank of a lake or river exactly? In New Zealand, most property owners have to allow people on the riverbanks of rivers, where as on the Snake River in Wyoming USA for example, you're barely allowed to dip your toe in the water from a drift-boat, let alone get out on the bank and fish. And on the east coast of the USA, oceanfront property ownership extends across the beach down to the low tide mark. They own the littoral zone; the starfish are theirs, and in the north-easternmost state of Maine, it's not uncommon for property owners to have the weed removed from their waterfront rocks. Were pockets lined when these zoning laws were introduced? I suspect so! It often makes me wonder what the American taxpayer thinks when their hard-earnt money goes into the rescue and relief of coastal hurricane 'victims'. New Zealand and Australia aren't entirely innocent to this phenomenon either, but generally a road and some green space separates houses from the coast,

particularly with newer developments. I hope this common sense
prevails well beyond my lifetime.

As I further explored New Zealand's South Island that summer, I
would begin to realise that the primary issue restricting anglers, was
whether or not properties would allow access to the rivers.

New Zealand's waters definitely attract large numbers of foreign
anglers, but added to the foreign anglers in New Zealand there is also
a relatively large population of local anglers. And with over sixty
thousand immigrants arriving per year at the time of writing, the
number of New Zealand residents wanting to fish was definitely
rising. With New Zealand's total landmass a quarter of the size of
Patagonia (NZ: 268,021 km² vs Patagonia: 1.043 million km²), it
doesn't take long to get from river to river or lake to lake, and as I
was quickly discovering at the onset of summer, there were many
other anglers out there travelling the South Island. With a bit of luck,
and good old-fashioned hard work, I was hoping I could put a bit of
distance between them and me. I had definitely managed to do so on
that first day at the Rakaia River and I must say that I was at a loss as
to where the fish were.

The tributary proved to be another dusty riverbed, full of braided
streams burdened with a heavy load of glacial silt and flowing both
turquoise and grey in colour, depending on depth and rate of flow.
Perhaps the fish were there amongst it, but I didn't spot one, and I
failed to find them by fishing the black streamer.

I re-joined the Rakaia River a considerable distance upstream on
the clear-flowing side stream. Dark clouds were drawing the blinds to
the west, and with the wind still howling, it was obvious that a severe
weather system was knocking on the backdoor of the Alps. Even so,
I wasn't about to give up. Before heading back for the day I decided
I would fish downstream through the clear side stream one last time
– the deep chutes next to the yellow, flower-clad banks looked too
good not to.

The tight channels between the vegetation were like corridors, often too narrow to cast in; I quickly realised that I wasn't going to be able get a fly to the fish, even if I wanted to. I overcame this problem by making a cast in the open, and then walking the fly downstream. This allowed the streamer to edge backwards ahead of me as though it were a small fish struggling in the current, 'walking the dog', as it were. I found myself practically willing a fish to be under one of the undercut banks. How couldn't there be?

Eventually I reached the water I had covered earlier that day; only this time I was fishing a far larger fly, a big rabbit fur streamer; also black. Spotting another undercut bank out of casting range beneath the vegetation, I cast the fly downstream and waded in. With the water around thigh to waist deep, it was flowing slow enough to easily maintain my footing, the fly frantically swimming ahead of me, doing its best to keep from being swept under the bank. The side stream looked especially good here, and although I felt like I was kind of cheating with this technique, I was confident it might work. If only there was a fish there . . .

Even submerging the rod tip in order to get the streamer right in against the bank, the fly got hung up on the bottom about halfway through. I was boxed in on both sides by quite steep banks, and with hedgerows of gorse on top of them; it was almost claustrophobic. I moved the rod tip out away from the bank in an attempt to dislodge the fly, and ended up getting the surprise of my life. This simple movement appeared to be all that was needed. Perhaps the fish had seen the fly stuck on a twig or something. Had the fly's sudden movement made the fish think it was about to get away? Get away it didn't!

Whether or not the fish had attacked from under the bank or the open water, the slight bend in my rod suddenly doubled. It took a few seconds for me to realise what was happening, I was onto a fish!

I could barely believe it, I hadn't seen a fin or a fish scale all day, I hadn't even spooked a fish while making the umpteenth number of river crossings I had made. But there I was; getting raked by near gale-force winds beneath darkening skies, still four kilometres from my camp and hooked up to a leaping fish whose shades of pink momentarily had my mind back on the salmon rivers of Alaska. In the back of my mind was the fact that I had hooked this fish with my rod held sideways; a nine-foot six-weight, the hook definitely wasn't likely to be set very well.

Seconds into the fight, to make matters even worse, the fish ran straight at me. The fly had already been a good ten-metres or more downstream when it had been taken and I wound on the reel like a man possessed, frantically trying to keep up with its headlong charge. I quickly gave up, and stripping by hand, I caught up to it. Expecting the weight at the other end to suddenly disappear at any second, extraordinarily, it remained; the fish continuing with its clean, splash-free jumps in tight confines. I was onto a rainbow trout I realised, and quite a good one, easily over four-pounds. Eventually, with the fish at my feet, our theatre of battle suddenly seemed even more cramped. With the steep banks sequestering me as though confined to a cell, I edged it into what shallows there were.

Getting well ahead of myself, I was contemplating the possibility of trout for dinner, when the hook suddenly pulled free, and the first fish of my trip swam off unimpeded. I guess it was a clean release, but it was bittersweet – it's always nice to get your hands on your quarry, particularly after such a long and trying day.

This was the one and only fish that I saw on the Rakaia River that day and with those kinds of odds, it was enough to confirm that I would be moving on the following morning.

I was hoping I might find better luck in the Lake Coleridge region, just a little further north. That was the plan anyway . . .

ˡ₁ ▲ ∝

Greeted with rain in the morning, my plans were looking a little shaky. The front that had been knocking on the backdoor of the Alps had waltzed straight through the house overnight, and was in the process of dumping its load of bad weather on my front yard. With river braids overflowing like runaway concrete pours, it didn't look like the rain was going to relent anytime soon. Fishing locally was definitely out of the question. A good excuse to sleep in I decided.

By eight o'clock I was wide-awake and the rain was still pitter-pattering on my van, which thankfully, appeared to be relatively waterproof. The rain didn't let up until about ten o'clock and it was only then that I finally emerged.

Long gone was the beautiful turquoise colour of the upper Rakaia River; the multitude of braided streams had amalgamated to just two or three and had adopted the colour of the mountain peaks and silt coated valley floor; glacier silt deposited there after millions of years of ice movement in the mountains had grinded the rock to a grey talc. Knowing it may take a number of days for the Rakaia and other local rivers to settle, I decided it was a good time to fish some lakes.

Driving up out of the Rakaia River Valley, passing sign after sign naming the multitude of sheep stations along the way, the very southern tip of Lake Coleridge eventually came into view. Unaffected by the evening's rain, Lake Coleridge was as blue as the sky; which was miraculously clearing. None-the-less, the northwesterly wind was still prevalent and as I drove past a little lake right beside the gravel road, I spotted a fellow fly fisherman. With a cigarette hanging from his mouth, he was an elderly man, and was getting the wind across his left shoulder on the roadside bank. He had quite a well-established campsite just a short stroll away, his caravan pulled in behind a row of pine trees.

On the spur of the moment, I pulled in past his caravan and continued around to the other side of the lake to the beginning of a sandy beach. The lake was mostly lined with small reddish coloured rocks, and with stunningly clear water; it looked surprisingly good. The regulation booklet stated that both spinning and fly fishing were allowed here; this and the lake's close proximity to the road told me that the fish were going to be of the educated variety.

I didn't bother donning any waders, but laced up my boots, grabbed a rod, and headed off down the beach towards the rocks.

Keeping a sharp eye on the water, I didn't see much along the beach, as I had expected, but when I came to the first weed bed prior to the rocks, I was almost shocked to see a rainbow trout of two to three-pounds. I froze to the spot like a deer in headlights, the fish just metres in front of me, and watched in disbelief as it casually rolled over and picked up a nymph or some such. Wishing I was invisible but knowing all too well that I wasn't, the trout knew I was there, and within seconds, it was gone. Yep! Educated!

This blunder of mine wasn't the greatest of starts, but it was good to see that there were fish there. Despite the fact that I knew they were most likely stocked fish, this first five minutes had me more optimistic than at any stage during the previous day on the Rakaia.

Opting to fish a nymph, I back-cast my way along the rocks towards an almost identical beach, in the opposite corner of the lake. The water dropped away into deep, dark blue water, where healthy beds of weed were present. It looked particularly promising off these rocks, and I did spot another rainbow roughly halfway along. In comparison, this fish would have easily been four, or even six-pounds. Much like the first fish, it wanted nothing to do with my nymph. In retrospect, perhaps a big, black streamer similar to what had proven effective the day before might have been a better option. All the same, I stuck with nymphs to the end of the rocks, when, on sundown, the wind swung a complete one hundred and eighty degrees. In the calm conditions, I tried a Parachute Adams dry fly, with little success. The fading light told me it was getting close to ten o'clock and high time for dinner – I called it quits for the day.

As I had suspected, two other people had arrived at the lake that evening, and they too had been fishing. So with the two extra spin fisherman and the elderly chap out for an evening session, there had been four of us fishing this little lake. Without a single fish secured by any of us, it appeared we were fishing a lake that was full of Rhodes Scholars. Come morning, I would move on.

If I could have found such a beautiful lake at the end of a long hike, I might have hung around for a week, but with no shortage of people pulling in and fishing, it wasn't for me; I wanted to find water that would slip under the radar of the average angler.

ᶠᶾ ▲ ∝

I managed to find the less heavily fished water in a small stream the very next morning, and with a small brown tout quickly spotted, I was hopeful of a good morning of fishing.

That sense of hope quickly turned into pure excitement, as a huge trout suddenly revealed itself. Annihilating some form of prey off the surface, a dragonfly, or even a mouse perhaps, it breached clear of the water like a submarine blowing ballast water. I found myself torn between fishing a dry fly, or a wet pattern.

Being close to midday by that stage, I had suspected the majority of trout would be holding deep, and unlikely to venture to the surface. Despite this logic, that one rise was enough for me to opt for a dry fly.

I tried a variety of flies as the sun shone overhead, but with grey skies and rain threatening all morning, I found myself ducking in and out of the shelter provided by some willow trees. Eventually the heavens opened entirely, and I promptly found myself trudging back – my head hung low – once again . . .

With typical 'NZ' four seasons in one day, the weather cleared that evening and offered views of nearby mountain peaks. They'd received a dusting of snow for crying out loud – it was mid-to-late December!

I found myself on a stretch of Lake Coleridge shoreline around dusk. Two spin fishermen also ventured down to try their luck, but thankfully, everyone gave each other space. Thinking I would wander back to prepare dinner at a reasonable hour and then possibly fish again after eating, I passed one of these spin fishermen on the way back to my van. He had quite a nice rainbow trout of about four-pounds, cleaned and gutted, sitting on the bank. This man later passed my van, wrapped in a headscarf under a broad brimmed hat to keep the sandflies at bay. I guessed him to have been around fifty-five years of age. I never did catch his name but I detected a Kiwi accent as he spoke of previous success on the lakes in the region. By the sounds of it he had lucked onto a brief flurry of action that evening, just as the sun had been shining at its brightest, before it dropped behind the mountains. Fishing a silver spoon, he claimed to have released another smaller rainbow, and lost another, which he suspected to have been bigger than that which he had kept. I was glad to see there were fish there to be caught and that they were willing to take an artificial offering. Over the first few days I spent on these lakes, it seemed like the summer was only just warming up, at times there was quite a bit of insect activity, but generally the fish appeared to be somewhat sleepy. After all, I guess it had snowed on the mountain peaks that morning!

Perhaps my luck would improve the following day . . .

꜔ ▲ ∝

It was getting late in the day when I arrived at Lake Pearson. The wind was typically strong, and from the west.

This large and long lake was right on the main road and ordinarily wouldn't have interested me very much, but with it being close to four o'clock, I figured it would suit me for an evening session.

There were nice easy wading conditions to be had on the eastern end of the lake where I had arrived, but with the westerly wind blowing straight into it, it wasn't on the cards that day. Besides, I told myself, this was where everybody would fish.

It was the northeastern bank that held my interest this afternoon. Backed by a near vertical rock scree, held together by little more than the thorny, invasive vegetation that plagues Canterbury, I suspected it received minimal fishing pressure. A few hundred metres along this bank, the shoreline curved into a low-lying headland that would also provide great shelter from the westerly winds. After the dismal few days I'd had, I trudged off on foot with low expectations.

Once around to the opposite bank, I realised I was going to make slow progress along the shoreline; it dropped away quite steeply and the vegetation at water level was far too thick to be negotiated on foot. Nevertheless, I was eager to get up to the sheltered side of the tree covered headland, and then fish my way back with the wind, wading along the base of the rock scree. Motorised boats were not allowed on this lake. I knew that very few people would climb up the scree and traverse it; the headland could effectively be un-fished, so up I went, high enough to get above the vegetation and then scamper sideways like a mountain goat – rocks tumbling down with every step.

It was far from user-friendly countryside to be keeping holes out of my waders, and I was grateful the ones I had brought with me were well past their used-by-date. Far below, the water looked beautiful, sublimely clear as usual, and a perfect turquoise colour. The hike would be worth it, I was sure of that!

Eventually it came time to negotiate my way back down to the water; no easy task with thickets of thorn bushes doing a better job than barbed wire, but just behind one last thicket, I finally made it down into the corner of the headland. Sweating, and clad in a paste of sweat and dust, I stepped into the water.

At the exact same moment, there was a loud splash behind the thicket of bushes. It was as though someone had thrown out a bucket of dirty dishwater – I just about fell over in fright! The blood was pumping! What was it? Was it a fish? What had it fed on?

Tiptoeing around the bushes, rod poised and ready to make a back-cast with a streamer – all hell suddenly broke loose!

The bushes shook and water flew, as two water birds erupted from their hiding spot in a cacophony of feathered fright. It scared the living daylights out of me!

My first possible fish had literally turned out to be a wild goose chase, but surely there were fish there too.

With vegetation so close to the water's edge, it looked ideal for bugs and the like to be falling out of. It was the kind of scenario that would have been ideal for a Chernobyl Ant bug imitation, if fishing in Patagonia. I wouldn't say the Chernobyl Ant is regarded as a go-to fly in New Zealand, but the likelihood of fish feeding in this manner was too probable to ignore. I wasted no time changing to a dry fly, opting for a little rubber-legged stonefly pattern over the Chernobyl Ant. Being slightly smaller than the Chernobyl Ant patterns I had, I felt it could be mistaken for pretty much anything.

I began working my way out along the sheltered water of the point, but with nothing showing any interest in natural surface prey, let alone my rubber-legged version, I eventually decided to go back to a bead-headed streamer. Perhaps probing the depths along the drop-off would uncover a few fish still sitting down there after taking shelter from the midday sun. Maybe I could get a fly in front of their noses as they started thinking about entering the shallows for an evening meal.

On my first cast, I detected a solid bump – my hopes soared! But, a few hours later, trudging back to my van, rewarded with no action for my efforts other than a few extra holes in my waders, I questioned whether the bump had been a rock; much like a number of others I had felt during the afternoon.

As I said, I hadn't been expecting too much, but after climbing and bashing my way up and over the scree, I must say I thought I was in with a chance, I thought I deserved something for my efforts. Unfortunately, however, the fish deities didn't appear to see it that way, and I ended another day of fishing with little to show for it.

There are many other lakes in this area and after a long, dusty drive into the night (on Christmas Eve); I parked for the night near one of them. I had fished this lake some ten years earlier, how would it have fared over the decade of Dairy Boom gluttony, I wondered? I hadn't caught anything that day all those years ago, but I had been totally cleaned up by what must have been an incredible fish. Belting a black and red Fuzzy Wuzzy streamer on dark, it hadn't missed a step in its attack and I'd hung on a split second too long. I had been lucky enough to have the lake to myself that day and, with the following few days being Christmas Day and Boxing Day, I was selfishly hoping for the same.

ᚠ ᚪ ᚪ

The lakes here were no secret, they received more than enough fishing pressure, but as I started hiking in on Christmas morning, there was no one to be seen. The brief hook-up that had destroyed my ten-pound tippet years ago was still clear in my mind – I couldn't wait to get on the water!

As I edged down towards the somewhat circular shaped lake, a light breeze was wafting across it from the north. I decided I would walk to the rocky western shoreline and work my way along it. But, I didn't get that far!

From up high, long before I got down to the lake, I spotted a trout in the shallows. My plans changed . . .

Once down at water level, I carefully crept in towards where I had seen the fish. It was nowhere to be seen.

If the lake a few days ago had been home to educated fish, the wild trout of these lakes were Oxford and Harvard graduates — assuming money and prestige garners a better education of course . . .

Once on the western shore, I had fished no more than twenty metres along the rocks, when the wind swung a complete one hundred and eighty degrees. I wasted no time battling it and wound in, bee-lining my way to the shelter of the southern shoreline.

Sullen clouds were sweeping in on the wind and before I knew it, it was a cold dark day. Merry Christmas!

Drizzle quickly set in, but with it came what appeared to be caddis moths getting blown off the bank of loose river-stones; the trout were taking an immediate liking to them. Merry Christmas after all!

I had been persevering with a variety of nymphs and small streamers, but as the audible slurps grew in number and regularity, I realised I had to come to the party. Unfortunately, I had no idea what to wear.

They weren't the white caddis moths I was used to and might well have been mayflies. It wasn't a huge hatch and in the strong wind they were quite hard to see. The trout were sitting beyond the calm water, in a stretch of water where the wind was blowing their prey along the surface. I would have thought the trout might have picked up their prey easier in the twenty-metre wide field of calm water, but instead they sat beyond it, just out of my casting range. Did they know they were safer there, or did they prefer to feed where the wind was stronger and their prey perhaps more vulnerable?

Occasionally they approached the calm water, seemingly gathering the troops and attacking in waves, two or three fish at a time, charging in towards the shore and boldly slurping down their prey. But what was their prey; nymphs rising to the surface and metamorphosing into moths (emergers), or terrestrial moths of some kind that were doing their best to stay off the water, I couldn't be sure.

To reach the fish beyond the length of my fly line, I allowed the offshore breeze to drift the line and fly across the lake, well into my backing. Despite what I thought to be an infallible approach, my selection of caddis, mayfly, and emerging patterns, were totally ignored.

By the time the day started drawing to a close, I was frustrated beyond belief. I reverted to nymphs, and also dabbled with a few dark coloured streamers. It's not the way I like to catch fish, fooling them into taking their prey when low light sees them letting their guard down, but after twelve hours on the water and twilight setting in at ten p.m. – I was willing to gain an edge any way I could.

It still didn't help my cause, and eventually it came time to stumble back, in what had become the dark of night. My Christmas day had ultimately been one of frustration, but at least I had been able to fish the lake alone that day. I planned to fish here again the following evening, but throughout the morning and middle of the day, I would investigate another nearby lake reported to hold both brown and rainbow trout.

ﬁ ▲ ∝

Boxing Day saw another vehicle parked nearby when I woke, and I realised I wasn't going to be lucky enough to have the water to myself that day. Promising to be a sunnier day, I wasted no time hiking through the tussock grass clad hills, directly to the second lake.

Unfortunately, from the top of the hill, I could see that there was already a canoe out on this long slender shaped lake. Sitting precisely in the middle of the lake at that stage, they seemed to be drifting the length of it, on a light northwesterly breeze. I made my way down to the southern end of the lake, and began stalking my way along the eastern shoreline, doing my best to spot a fish through the gorse and flax and willow trees.

Just as I sat down to pull on my waders, another angler walked past from the opposite direction, and paused for a brief chat. Having spotted just one brown trout for the morning, he claimed conditions to be 'quiet'. In our brief passing, I noticed he wasn't openly willing to divulge what pattern he'd attempted to fool the fish with, but whatever it had been, it hadn't been successful.

Having seen little myself as I'd made my way along the bank, my intention was to wade back along the knee-deep rocky foreshore and work a variety of wet flies. Out beyond the rocks was a patchwork bottom of weed beds, filling in the blanks between the rock and sand. I knew the probability of a few trout concealing themselves in this slightly deeper water was high, especially with the day warming as quickly as it was.

Starting with the small black streamer I had finished fishing the previous evening with, my first cast saw a brown trout of at least four-pounds, quickly appear behind my fly. It followed the fly a lengthy distance, right into the shallows. Instinct tells us to stop the retrieve when this happens, but my usual tactic is to do the opposite; I'll increase the speed of my retrieve with the intention of enticing a take based on common dog psychology – 'If you run, I'll attack!'

Of course, when it comes to the wily old brown trout pursuing a fly, there's no rule set in stone. If the water were deep enough for the fly not to fall straight to the bottom, perhaps stopping the retrieve would also work. But in this case, in the crystal-clear water of North Canterbury New Zealand, the trout in question wasn't remotely interested. I knew I probably should have changed flies and dished up something different with my next cast, but I also knew that getting a second chance with these fairly heavily fished trout was rare, so a combination of laziness and wishing to strike while the iron was hot, saw me fishing on. Maybe the trout wanted a second chance too.

In the end, this was the only fish I saw along this side of the lake, and by the time I eventually stepped out of the water where I had stashed my six-weight outfit amongst some willows, I had little else to show for my efforts.

Standing there on the bank concentrating on my blood knots while retying a leader, a fellow by the name of Dean scared me half to death, as he quietly wandered past behind me and asked how I was faring.

We shared news of our mutual lack of success for the morning, and much like the other angler, Dean suggested there were fewer fish to be seen from the bank than usual. Being late in the morning by that stage, and a nice sunny day. I wouldn't have thought this to be unusual; I was surprised anglers were unwilling to get in the water and prospect a little further into the lake.

"Is there anyone else fishing at the other lake?" Dean asked.

"I'm not too sure," I replied. "I took a shortcut over the top and didn't look there this morning. There was another vehicle parked near me when I left, though, so I presume there's somebody fishing. They're smart fish over there! I fished from eight o'clock in the morning to ten o'clock at night there yesterday, I didn't even get a take. They were feeding too, all over the place! Big fish too! A high IQ, that's for sure!"

"Yes. They get flogged," Dean said quite simply, confirming what I suspected.

"Yeah, I figure that to be the main reason why, but the thing I don't understand, is where are the scrappers? Where are the smaller fish that are more likely to throw caution to the wind? If you came across water like this in Tasmania or Patagonia," I said, indicating towards the lake in front of us with my rod, "there might be some big fish, but you're also likely to get smaller fish that aren't so smart."

Apart from the likelihood that anglers catch and kill the smaller 'pan-sized' fish, and the big trout also prey on their own offspring, neither of us could come up with a reason why. We eventually wished each other all the best, and continued on in our separate directions for the day.

There was a considerable amount of flax and gorse lining the opposite bank, and, as a result, it was my suspicion that it probably received less attention – so off I went!

Down on the water's edge, there still appeared to be a solid bed of rocks along this western bank, more than a suitable platform to be wading on so as to get clear of the vegetation. Getting upwind on this side of the lake was no easy task due to the thick flax and gorse, but as you might have gathered, I'm always willing to exert a little extra energy and endure a bit of hardship if it means reaching less readily fished water.

The occasional sheep had helped me out with a trail of sorts for the first thirty metres into the vegetation and, thankful for my old waders, I clambered over the last of the gorse and down onto the river stones at the water's edge.

Sitting there buried amongst the flax, eating some lunch and drinking tea while gazing into the shallows, it didn't take long to start spotting numerous numbers of small fish; it was like looking down into a fish bowl. Some were slender and light in colour, while others were short and stocky with dark colours; a variety of native galaxiids

I presumed. There were even silver coloured fingerlings that tended to school together; barely bigger than matches, I believed them to be juvenile trout. With their dorsal regions slightly darker in colour, their camouflage was impeccable.

Surely there's the odd larger fish hoping to prey on them, I thought to myself, and I wasted no time tying on a tiny brown coloured Matuka pattern – identical to the smaller slender fish – or so I believed.

No longer than my little finger, I fished the little size six Matuka all the way back to the beginning of the flax, where I had stashed my six-weight. The water looked excellent and considering the strengthening wind and lack of surface activity, I reasoned that my fly choice was ideal, but once again, my efforts had gone unrewarded.

I hadn't even seen a fish here and I found myself wondering where they were. The fish had predominately stayed at a safe distance in the middle of the lake the day before and I realised this was quite possibly happening on this lake too, particularly considering it was around midday by that stage.

Call me stubborn, but I was certain my strategy was sound. I decided to push even further into the flax and gorse, to give this stretch of lake one last chance. I would then 'clock-in' for the evening session at the neighbouring lake. Would it provide me with the same frustrations as the day before . . . ?

As I sat down for some tea before putting this plan into action, I was watching multitudes of little fish gathering at my feet when I noticed Dean making his way down the hill on his return from the neighbouring lake. Interested to hear how he had fared, I waited for him to arrive.

It turned out that the fish had been surprisingly quiet according to Dean and there were four other fly fishermen trying their luck. Wow, it was a small lake for five anglers.

Although I would have been happy to hear of Dean having some success, a part of me took comfort in the fact that neither he, nor the other four anglers had managed to tie into a fish there either. I wasn't so incompetent after all. With the wind having prevailed from the south the day before, perhaps that was all it took. Things had been quiet on the surface for me as well – until the wind had swung that is.

"You know," I said, "even though the fish aren't rising here today, I've enjoyed the fishing here better than yesterday. I pretty much went through my entire fly box yesterday, there were fish rising just out of casting range all over the place; I even fed my fly and line out across the lake on the wind, well into my backing. They wanted nothing to do with any of it." To this Dean gave a knowing chuckle.

As we stood there chatting, I filled him in on my tactic of trying to match the little fish in the shallows. In various shapes and sizes, I pointed them out to Dean, the trout fingerlings again easily distinguished as they stuck together in their small schools. The galaxiids on the other hand appeared to be somewhat solitary, even if they were numerous. Some of the galaxiids were slender and others stockier. Much like the native galaxiids in temperate Australia, the slender subspecies was easily mistaken with the trout fingerlings

"There's a few different species I think," Dean said. "See that one there that just went under that rock, it's almost black in colour."

Dean also spoke of a native fish similar to a grayling that is now extinct. This intrigued me at the time and a bit of online research revealed that Dean was right, there had been a native New Zealand grayling (*Prototroctes oxyrhynchus*), a smelt species whose records online look remarkably similar to a cross between an arctic grayling and a bonefish due to its smaller dorsal fin. Spawning in freshwater but reaching maturity in the saltwater estuarine stretches of rivers, it's unlikely we would have seen it in the lake. Reaching forty centimetres in length, they were in good numbers during early colonial years, but due to deforestation (still an issue in NZ and perhaps even more so, in Australia), overfishing together with competition, predation and disease after the introduction of trout, their numbers declined rapidly. The last recorded sightings of the New Zealand grayling were around 1920-30. In 1951, some twenty-one plus years later, the New Zealand government classified the species as having 'full legal protection', whatever that meant. Not much, as it turned out, as by 2018 the New Zealand Department of Conservation reclassified the species as being extinct.

Incredibly, the Australian Grayling *Protroctes maraena*, another species I was unaware of, although suffering similar disease issues due to the introduction of trout, has somehow managed to survive in Australia and currently appears to be at the heart of rehabilitation projects. Unfortunately, similar initiatives of awareness and action arrived too late in New Zealand.

With Dean and I standing there pointing out the fish with our rod tips like children holding dip-nets, it eventually came time for Dean to head off for his drive home. I turned back to the north, ready to do battle with the gorse and wind one last time.

I pushed on three times as far this time, my progress coming to an end as I virtually rolled over the top of the lower gorse bushes and onto the water's edge. I continued edging northward along the rocks in the water, negotiating overhanging flax, and doing my best not to disturb the water too much. I'd only gone ten metres into the wind, when I spotted a massive rainbow trout; lying like a log, easily in excess of ten-pounds. With a six-foot-two person frozen to the spot directly in front of it, the fish knew something was wrong, and unsurprisingly, it was the first to break the standoff. Vanishing into the depths like a ghost, this was by far the biggest fish I had yet seen in New Zealand on this trip. I had known there was no way I could cast at it while we ogled each other, but as I crept further along the bank as quietly as I could, I planned to get another thirty or forty metres along the shore, and then fish my way back. With a little bit of luck, this massive fish might have settled by the time I returned, and with even more luck, it would be hungry and looking for a meal – a small galaxiid imitation perhaps . . .

Back-casting my way along the bank, letting the fly sink on the leader and tippet at the end of the floating line, I made small strips, similar to those I would impart on a nymph. As you might expect, anticipation was high, there was at least one big fish out there . . . surely there must be others.

Even if the fish were there, that didn't mean they were going to throw themselves on the bank and in the end, I fished straight past where this huge rainbow had been and there was no sign of it whatsoever. In fact, I worked my way along the entire bank, past where Dean and I had previously been chatting, and all the way to the very end of the lake. I couldn't believe it, the little wet fly looked perfect in the water, even I occasionally mistook it for a fish when stripping it close to check on it. How could a little fish flirt with danger out in the deep water along virtually the entire western bank, and not have a larger fish at least take a snap at it? Assuming the fish to be extremely fussy, I was even fishing a six-pound tippet; something I would ordinarily never dare do when fishing a streamer styled wet fly, especially with the knowledge that there were such big fish in these lakes. Going against this rule of thumb of mine would end up letting me down in the days ahead, but not that day.

This was it for me on that lake and I wound in, ready to hike over to the neighbouring lake, hopefully I could set the record straight before dark.

There was nobody on the water when I arrived, but knowing I was the sixth angler on the water there that day, I didn't like my chances. In support of Dean's earlier report, there was also very little surface activity on the lake that evening. Moreover, it wasn't until just on dark, in the southeastern corner, that I finally spotted my first rises. They were audible, large swirls, made by big fish that were feeding confidently. Although not as regular as the day before, they were feeding in a similar fashion. Again, it was difficult to see what was being fed on. There was no clear hatch in progress, but the confident aggressive boils suggested that the prey wasn't making life easy for the fish; usually a good indication that some form of nymph is 'hatching'. I tried some emergers and, with the hope they might silhouette well, I tried some darker flies such as a Craig's Nighttimes and large black spinners. I hadn't planned to fish very late that day, but as I went through a variety of nymphs and streamers on dark, before I knew it, it was ten o'clock again. I still had nothing to show for it.

Somewhat fed up, I hiked out, looking forward to moving on to some rivers. Although the upper Rakaia River hadn't been easy fishing, the lakes had been proving to be even less productive.

It was well and truly dark by the time I got back to my van, but I was eager to put some distance between me and these lakes and so as to not waste any time the following morning, I was happy to drive into the night in order to reach the first river I wanted to fish.

ʕ ▲ ∝

The only problem with driving to a fishing spot in the dark is that, sometimes, you don't get to the exact river you're looking for . . .

At the end of a little dirt track, I had parked for the night next to a trickling stream that had looked beautiful under starlight. There hadn't been a breath of wind by that stage and I'd even had a wash. That morning, however, the wind was back with vengeance, whistling through the trees overhead and having me somewhat worried about branches falling. I ended up spending most of the morning in the van, tying a few flies and sorting out my fly boxes.

By about midday, I finally emerged. The wind was still blowing, but the sun was coming out and made the conditions more appealing. I was under the impression that I had camped on the right river; if I followed it downstream a kilometre or so it would deposit itself (and me) into the actual river I was hoping to fish – easy!

I happily headed downstream along this creek, fishing the few small pools here and there with a Royal Wolf dry fly. I spotted a few small fish along the way and I thought I was doing great, but as the gradient steepened, the vegetation became thicker and thicker and the rocks became boulders. I quickly realised the fishing opportunities on the little stream were finished and that I would make better progress if I got to high ground.

After a steep, plant-clutching climb up the shingle bank, I finally got onto terra firma, and began making steady progress. My mistake in following the stream became all too clear from this higher perspective and after a few kilometres, I came to the confluence I was looking for. Sliding my way down the valley wall to a far larger river, I reached my primary goal.

The wind was blowing downstream here and basically wrote-off my hopes of indicator nymph and dry fly fishing. The main channel was little more than five metres wide where I reached it and as I waded across to reach the open riverbed, I realised how high and fast it was flowing; this in itself made for inadequate nymph fishing conditions.

I tied on a black streamer and decided to fish my way downstream, swinging the streamer in the current. Although young trout fingerlings were feasibly being targeted by adult trout at that time of year, along with galaxiids, it still wasn't the classic New Zealand dry fly or indicator nymph fishing that I was hoping for, but with the snow-capped Alps offering a hydrant of water in early summer, it was the only feasible technique. It also quickly proved to be quite productive!

In the very first pool, downstream from that which I had crossed, an acrobatic rainbow of a few-pounds quickly took a liking to the streamer. Bouncing its way downstream, it did its best to rid itself of the hook. Growing somewhat tired of canned sardines and my pasta meals, I wasted no time getting it on the bank; my first successfully caught fish of the summer. About time!

An inspection of what it was feeding on revealed nymphs and possibly willow grubs had been its primary prey that morning, none of it longer than a centimetre. I guess it had spotted my offering, mistook it for a small fish or big nymph, and thought all its Christmases had come at once.

With the sun shining and the wind occasionally looking like it might swing to an upstream direction, I continued downstream, negotiating my way along a beautiful flower-filled valley floor, fishing the likely looking pools and runs when they appeared. I missed a similar sized fish behind a midstream rock some four pools down and then picked up a courageous little rainbow that cartwheeled all over the pool before being quickly subdued and released.

After covering perhaps two kilometres of river, I decided to head back and explore upstream so as to decide on which direction I would fish the following morning. If it were to be downstream, I would hike straight through to where I had just finished, and start fishing from there.

Upstream from where I'd reached the river, it quickly thinned out into almost endless rapids. I hiked directly, covering perhaps another two kilometres before I even bothered to fish. I was sure there might be the occasional deeper pool further upstream, but for the following day, the odds definitely seemed to be in my favour in a downstream direction.

I fished just a handful of the deeper runs on my way back downstream to where I had reached the river, and it was only at the very last pool that I missed a take from what felt like a reasonable-sized fish. Downstream it would be the following morning!

ʄ ∧ ∝

Once on the riverbed, the wind was still there, persistent as ever, hounding me like an angry dog. I turned downstream and hiked directly through to the pool I had finished at the evening before. From there I started fishing, progressing deeper and deeper into the rocky gorge country. Some of the river crossings were a little nerve-racking at times, but by picking out the shallower stretches and going with the flow when crossing, it was a relatively comfortable river to fish.

The deeper, back-eddying pools on abrupt, ninety-degree bends in the river hadn't been productive as yet, but that morning, it was at one of these where I picked up my first fish. At little more than thirty centimetres, it wasn't a big fish, but considering my lack of success until this river; it was nice to get on the board for the day. I was under the impression that there should have been brown trout in this river as well as the rainbows, but so far, they were nowhere to be seen.

The next fish I encountered was on a ruler-straight stretch of river, a steep bank of shingle on one side and solid bedrock on the other.

Swinging the streamer out from the faster current flowing along the bedrock, the fly was taken at the head of the pool, midway through its swing. This was possibly the largest fish I had yet encountered on this river, and upon taking the fly it wasted no time blasting downstream, executing jump after jump, all the way to the end of the pool where it finally threw the hook. I didn't get a good look at this fish, but judging by its silver sparkle and its aerial routine, I was almost certain that it too had been a rainbow. I was so delighted with its performance that I almost forgot to be disappointed in losing it. Easy come easy go; there appeared to be plenty of fish to go around, and the further I got away from where other anglers were willing to walk, I knew the fishing would only get better.

The deeper into the gorge I went the more shelter from the wind I found, but as the day warmed, I knew the hot air rising off the plains downstream would potentially suck the cold alpine air down the valley.

It was early afternoon when I reached a beautiful looking pool. Backed entirely by vertical bedrock, a shallow entrance to the pool was followed by one of the longest and deepest pools I had come across. Waist to thigh deep throughout, it wasn't as deep as some of the churning holes on the abrupt ninety-degree bends; but thinking like a fish, it was one of the nicest looking spots I had seen on this river.

I crept towards the narrow entrance at the top of the pool, and made a cast into the rapid, swinging the fly into the clean chute of water against the cliffs. On my side of the chute, the shallow stretch of water lay like a long dinner table. The little black streamer was just on the very edge of this, on that very first cast, when I watched a long fish seemingly snake its way out of the depths and clamp onto the fly. Appallingly, the hook didn't find its mark! I stood there in the shallows, stunned!

For a brief moment I debated changing flies, showing it something different, but as I had a few days earlier, I decided to give the fish a second chance, and simply lay out another cast. Who knows I thought, perhaps it's angry at itself for missing a meal, or perhaps there's more than one fish? Perhaps there was more than one trout fingerling flirting with danger in the area too.

I eagerly anticipated the fly swinging out of the current, my eyes zealously locked on the 'dinner table'. The black fly swung onto the table in plain view, it had made it to safety. But then . . . as if in slow motion, the fish climbed up onto the table behind it, cocked its head like a chicken about to peck at scraps, and snapped at the fly. The little fingerling imitation went no further!

This was by far the biggest fish I had encountered on this river, and similar to its almost lethargic attack, it dejectedly rolled back off the table as though climbing off a couch, turned, and laboured its way downstream into the main pool. Assuming the fish in this river to be relatively small up until then, and still with my mind set on the overfished trout of the lakes, I was still fishing a six-pound tippet. Up until then it hadn't been a problem, but now that I'd hooked a fish that was easily four-pounds, it was 'game on'. Like so many larger trout I've hooked over the years, this fish didn't jump once, instead, it drove its way around the pool with 'top dog' authority; it went where it wanted, when it wanted. Generally I think resident trout also like to go for a bit of a walkabout every now and then; they like pools that offer cover in the form of: bankside vegetation, rock, weed, or fallen debris, and they like a steady rate of flow, fast enough to drift food towards them at a manageable speed, while sheltering amongst the cover. The shallow, slow flowing tail end of the pool is another area where the dominant fish of a pool will often feed, particularly late in the day when they can camouflage themselves more effectively. This fish I had hooked had hoped to get first priority over anything flowing into the pool by sitting at the head of the pool, and it was adamantly uninterested in the idea of being drawn into the shallows! Nonetheless, eventually it tired and I was able to get my hands on a beautiful rainbow trout, which would have easily been half a metre or more in length. (50cm = 19 137/200 inches)

As it swam away strongly, I couldn't have been happier, there's nothing quite like getting off the beaten track and having your efforts rewarded. On this high note, I decided to hike back out, and give myself plenty of time to drive towards the next river I planned to fish.

It was a considerable drive to reach this next river and, once more, I found myself negotiating dirt tracks, river crossings and gates in the dark.

ᚠ ᚠ ∧ ∝

Even though it had been close to midnight by the time I had arrived the night before, I had a far better idea that I was in the right spot. This river was considerably larger and just a fifteen-minute walk away.

Like so many of New Zealand's South Island rivers, I found myself on another braided watercourse; quite a bit larger than the previous river, but nowhere near as big as the Rakaia.

Much like on the Rakaia River, I doubted I would find fish in the open braids of this river, but after the immediate success I'd experienced on the river I just departed, I couldn't help but try. Some of the pools looked perfect, and with my mind flashing back to Alaska, I could clearly imagine schools of salmon making their way upstream. Salmon were out of the question that early in the summer but would the trout sit out in the open with no cover, no form of protection other than their camouflage, their ability to blend into the river stones? Bears weren't a threat to them, but there are more than enough birds of prey in New Zealand that could be. Arguably, their biggest threat was humans, but on that morning and on that river, there was no one else to be seen.

Mountains loomed ominously in all directions from the valley floor, but with the highest peaks standing proudly at the river's headwaters, it was from there that the wind prevailed over my two days fishing.

I hiked upstream along two or three pools, scanning the water from a safe distance, before fishing my way back down through them. Regardless of how good it looked, there wasn't a fish to be seen.

As the riverbed eventually started to narrow slightly, the river split in two, both channels hugging bedrock on either side of the valley, an island of river stone and shingle between them. I chose to follow the inside bank of the right-hand channel; wider and deeper, it looked to be the better of the two.

Mixed with the jumble of rock along this branch's outside bank was the first vegetation I'd seen near the water for at least two kilometres. There's a lot of prey for trout to find amongst New Zealand's free-tumbling river stones, but there is no doubting the fact that the presence of both terrestrial and aquatic vegetation increases the depth of their food chain tenfold.

I was starting to doubt if there were fish in this river at all; when suddenly, I spotted a huge fish, out in the open, as bold as a boxer. I froze to the spot as though hearing the click of a landmine pressure plate, willing myself to disappear, again. It wouldn't be the last time for the summer!

This fish hesitated as it sensed danger, and then just as I thought it was going to settle so I could slink out of sight, it drifted off, and vanished like a date on prom night.

I decided I would continue upstream, and fish my way down the left-hand channel. Hopefully that would allow enough time for the fish to settle, before then fishing back upstream through its haunt.

A complex arrangement of boulders sat at the top of the left-hand branch, creating a nightmarish complexity of currents. Keeping my distance, I skirted around them, struggling to work out the best approach. I chose to attach a heavily weighted black streamer, and began fishing my way down, doing my best to get a clean swing through the multitude of undercurrents and eddies. It was no easy task, even with a streamer, but below a long, midstream boulder splitting the flow in two, I spotted a large dark shape. It suddenly appeared behind my fly like a submarine rising from the depths to pounce on its target. Unfortunately, it didn't!

This inquisitive fish took a lengthy look at the black streamer, but then aborted its pursuit like a distracted dog. It appeared to resettle in the slack water provided by the boulder. Perhaps this was where it had been sitting all along. It was a big fish; darker and perhaps larger than the one I had just walked away from, another attempt at it was definitely in order.

To swing my fingerling imitation down onto it naturally, I decided my best option was to crawl out onto the long boulder and then cast across to the far side of the split stream.

Wading to the upstream end of the rock, I clambered onto it and keeping low, leopard crawling with my quarry oblivious to the threat, I edged towards it. Lifting my head up, I could just see the submarine-like shape sitting in the slack water, poised in the middle of its safe harbour to feed on any morsel of food that came its way. My focus was on the outside channel to my right, the largest and fastest of the two.

Casting from my prone position with my head lifted up as though lying on a surfboard, the line and fly landed in the turbulent water, and was quickly drawn into this massive trout's private domain . . . surely it would take it this time . . .

I didn't have the best vantage point from where I lay, but I could see and sense enough to realise that this fish was no fool, and upon seeing my fly for the second time, it hastily left the premises. After all, what young fish in its right mind would swim into its lair twice within the space of fifteen minutes?

I took comfort in the fact that there was another fish, hopefully now settled and confidently feeding, in the adjacent branch of the river. I wondered if they were both aware of their nearby neighbour. In a roundabout way, they could have quite easily swum over for a visit. These were extremely large fish and I suspected them to be solitary in nature; fish that had individually commandeered these two branches
of the river, water that offered gentle flow, deeper water, and the cover they were partial to. Extraditing them from their preferred abodes wasn't so easy it seemed.

Seeing that the black streamer had enticed at least partial interest, I decided to persevere with it and start fishing the other branch from the top down; I was confident my fly would cross paths with the fish there, all too soon. Unless of course it had decided to cross the channel and wait out the day under the cover of the rocks and bankside vegetation. Somewhat surprisingly, quite the opposite turned out to be the case . . .

I covered a good forty-metres of river and was just nearing the end of the deeper water off the shingle bank when I spotted the fish. Only this time it was another twenty metres downstream, in shallower water, just below a trickling stream that was dribbling into the main river. Had it not risen to take a natural 'dry' drifting from the rivulet, there's a good chance I wouldn't have seen it. Having seen how the previous fish had ignored the streamer in the bright daylight conditions, I decided to do away with it; I would try my best at playing the 'match the hatch' game. The only problem was, there didn't really appear to be anything hatching. I watched for a while and saw nothing, but it was clearly taking something off the surface. I looked through my fly box before finally opting for a tiny caddis pattern.

Now came the question of presentation, do I drift the fly down the rivulet to the fish and no doubt spook it once forced to lift the line and fly off the water, or do I sneak around the fish and cast upstream and over it, no doubt spooking the fish as my line falls to the water? The life of a fly angler – it can be a tough life at times!

In an ideal world, there would have been a bank just off to the side with a nice hedgerow of tussock grass I could have hidden behind, I could have then cast above the fish on an angle, and drifted my leader and fly straight through where it was sitting. Easy. But, back in the real world, I found myself crawling downstream towards the fish, exposed as a rabbit entering Baghdad.

Trying to get as close as I could to limit how much line I would need to feed down to the fish, I finally got into position and got my line sorted out. The time of reckoning was nigh.

I flicked the little caddis imitation out into the current, feeding line out to it as it drifted in the rivulet towards where this huge fish had been quietly sipping down dries of some kind. With a back eddy and the current of the main river to deal with, the unpredictable flow quickly proved a bigger burden than I had anticipated; my best laid plans suddenly irrelevant as the fly was drawn under the surface, right when it was in the 'zone'. With a fish of this size, with years of experience, know-how and instinct locked in its brain and DNA, this was all it took. I lifted the fly and line off the water and sat there, waiting for another rise, which never eventuated. A part of me knew it never would, I knew a fish of this magnitude would spook at far less than this, and eventually, after an hour or more spent on these two fish, I got up and moved on.

It was mid-afternoon, and I was at least another four or five kilometres upstream before I spotted another fish. Up until that point, I had assumed the previous two dark coloured fish to be big brown trout, but were they?

With the afternoon breeze funnelling down the valley as I had expected it to, I spotted a fish sitting in an unruffled pool behind a large boulder. It was otherwise a very fast flowing stretch of river and this was another dark fish, easily close to ten-pounds. From my vantage point, I could clearly see the flashes of pink as it happily finned in the gentle current it had found. There was no mistaking it to be a big rainbow trout. Again, this fish had taken up residence in what was the optimal spot on a long stretch of river, and once more, it also sat sheltered from the main current in a position where the current flow, from all angles and variations, would deposit food on its doorstep. My guess was that it had this fifty-metre stretch of fast water all to itself.

I had as much chance of presenting a natural drift with a dry fly to this fish as I might have in a gold pan. I had already seen it take two dries off the surface, though, so make an attempt with a dry fly I would; a Royal Wolf. Often passing as a variety of prey items, from beetles to various moths, the Royal Wolf pattern is regularly my fly of choice when I can't decipher what's being taken, particularly for rainbows, which, at times, appear to find the splash of red in the fly irresistible. Besides, in a situation such as this, there was a good chance this trout was taking pretty much anything that came its way.

One thing was undeniable, though; it wasn't partial to a submerged Royal Wolf! With the disorganised array of currents and back eddies, as I had thought it might, my fly was quickly drawn beneath the surface. The trout disappeared with even more haste.

It's easy to look back and question, 'what if', but it would have been interesting to see what might have happened had I dropped a weighted nymph into one of the back eddies. Sometimes, however, there's simply no right or wrong and before my summer was out, I would even see that even the wise brown trout would sometimes take a submerged dry fly.

On this occasion, I wound in and continued upstream, hopeful for a fourth chance at a fish.

The shadows were well and truly creeping up the walls of the valley by this stage, but it was difficult to gauge exactly what the time was. In the distance, on the right-hand side of the upper valley floor, I picked out a patch of green vegetation and told myself it would be my turnaround point. For the following day, I would hike directly upstream and start fishing from that same point.

There was very little structure in the braids of the river for the remainder of this stretch and I didn't bother fishing much of it. On reaching my turnaround point, I removed the dry fly and attached a large black streamer; my plan was to try and fish back downstream, on the opposite bank of the streams I had fished on the way up. With the conditions darkening into the evening, I knew it was a good option; there were trout fingerlings and galaxiids in the river and on dark I hoped there might be a little less feeding inhibition amongst the adult trout.

In a deep, bubbling hole on a bend in the river, I finally felt my first touch on a fly in this river. It could have easily been a small fish, but at the same time it could have easily been one of these monstrous trout, hesitantly having a peck at a form of prey it wasn't quite certain about. With nothing interested in the fly on my second and third cast in this hole, I suspected I might have just missed one of the big ones.

Continuing downstream, the wind was howling by now; it was getting dark and it was getting cold. If I'm honest with myself (and with you the reader) after such a long and trying day, I really was just going through the motions; I was thinking more about getting back to my van and getting out of the wind and my wet waders than catching a fish.

I slipped my way up and over some high ground and came down to a stretch of river that had looked promising from the other side earlier that afternoon. With a handful of large boulders along the water's edge, I positioned myself just behind the upstream boulder and took a much-welcomed seat on a smaller rock. By this stage of the day, I probably should have double checked my tippet, tested my knots and perhaps changed from a six-pound tippet to one more suitable for stripping streamers, particularly when ten-pound fish were on the cards. Instead, I wearily laid out a cast directly behind the boulder in front of me. The fly swung no more than two metres below the rock when it stopped dead. It took me a moment to snap back to my senses and the job at hand. In retrospect, I would have had a better chance of success had I been more off my game. Instinct took control, and I hung on for a millisecond too long. In what seemed like the blink of an eye, a massive fish broke the surface behind the rock with a formidable swirl – the knot to my fly gave way as if it were tied in silk.

I couldn't believe it, I must have covered at least ten kilometres that day, and in the fading light, I'd finally outwitted one of these impressive fish, only to be undone by my own carelessness. Mentally (and verbally) kicking myself, I knew I should have replaced the lighter tippet with a ten-pound tippet back at my turnaround spot, I had seen that there were fish over ten-pounds in this river, but from my experience, a ten-pound tippet can withstand most takes on a wet fly from trout up to any size. Assuming of course that you let it run as quickly as possible afterwards. Six-pound tippets on the other hand tend not to last long at all.

I hiked on mumbling to myself, angry at my slackness and angry at the fact that I'd kind of conceded defeat, right at the optimal time of day to be fishing; it was on dusk that I should have had my wits together.

As you'd expect, I didn't encounter another fish that evening and it was dark by the time I waded back across the last stretch of river towards my exit point, I couldn't get there quick enough.

Somehow, I managed to find my way through the gorse and back to my van. It had been an incredibly long day and it was midnight by the time I had something to eat for dinner.

The following morning my plan was to head directly upstream to my turnaround spot, and then continue fishing further upstream. I had no idea what I might find, my only concern was that the river might thin out too much. Given time, and hopefully some decent weather, I was looking forward to finding out . . .

ᚠ ᚪ ᚳ

The weather had improved from the evening before, and I wasted no time hiking directly upstream to where I had turned around. The fact that it took me two hours to do so was a good indication of just how much water I had covered the previous day. I continued upstream from here, eagerly scanning the water in search of my first trout for the day.

I didn't see any fish for quite some distance, before I finally spotted a small one, which I actually supposed to be a brown. Deciding to persevere with the streamer from the evening before, I double around it with the intention of fishing down through the entire pool. Reaching the top of this long and relatively wide pool, I couldn't believe my eyes.

For a moment I thought the first dark shape I saw was a rock, but then I saw another and another and another… There must have been close to five big trout sitting in various spots along either side of the main flow entering this pool, the majority of them hugging the opposite bank. I was utterly stunned by the size and number of them, but still I decided to leave them for the time being, and to fish back downstream on my side of the river. They can wait, I told myself. I also figured that if I caught a fish in the lower end of the pool on my side, I was less likely to disturb the big boys at the top.

As I worked my way downstream, I started spotting a few more fish; they were against my bank, the opposite bank, and in the middle, I was like a kid in a chocolate store with no cash, I didn't know which way to turn. None of them were rising and, adding to my bewilderment, they wanted nothing to do with my streamer.

I was approaching where I'd spotted the small brown, when right next to the bank just ahead of me; a larger fish of about four-pounds clearly sipped a dry off the surface. Thankful for a positive indication they weren't all on a hunger strike, I chose not to waste this opportunity; but once again, I couldn't be sure what was being fed on. I had seen a number of sedge caddis on the rocks while hiking in that morning, and I decided they were as good a choice to imitate as any.

I attached a size fourteen deer hair sedge caddis that had been in my fly box, for years it seemed. I stripped out five metres or so of line, cast the fly, and began feeding it downstream towards the feeding fish. Gracefully finning over some light coloured gravel less than a metre from the bank, I could just make out the fish from where I sat, hunched over and also doing my best to not be seen.

As I've already said, you rarely get more than one chance at a trout like this in New Zealand, particularly if feeding a fly down onto it, but in this case, one chance was all I needed.

The fish elegantly rose up to the fly, as unassuming as could be, opened its mouth over the fly, and closed it. I struck!

I had timed things well and I instantly felt the fish . . . but oh so briefly. Instantly breaking the surface, the fish felt the hook too, or so it seemed; at the very least, it realised its morning sedge caddis meal wasn't quite what it expected. It spooked into deeper water, and left me standing there, gob-smacked. What on earth had gone wrong? After what I was certain to have been a clean hookup, I have never seen a fish rid itself of a fly so quickly. Luckily, there were plenty of other fish to turn to . . .

A few rises on the other side of the shallows in the lower end of the pool caught my attention and I fished on, carefully wading out towards them. After making four or five unsuccessful casts, I finally did what I should have done after missing the previous fish. I thought I had missed it . . . but on inspecting the fly . . . it seemed that wasn't the case.

As I said, the couple of sedge caddis flies I had floating around my fly box had been doing so for years. The hook had broken in the fish's mouth. No wonder it rolled on the surface and fled. The old 'long-term tenant' in the fly-box story! The fly had looked okay when I had tied it on, but looks only tell half the story about the state of a hook.

Once on the opposite bank, I doubled back upstream to the big fish at the head of the pool. They weren't quite so easily spotted from this side, but with a few fish still visible, I drifted an elk hair Stimulator over them, hoping it might be mistaken for a stonefly.

They paid no attention to it, so I attached a nymph-dropper to the bend in the hook; if the nymph was taken the dry fly would dip under the surface, and I would strike accordingly – indicator nymph fishing with the dry fly as the indicator.

Still these fish showed no interest in my flies. It was quite a deep pool and even though it was a bead-headed nymph, there was still a good chance it was drifting too far above the fish; this in itself will send alarm bells to the wary trout of New Zealand's rivers. Nymphs usually trundle along near the bottom in the benthic zone of a river, where they too no doubt hope to rely on their camouflage, and are close to the rocks they hide under. Obviously, it's also here that the trout feed on them; if your nymph isn't down there with the 'naturals', your chances of success rapidly diminish.

Hoping to escape a strengthening wind coming down the valley, I took a gamble and turned off the main river onto a large tributary flowing from a much narrower valley. It was a beautiful stream, definitely large enough to be home to a few fish, but even while having lunch overlooking one of the larger pools, there were none there that I could see.

I got back on the main river and continued upstream into the breeze.

Considering the number of fish I had just seen in the one pool, I didn't see any fish for quite a distance. Had the trout been sitting below the tributary feeding on something that was being washed into the main river, I wondered, or was it optimal water temperature that had them congregating there . . . ?

In a similarly disorganised, current-filled pool, I finally found a fish sitting behind a big boulder on the side of a fast-flowing run; once more, it was in a location suitable for conserving energy and having its food 'home-delivered'. Of course, it was also very awkward presenting a fly to it. All the odds were in the fish's favour, and as I partially expected, I ended up spooking this fish too.

On the side of another fast run, just a little further upstream, another opportunity presented itself.

This was a huge rainbow, dark in colour and easily over ten-pounds. It was sitting right on the edge of the river, in remarkably shallow water, sipping down the occasional dry, which again, were so small I had no idea what they were. Midges or sandflies, perhaps . . .

I probably should have changed to a small fly on the spot, but again figuring it was taking anything that came its way, I fed the dry fly and dropper down towards it. It spotted the dry, took a double take, and looked like it might actually move to investigate. Heavens forbid; it's actually going to take it . . .

No! The nymph hit the bottom, the dry fly dipped under the surface, and this fish of a lifetime vanished like a distant dream. Between crawling into position and then dealing with the wind, it had taken a good fifteen minutes before even flicking the flies out to this fish, but in the end, it had all come to a close in seconds.

At that moment, sitting there on the bank in disbelief, I thought my life had come to an end. When would I get another opportunity like that?

Little did I know, there would be many more encounters like this that summer; some would end on a high note and others in equally bitter disappointment.

Thankfully, I eventually came to a long and large pool, similar to that which had held so many fish earlier that day. It was here that I found another good number of fish.

Sitting in deep water roughly two thirds of the way downstream, it appeared to be the point in the pool where the river flow slowed to what was an optimal speed for them to conserve energy and pick off their prey. I had never before seen such big trout appear to be schooling like this. I sat well back from the edge of what was quite a high shingle bank, and watched, doing my best to keep an eye on the fish while lengthening the dropper on the brown nymph I was fishing. I also replaced the Stimulator dry fly 'indicator' with the largest Royal Wolf I had in my fly boxes.

Crawling into a casting position, just upstream from the fish, my plan was to cast above them on an angle and let the flies drift down through them. With my leader and tippet around twenty feet in length, I would hopefully be able to present the flies, and then lift them out without spooking the fish if unsuccessful. As I've said in previous books, if a trout is going to take a fly, they will usually do so the first time they see it, particularly if, as in this situation, there's competition from other fish. Sometimes, however, consecutive presentations are what are required, to convince, or frustrate a fish into feeding. If presented carefully, consecutive casts of the same fly might also fool fish into thinking there's been a hatch further upstream.

At a guess, I suspected these fish were sitting a metre and a half below the surface. Even though I had lengthened the nymph-dropper to over a metre, I still doubted that the weighted nymph would hit them on the head; as I knew it needed to. My first two presentations drifted through seemingly unnoticed and I managed to heave the twenty metres of line out, and back upstream, without unsettling the fish too much. My third cast from my seated position resulted in the back cast getting blown to the ground. As I crawled around picking my leader out of the grass and rocks, my patience was wearing thin .

Despite my impatience, the fish were still there – I couldn't not attempt a fourth cast!

The white 'wings' of the Royal Wolf sat high on the water, easily visible as it drifted towards the fish. I was expecting very little by this stage, but then . . . quite suddenly . . . I watched in disbelief, as one of these trout broke from the pack and casually rose towards the surface. Confidently, and deliberately, as if in slow motion, the rainbow trout engulfed my dry fly indicator.

"Gotcha!" I said out loud as I struck, and got to my feet in the one motion.

The fish heard me loud and clear, but clearly didn't wish to hang around for a chat. It took fright and shot off on a blistering run, upstream and across the pool, my drag screaming, my paces precarious on the shingle bank, and my backing seeing the light of day. As with the larger fish I had caught and released a few days earlier, this fish didn't jump once during the fight. This rainbow, however, was a different kettle of fish entirely; it was far larger, a jump or two might have been just what it needed. Finding no solution to its dilemma in an upstream direction, I gradually persuaded it back downstream. The bank from which I had been casting was quite high; it was because of this that I'd had such a clear view of the fish, but I quickly realised I would need to get down in order to land it.

The lower end of the pool split into two branches, the smaller of the two on the other side of the river. The shallow water and slower current in the smaller stream looked to be the ideal spot to hopefully draw the fight to a close. With the fish heading that way, I got in the 'drink' and followed.

Luck had definitely been on my side for this fish to take the dry fly like it did, but that's sometimes the magic ingredient when fishing; I could only hope that my luck would hold until the fish was safe in my hands. Its panics in the shallows had me anticipating the multitude of things that could go wrong in the latter stages of fighting a trout on a light tippet; kind of like someone pulling out of a deal before signing on the dotted line, or the girl who steps outside to take a call, but is never seen again . . . close but no cigar. That wasn't the case with this fish and eventually it succumbed to the imminent predicament it found itself in, and I led it safely to the shallows. Not flapping around in a net or on dry rocks, but safe at my feet, in the water, where I could get my hands on it and remove the hook.

And what a beautiful fish it was; easily eight-pounds or more, sparkling bright pink and silver and covered in countless black dots, it was in superb condition for early summer. The sun was shining, the water beautifully clean and clear, and after two days of toil on an astoundingly difficult river, I'd finally been rewarded with a remarkable fish.

I was well over two hours upstream by this stage and it was well past time for me to be heading back. There was no way I could bypass the pool where I'd encountered the multitude of fish earlier that day, though!

Despite my high expectations, there was little activity on the surface and my flies did nothing to promote any. Incredibly, I didn't even see a fish, and with the valley now filled with shadow, it was high time to make tracks.

It was dark and close to midnight by the time I followed my nose directly up to the fence near where I'd parked my van. It took me a few moments to realise that I'd missed the gate, but stepping through the fence – I'd made it!

꒷ ▲ ∝

My next port-of-call would take me a considerable way north into the 'North Region' of the South Island and once there, I was looking to fish another river. New water, on a new river, in a new region – I was excited – who knew what I might find . . .

2. NORTH & WEST COASTS

2

The weather looked threatening on the drive along the dirt track from which I planned to hike onto the Clarence River, but a good forecast for the next three days had me excited about the fishing possibilities that lay ahead. My plan was to hike along the river for half a day and camp for three nights, hiking back out on the afternoon of my fourth day.

The river looked good where I parked for the night, but with a keen eye kept on the water as I loaded my pack for an early departure, I failed to see any evening fish activity. They would be keeping their distance from people accessing the river on the dirt road I told myself; ten kilometres or so downstream on foot and I was confident I would find the fish I was searching for.

ʄ ▲ ∝

Sunshine greeted me in the morning but so too did a strong wind, gusting downstream along the river. I wasn't even going to be fortunate enough to have an early morning calm period, as had regularly been the case. Nevertheless, with my rod tubes and tent strapped to my pack and my billycan hanging from a strap, it wasn't long before I was chiming my way downstream like a cow in the Swiss Alps.

It was a verdant but dry landscape here on the southern border of Molesworthy Station; New Zealand's largest property at over 1,800km², and the seeds from the various grasses took a quick liking to my socks and bootlaces.

The Clarence River generally wasn't braided like the previous rivers I'd been encountering; instead, the upper reaches I was hiking along had rather sturdy banks. It turned out that by the time I decided to stop and pitch my camp, I had ended up reaching a rock gorge, it's banks unchanged for thousands of years. Pockets of willow trees had occasionally been present along the river, and it was at the base of some willows on some green grass that I decided to camp. I wouldn't get shade in the late afternoon, but I would get a welcomed wakeup call with the sunrise.

It had become a warm day by this stage, even if the wind was still strong, and I jumped straight into a nice pool to cool off. I then sat on the bank and spent a good half-hour picking grass seeds out of my socks and boots.

With my tent pitched and rod rigged, I continued in a downstream direction, expecting good things.

From the top of the cliffs on the hike in that morning, I had seen a big fish sitting at the tail end of a deep pool. I'd taken it as a good sign, but as I continued downstream scanning the water, it seemed the big fish weren't as prevalent as I'd grown used to over the previous few days. In contrast, there did appear to be a reasonable number of small fish in this river.

I must have covered at least two or three kilometres of water that evening and, in the end, the only decent-sized fish I saw was one sitting at the very spot a trickling stream gurgled into the main river. Sitting there like a drunk in front of the beer taps at a bar, this fish promptly fell off its stool and shot out the door.

The Clarence River is one of New Zealand's South Island rivers which has been, and sadly probably always will be, affected by didymo. Known colloquially in New Zealand as 'rock snot', it's an introduced alga that looks exactly like that, snot. This foul stuff has found its way into many of the South Island's lakes and rivers and, in my view, has largely destroyed them in comparison to what they once were. New Zealand's officials, and the generally conscious water users in New Zealand have somehow managed to keep it out of the North Island. The arrival of didymo to New Zealand's South Island has been traced back to a Canadian tourist, who brought the dormant spores into the country on a canoe. Even when dry, they still manage to survive for a period of time and the spread of it can only be prevented with the use of detergent and prolonged drying. As the signs all around the South Island plead with lake and river users: 'CHECK CLEAN DRY!

On my trip to New Zealand ten years earlier, the didymo was only just starting to spread, but by the end of my summer I would realise it was now pretty much all throughout the South Island. Rivers like the Rakaia that 'flush' well during flood events seem to handle it better than those that don't. There's no proof didymo directly kills trout, or even native species such as galaxiids, but with the amount of gunk drifting downstream in some of the rivers, it must surely make for difficult feeding conditions; the trout required to spot their prey amidst a hailstorm of snot. Blanketing the bottom of lakes and rivers like a snotty carpet, it might also clog up the crevices in which nymphs and other forms of trout prey are trying to live, therefore limiting insect populations.

It definitely makes for a slippery and frustrating fishing experience, and due to the amount of crap your nymph picks up, it virtually disallows the use of indicator nymph fishing tactics. The only positive I can see is that its presence makes it quite difficult for an angler to spot the fish, and due to the regular fowling of your fly, lure or bait, it generally makes already difficult fishing even harder. In other words, the fish have a better chance of avoiding overfishing. Perhaps!

I myself was struggling to spot the fish in this river, I found myself wondering if there were any larger fish there at all. Smaller fish were rising to substantial insect activity on dark. But when I say smaller, I mean no bigger than my hand. It was like the larger fish were being treated to some fine-dining elsewhere.

I resorted to swinging a streamer, but in pools that looked like they could do me no wrong, even that approach failed. The following day I would fish upstream so as to give these downstream stretches a bit of a rest, and on my second full day I would fish downstream again.

The wind continued blowing into the night, and as I lay there trying to fall asleep, I could hear rocks getting blown off the cliff faces, bouncing down the nearby screes and, on some occasions, falling straight into the river with a plop.

ℾ ∧ ∝

Similar to the previous day, there was a steady downstream breeze blowing first thing in the morning. By the time I'd finished breakfast it had failed to abate. If anything, it had strengthened. I headed upstream regardless, straight into the twenty-knot headwind. Talk about starting behind the eight ball!

Apart from the didymo and additional green slime that was possibly due to high nitrogen levels as a result of upstream farming, the river looked perfect. But, as I took a bird's eye view traversing a few hundred metres of river from atop some cliffs, I spotted just two fish. Fairly certain they were browns, they weren't holding in the main flow against the bedrock banks, but were instead resting out in the open, halfway across the river, camouflaged over the kind of shingle sediment you dream of finding in New Zealand. In water that might have been about waist deep, they weren't big fish, individually perhaps just two-pounds. In such a large river, they almost seemed out of place, I couldn't even be bothered fishing for them. The one big fish I had spotted on the hike in was a definite rarity, had it been a salmon I wondered?

I got back down on the river, crossed it, and continued upstream on the opposite bank. In calm water along the very edge of the river, I spotted another trout, this time perhaps a touch under two-pounds. It was quietly sipping down miniscule insects off the surface. The usual so small to be indistinguishable variety: midges, sandflies, mosquitoes – I had no idea! Considering what I thought the river should have had on offer, I again found myself struggling to get enthusiastic about targeting such a small fish, but I eventually knuckled down, and got onto the task at hand.

Having been bothered by a number of blowflies while having breakfast, I had tied on a blue Humpy before setting out; I knew it would be the perfect imitation. As I sat there watching this little trout sipping down the miniscule dries, I honestly couldn't be bothered changing flies. I also couldn't justify the wear-and-tear on my limited selection of tiny flies. I flicked out the blowfly imitation, feeding out line as it drifted towards the unassuming fish. Boldly moving towards my offering (or stupidly), the trout broke the surface near the fly as though attempting to eat a meal larger than its mouth. I struck half-heartedly, turned my back, and continued upstream with the wind now blowing a steady thirty knots.

At one of the deeper holes I reached, with water coming into it at various angles, I got an inkling that a Chernobyl Ant might be worth a try. It wasn't like I had much to lose, and I was tired of trying to present dry flies with a natural drift, especially in such strong wind and on a river whose pools seemed to lack any kind of uniformity.

This one was a mixed bag of fast-flowing rapids, slow-flowing back eddies, and inflowing side-stream chutes, all virtually on top of one another. I reasoned that the Chernobyl Ant could swing across the top of this mess, like a helicopter avoiding rush-hour traffic. And to a certain extent, it could do so naturally; dragonflies, stoneflies, damselflies, and various other insects often skate across the surface when trying to take off, and when trying to avoid being swept downstream on a river. Granted, however, it does take a very aggressive trout to attack this kind of prey, and with New Zealand's trout known for their extremely high IQ and cautious nature, the Chernobyl Ant is definitely not as commonly used as it is in Patagonia. Nothing else was working on this river in New Zealand though, so why not?

My first cast went into some fast water at the head of the pool, sideways, an unequivocal no-no in the standard dry fly fishing 'textbook'. Despite my seditiousness towards doctrine, it swung out sideways, skated across the surface into calm water next to the rapid, its rubber legs wriggling, invitingly bringing the fly to life, when a small rainbow trout promptly took a snap at it. Suggesting it was also a free-spirited nonconformist marching to its own beat, it missed the hook entirely.

After this brief moment of triumph; the rest of the afternoon didn't follow up with the fish climbing all over the fly as I had hoped, however, the Chernobyl ant did manage to draw the attention of a few other fish. It was more action than any of my other strategies had produced. Even so, considering the distance I'd hiked in, it was nothing short of second-rate fishing.

Once back at my camp, with the sun sinking towards the mountains to the west, I sat down and decided that enough was enough, I'd come out to fish and camp for four days and three nights, but instead, I didn't even continue fishing that evening. I had a wash in the river and started getting my things together for an early departure the following morning. I couldn't understand what the problem was; this was a long and large river; there were clearly fish in it, but not that many, and not many of any size, was I just in the wrong spot on the river, or would I also be struggling elsewhere? Like a malignant cancer, the didymo was definitely going to be strewn throughout the river system. Was that the problem I wondered?

I sat there eating my dinner at a respectable hour for once, and feeling somewhat crestfallen, I glanced up towards the mountains to the south. An eagle hung in the air, its wings spread wide as it soared on the late afternoon thermals, searching for a meal far below. It was nice to be out there, but with relatively easy dirt road access and any number of raft trips utilising this river, there was a good chance that I had hiked ten kilometres downstream on a river that simply got too many anglers on it. I hadn't seen any over the two days I'd been out there, but all it takes is the occasional group raft trip with half a dozen fishing rods amongst them. Judging by what I had already seen in North Canterbury, somebody would have been cashing in on that opportunity – it sadly now seemed par for the course in New Zealand – money, money, money!!!

f﹐ ▲ ∝

Sure enough, as I started throwing things out of my tent ready to pack my gear and start the hike out, I might have thought I was in a combat zone!

From a distance I had heard it, and as I dug around inside my tent it grew louder and louder, until I thought it would land on top of me. The chopper put down on a flat stretch of river bank no more than thirty metres from my campsite.

With a middle-aged couple on board, the guide was eager to know if I had fished up a nearby tributary. I let him know that I'd had a look at the first hundred metres or so, saw very little, and had turned around. He suggested that there were only a handful of fish up there and that it was a good spot to get out of the wind. It seemed perhaps I hadn't looked far enough. It was a good thing I hadn't seen the chopper drop them off on the day I arrived, as I would have wasted my time hiking a lot further downstream. Par for the course on the Clarence River increased even more on my hike out . . .

As I had suspected, I came across a flotilla of half a dozen red and blue rafts making their way downstream. Sure, it was a nice way to see the river, and no doubt made someone lots of money, but I'd be lying if I said I was happy to see them. I wondered how many of the people were looking to bag a fish for dinner instead of freeze-dried meals; hurling lures at every stop, or even mid-drift as the thousands of drift boats anglers do in the USA. Apart from the fish, who could blame them I suppose?

An hour or two later and I was back at my vehicle, this time with no fish spotted along the way. I decided to head up another tributary near where I was parked.

The dirt track was more than suitable for my two-wheel drive vehicle and as I covered about thirty kilometres, I kept a keen eye on the river straight out the window, but again, I didn't spot a fish the entire way. Never have I seen rivers look so good, yet fish so poorly. Not that I ended up actually fishing this tributary, but had I, I suspect my efforts would have offered little more than casting practice.

Seeing that New Zealand's largest station (farm/ranch) had become somewhat of a tourist attraction, and in a sense a national park, had it also become a victim of its own success – much like what I believed was happening to New Zealand? Crisscrossed by good dirt roads, hiking tracks, sleeping huts and even self-composting toilets, it seemed to me that New Zealand's Department of Conservation and the station itself hadn't done themselves any favours; it was now so easy to get to it all. Even so, they hadn't created problems that a few locked gates wouldn't have fixed. Then again, even if it wasn't easy to reach by vehicles, I guess it still would be by helicopter. 'Making it easy' . . . sadly, it seems like this is what life is all about for many folks these days, prompt self-gratification. And making lots of money of course! Unfortunately, and unjustifiably, the environment and our fish stocks tend to suffer as a result.

I'd had enough of this area and I returned to the tourism-flogged town of Hanmer Springs, to track down a weather report.

The forecast suggested I was in for a few days of wind and the possibility of torrential rain. Optimistically, I told myself the wind was most likely accurate, but the torrential rain would end up being just a few showers here and there; I liked my chances of getting the wind behind me at a couple of nearby lakes, a rise in the rivers due to rain hopefully wouldn't affect them much.

ᚠ A ∝

Out at the lakes, rain set in for the entire following day, and washed my optimism straight down the drain. I spent most of that day cooped up in my van, catching up on some writing and tying flies. I drove back to Hanmer Springs later that afternoon to get some fuel and another weather forecast. I was hoping for a miracle, but it looked like there really was torrential rain on the way.

ᚠ A ∝

I woke to heavily flooded rivers, and incredibly, sunshine. A few months' worth of rain had fallen overnight and judging by the radio, it had hit most of the South Island; roads were blocked with landslides and flooding, and as I sat in my van overlooking the swollen Waiau River eating breakfast, I realised that most of the South Island rivers were likely to be unfishable for weeks. I hadn't planned to, but I decided it was a perfect time to hit the coast.

With the weather in the very north of the South Island quite often better than elsewhere, and the remainder of the island sounding like a crumbling sandcastle, it was to the north I went.

After a day of driving that saw the roads equally flooded with traffic, I finally reached Golden Bay.

Sitting on the very north-western tip of the South Island, the twenty-six kilometre long sand spit creating this massive natural harbour also creates a vast nursery for a multitude of fish, in particular, yellowtail kingfish. With a bit of luck, I was hoping to cross paths with these speedsters on the sand flats with a fly rod.

As I travelled further north into the bay, crossing a few of the local streams on the way, I realised their watershed had escaped the worst of the rain. Being rainforest streams rather than free-stone braided rivers, they were still flowing quite clear. There was more rain anticipated for the north coast in the days ahead, but seeing these clear rivers, it was enough to get my hopes up.

ƒ⟩ ▲ ∝

On my first full day up there on the north coast, I went to investigate one of the rivers, only to be disappointed by limited access due to privately owned land. Property owners often weren't home, and when they were, they spoke of their riparian ownership and told me I wasn't allowed to cross their land. I quickly gave up on that particular river, and decided to hit the saltwater. Unlike the east coast of the USA, surely nobody had laid claim to the beach and intertidal zone, just yet . . .

Stretching out to sea a good three hundred metres or more, there were plenty of baitfish in the shallows across the flats, and there were also plenty of stingrays. It's these stingrays that the Golden Bay kingfish fly-fishery is based on. Hovering over the stingrays like fighter aircraft supporting a B52, the young kingfish feed on baitfish the rays disturb while cruising the flats. No doubt people have been aware of this behaviour for years, but that summer, the word was well and truly out. On the drive out towards the spit enclosing the bay, I spotted a number of fly anglers in various locations. The spit itself is a wildlife reserve, full of roosting birds and even wading anglers aren't allowed too close. Knowing very little about the fishery, I postulated that by fishing close to the reserve, I would increase my chances of encountering fish and rays that hadn't been cast at.

The rays were there in good numbers, but I only saw one or two truly big ones (the ones that the kingfish like to use for cover). I never did see any kingfish, or kahawai, a one to two-kilogram pelagic species of New Zealand's coastal waters. The wind and cold water eventually saw me returning to dry ground.

Hoping to camp near some freshwater for the night, and perhaps locate some trout before the forecasted rain hit, I drove down more dirt roads, into fern-filled rainforests, in search of another river.

The coastal roads in the north of the South Island can be ridiculously busy with tourists at times, and it was great to get off the beaten track. Unfortunately, by the time I reached the river, I discovered it to be flowing through rural grazing countryside; not exactly the untouched watercourse I was hoping to find. It was still a beautiful looking stream by its own right, and looked worthy of a fish.

ᶠ₁ ᴀ ∝

In many respects, this river reminded me of some of the rural rivers in Patagonia, so much so with its overhanging vegetation, that I risked fishing the unorthodox Chernobyl Ant again. It was all to no avail though; I didn't even see a fish here. I decided to dedicate the next two days to hopefully finding a kingfish on the flats.

There were perhaps half a dozen or more other fly anglers fishing various parts of the flats, and I got talking to an Irish fellow around my age. He claimed to have been fishing the area for a week, and had managed to catch two. Another local kiwi suggested the water was still too cold and there weren't enough big rays hanging around. I figured I wouldn't catch much on dry ground, so despite a forty-knot southerly blowing offshore virtually all day, I got out there.

I briefly saw a fish feeding in the shallows amongst the waves, but I couldn't be sure if it was a kingfish or kahawai. The kingfish are said to average around seventy-five centimetres in length, with the occasional fish exceeding a metre. The fish I briefly saw break the waves in pursuit of baitfish was in the lower end of this scale, there was every chance it had been a big kahawai and not a kingfish.

ᚠ ▲ ∝

Looking across the bay the following morning, the ocean was surprisingly composed. I decided to go where no one else seemed to be interested in fishing; it wasn't like anyone else was finding the kingfish, so I figured why not think outside the box a bit, with the lack of wind there were options aplenty?

I waded across quite a wide inlet to a long sand beach. It wasn't as shallow as the rest of the flats in Golden Bay, but I thought it was shallow enough for the rays to still be in the area. More importantly, there was a lot of bait here. For all I knew, the fact that the beach dropped away into slightly deeper water might have been a good thing. As I arrived on the scene, the bait schools started to fidget like a mass of twitching fingers, and then suddenly, they took flight as something attacked. I might be onto a good thing here, I thought.

Despite the obvious potential, my run of bad luck continued. Well, it was actually bad technique in this case; a lack of concentration, which might well have been attributed to a lack of belief. If you can't believe when there's bait coming under attack right in front of you, well, there's something wrong. So yes, this missed opportunity was entirely my fault. It wouldn't be the last for the summer.

My blue and white deceiver was halfway back through its retrieve, when I paused to rid some stripped line that was getting tangled around my feet. This brief pause in my retrieve resulted in a sudden take. I detected it clear as day between my thumb and forefinger in my rod hand, but with my stripping hand clearing loose line, and my concentration elsewhere, the fish got a taste of the fur, and kept right on going. Under normal circumstances, I would have struck with my stripping hand in an instance.

I got a brief glimpse of a silver fish as it veered out towards deeper water. At about seventy-five centimetres in length, it could have easily been the kingfish I was searching for. Had it been a kahawai, it still would have been a nice reward for my days of uncompensated toil.

That evening I went back to the flats for one last crack at a yellowtail kingfish on the fly. Having hiked out across the flats, I'd barely made a cast, when, as if on cue, the beautiful sunny weather suddenly turned as dark as the ace of spades. With the wind and drizzle stinging in from the south sideways, no one else was foolish enough to be out there.

With the wind whipping the surface, I managed to spot a medium sized ray that would have still covered an average-sized dinner table; it had a blue-and-white fly decorating one of its wings. As the popularity of this fishery grows, and sadly I'm sure it will, I can see the poor old rays having to dodge more and more flies being thrown at them. I stood there, cold, and alone, everyone else seeming to know something that I didn't. I wound in and decided to cut my losses, there would be no fly-caught fish for me from the north of the South Island that summer. Towards Greymouth on the west coast I would go.

ſ₁ ▲ ∝

After sleeping the night parked beside the Montueko River, I woke up and decided to see what I could find tucked under the semi-submerged willows lining the banks.

With the water substantially high, I realised that the fish, if there at all, were likely to be deep amongst the willows, safely enjoying the impenetrable cover and possibly an abundance of food; well out of reach from my flies.

After a week of so much rain, it took just a few hundred metres of swinging a streamer in towards the willows to realise that if trout were what I was after, then lake fishing was my only option. Pretty much the entire South Island was likely to be in the same water-sodden state, but over the next two days, the west coast would show me it could take things even a step further . . .

It rained cats and dogs! On my second day south of Greymouth, I checked the forecast and learnt that rain was a virtual certainty for another ten days straight. I hadn't come to New Zealand to sit around waiting for bad weather to clear, so I decided to cut my losses again.

Although I'd only really just arrived, I left the west coast behind me, and began crossing through the Southern Alps to the Central South Island Region, and back onto the Canterbury Plains.

3. CENTRAL SOUTH ISLAND

3

As I reached the summit of Haast Pass, New Zealand's southernmost road crossing the Alps, the fog miraculously thinned and as I started descending, the weather progressively cleared with every metre I dropped in elevation. Once down in the town of Wanaka, the sun was shining and it was a beautiful summer's day. With a bit of wind of course. The boats were out sailing and the blue water sparkled, it literally was a breath of fresh air. I hadn't caught a fish in over a week and I'd be lying if I said my morale wasn't low, but oh how good it was to see some clear skies!

Driving in a northerly direction, I had my sights set on Lake Benmore, the largest man-made lake in New Zealand. Able to hold one and a half times Wellington harbor when at full capacity, it's an impressive lake network. The headwaters for many of the rivers feeding this extensive dam system originate in low-lying hills and mountains across the plains. With a little bit of luck, I was hoping they might have dealt with the recent rain quicker than those fed from the Alps.

I was still a long way from the lake by nightfall and I ended up camping the night in a river valley flowing from the Alps anyway.

ʕ ʌ ⸿

It had been an ice-cold midnight wash on the edge of the raging river, and in daylight, it was obvious that the glacier silt choked river was flowing well above capacity. Some of the rivers in New Zealand are so low these days they're unable to support native galaxiid populations, let alone populations of trout. As a result, and as I had been discovering on the west coast, there was so much floodwater around that it was difficult to gauge what the rivers might have looked like under normal conditions – perhaps they were usually bone dry!

I suspected this river was comfortably able to support a trout population, but with the river grey in colour and raging, it would have been far from a comfortable fishing experience, and most likely counterproductive.

I was experiencing a classic case of Antipodean feast or famine, drought to flood in the blink of an eye. Contrasting weather events like this aren't too uncommon in New Zealand and Australia, and are arguably becoming more common the world over, but it has often seemed to me that a lot of water goes to waste in New Zealand. It's hard to find a rural pastoral property in Australia that isn't dotted with dams due to the often dry conditions, whereas in New Zealand's dry areas such as Canterbury and Otago (Where the water intensive 'Dairy Boom' has arguably been most focused), it appears they are less likely to sacrifice land for a hole in the ground to store water. Instead, more often than not, the nearest river is sacrificed – basically for free no less!

Fishing on the river I had woken up on was out of the question and I got back on the road, continuing towards Lake Benmore.

The far smaller stream I found near Lake Benmore was relatively clear, but it was still flowing all over the place, bursting its banks in places, and making life generally difficult. Grass and other debris lining nearby fences suggested it had recently been a lot worse.

I decided that lakes were my best option, especially if I could find bankside areas that had flooded and created shallow sloughs. Trout, particularly brown trout, love scouring flooded plains in search of food, and complete with willows and tussock grass creating a perfect setting, I found just the thing I was looking for

Right on time, a steady afternoon breeze was blowing by this stage, but beneath ancient willow trees lining the bank, there was a narrow strip of calm water. With my four-weight rod rigged up ready for the possibility of close quarters stalking, I was surprised to quickly spot a trout, inches from the low bank and sipping down incredibly small prey. Yes, you guessed it, so small I couldn't distinguish what it was. The rises resembled and sounded like nothing more than gentle kisses on the surface.

Considering the abundance of overhead willows, I assumed it was picking off willow grubs getting blown out of the trees, but as would become progressively clearer that summer, New Zealand's trout are often partial to tiny morsels of food: sandflies, midges, mosquitoes, you name it. When feeding on such miniscule prey, they often become even more selective – another quality that makes them such a challenge to catch.

Little interest was shown in my dry flies beneath the willows, and once I got out on the flats, I found more fish feeding on indistinguishable surface prey, and my struggle continued. There were a number of fish working an oil-calm wind lane off the corner of the lake, and I suspected they were picking off dead midges that had been flushed out of a nearby flooded slough, feeding into the lake. I threw a handful of patterns at these perplexing fish, but achieved little.

I was hoping to cover a reasonable amount of the lake before the end of the day, so I reverted to a small Matuka, aiming to imitate any trout fingerlings or galaxiids gambling with their life on the flats that afternoon. Forging ahead, wading across the flats, my mind started wandering; how long was it going to be before I finally caught a fish and broke my own, personal drought; I'd driven so far and caught so little . . . ?

As though telepathically channeling success, a backhand cast out wide finally connected with something firm. Finally! And boy did it feel good!

I went on to pick up two brown trout of about three-pounds; plucky, solid little fish that hit hard, and fought admirably prior to well-deserved releases. The little Matuka had finally proven its worth! A third fish angrily nipped at the Matuka for the last half of another retrieve, before eventually connecting. It launched into an instantaneous jump, and threw the fly just as quickly. It had taken some doing, but I had finally got onto some fish!

I happily went to sleep that night with plans of exploring further around the lake the following day. Little did I know; it would be early afternoon by the time I dragged myself away from the swampy slough next to my camp.

ᶠᵞ ▲ ∝

In no more than knee-deep water, some beautiful brown trout were cruising the shallows of the slough and a game of cat-and-mouse quickly ensued. Hiding amongst the bankside foliage, standing in the mud, sinking deeper and deeper, I tried fly after fly on the two or three finicky fish here. Once again, they were sipping down prey so small it may as well have been invisible. I fished the smallest flies in my arsenal, on the lightest tippet I had; four-pounds at that stage, but by day's end, I realised I would need to go even lighter with fish like this.

I came across another brown trout, right at the end of the shallows; in fact, there were possibly two fish here. Seeing that whatever they were taking appeared to be stuck in the surface film of water, I dug out a green-bodied Spotlight Parachute emerger. With a hackle feather fanned out around some white calf tail to create the 'parachute', the body of the fly hangs beneath this parachute, and resembles a nymph attempting to hatch into its moth form, and free itself from an aquatic nursery. I hadn't chosen the fly to necessarily match an emerging nymph of any kind, I'd actually selected it due to the fact that it was one of the smallest emergers I had, and because I thought the green nymph body might get mistaken by an unassuming trout as a willow grub floating on the surface. The fact that willow grubs fall into the water and usually sink quite quickly meant that I was hedging my bets to some extent, but sometimes, that's what it takes to fool a fish.

There also appeared to be a larger fish right in the corner under some willows where a trickling stream fed the slough. This fish was pretty much out of range from where I was crouched, but the other fish was confidently feeding in the open. In water that was well below knee-deep, it was covering quite a lengthy beat. Much of the surface prey it was finding was quite close to the bank – right in front of where I was hiding!

Casting my fly just a few metres from the grassy bank, it took a number of minutes for the fish to venture back into my ambush. In doing so, it started sipping down a number of the unidentified naturals. It reached my fly. And hungrily, continued filling its belly. I had no intention of letting my fly reach its gut, and with a swift strike; I planted it in the corner of its mouth. At last!

This is the moment all dry fly anglers love; the moment the unassuming fish feels the hook, and the calm water suddenly explodes like shattered glass. It had taken me well over half a day, but I'd finally hooked one.

At perhaps a touch over three-pounds, this fish turned out to be larger than I had expected and I quickly found myself getting in the water to keep it under control. Well, as best I could anyway. It first fled down the slough towards the lake and, as I suspected it might, it did it's best to get its head into the weed and fallen branches against the bank. The maximum pressure I dared exert on my four-pound tippet was enough to persuade it away from the danger, and once out in the open, we were back on equal terms.

Pursuing trout feeding in such shallow water, and in such close proximity, had made for an exciting morning of fishing. On two occasions, fish had even chased large nymphs or fingerlings right to my feet. I had contemplated trying a nymph, but it was the gentle and more regular surface rises that had captured my attention. And now, finally, it had paid off – assuming I could get the fish to the bank of course . . .

Releasing it was my intention, and naturally I kept it off the bank, securing it instead with my hands in the shallows, before safely removing the fly and sending it on its way. Now I could explore more of the lake finally.

I chose not to fish the flats that I'd covered the previous evening, but instead cut across open ground towards what looked to be another inflowing river. Boggy ground made for slow progress, and once at the river, the effects of the recent rain was obvious there too – it was far from a tranquil, babbling brook.

Despite the raging river, flooded backwaters on the flats near the mouth of the river proved to be another promising alternative. The water in these shallow pools was incredibly clear and the handful of fish in them were incredibly smart. It seemed there was nothing I could do to catch them, but just as the sun sank behind the mountains, I did away with the dry flies and tied on what I now viewed as my faithful little Matuka pattern. My intention was to give the lower fifty-metre stretch of river a fish, and then call it a day.

The afternoon breeze had been gentle that day; quite possibly my first day with barely any wind, and now, early in the evening, the lake and river shimmered like sheet glass. I was perhaps just thirty metres from where the river splurged out across muddy sand flats into the lake, when a solid trout found my Matuka to its liking – no doubt assuming it to be a misplaced trout fingerling or galaxiid – 'miles' from safety. At about four-pounds and in superb condition, this fish jumped all over the lower stretch of the river. There was no real structure that I could foresee causing me any troubles, and it was great to fight this fish off the reel, to let it run and dance at will, but thankfully secure it in the shallows for a successful catch and release. It had been a long and challenging day, and although I would have preferred to fool such a fish into sipping down one of my dry flies, subsurface prey was still likely to be on the menu, and it was a nice way to finish the day.

Listening to the weather forecast on the radio later that night, it sounded like showers were on their way – AGAIN! As had been predicted, Fiordland and the West Coast had already had rain.

ʃ ⅄ ∝

I knew the lack of wind had been too good to be true the day before, and it was back with vengeance come morning. Whistling through the willows overhead, their branches banging like slammed car doors, I lingered in my sleeping bag until well past my usual wake up time of seven-thirty. I had guessed that willow grubs were being fed on in the slough the day before, and had tied a few imitations the night before – surely the wind would have them raining down!

A tiny grub, barely longer than two match heads, green in colour with a dark greyish coloured head, willow grubs are easily imitated on a small hook. Dropping them on trout in a natural manner is not such an easy task, especially in shallow water, where fish only have a brief moment to intercept the fly before it hits the bottom. Happy to accept the challenge, I endeavoured to give it a go that day.

By the time I got on the water in my corner of the lake, I was pleasantly surprised by the protection I had from the wind. Adding to the protection from the wind, the willow trees also provided a little bit of cover to sneak up on the trout feeding in the shallows beneath.

I spotted a trout quite quickly, even before I got to the slough. I sat down to observe it while replacing the lower end of my leader, but by the time I had finished, the trout had disappeared; no doubt working further along the bank in search of food.

I continued towards the shallow slough, wondering if there would be enough water, it appeared to me that the lake had dropped a foot or so. Surely just one sunny windless day and an evening with no rain hadn't been enough for the lake to drop this much? Lake Benmore was the second in a series of three or four dams, so for all I knew, perhaps water had been released to generate power in one of the lower dams.

I got to the little cove and in barely half a foot of water, I found a beautiful brown trout. Sipping down the seemingly invisible dries, it was prowling the exact same area I had been locked in a standoff the previous morning.

As I had seen one of the larger fish doing the day before, I watched this fish charge into the shallows chasing some kind of prey, either small fish or an incredibly fast nymph, it was too fast for me to see. My guess was that it was finding fish that were straying too far from cover. Its behaviour had me debating whether or not I should actually cast my Matuka at it instead of a dry.

If I'm honest, I'd virtually accepted defeat before stepping into the water, the better half of the previous day had shown me how difficult these fish were to catch and now there was even less water. Opting for a newly tied willow grub, I finally plopped it down, barely three metres from my rod tip, just as the fish drew near. As I had supposed it might, the fly sunk far too quickly, and the fish instantly spooked. So much so it chose to exit the slough entirely! I stood there dejectedly watching its bow waves as though it were a departing ship.

This was the only fish I saw in the slough that morning; no doubt it was too shallow for them, but as I waded out onto the lake, which was also little more than knee-deep, I found a good number of fish cruising the shallows off the slough - gently sipping down dries.

Although the majority of these fish were adopting the usual covert approach to surface feeding, there was still the occasional maverick who chose to leap clear of the water in pursuit of its prey; some kind of emerging insect or perhaps regular terrestrial insects that were just touching down briefly: dragonflies, damsel flies, or even just regular flies . . . who knew . . . not me!

The more prevalent, delicate sips, that's what had me baffled. I wondered if they were feeding on spent shucks from some kind of insect that was hatching further up in the watershed; perhaps their spent exoskeletons had accumulated in the corner of the lake beneath the slough. But as I scanned the surface directly in front of me, I couldn't spot anything in great enough numbers to give away what it was eating. The fish were there in good numbers, some coming incredibly close to my feet before spooking. I tried a Red Tag for a little while due to the fact that I'd seen a beetle on the surface two days earlier, but I knew I was clutching at straws.

Eventually I gave up with the dry fly approach and tied on a nymph. I told myself that I would work my way up to a lone willow tree, a spindly specimen, somehow managing to survive on a tiny mound of dirt. Standing proudly on the crest of its castle, it was stranded by an otherwise endless moat.

I worked my way slowly towards this tree, speaking to the occasional fish here and there as they sipped down their meals without a care. The tone of my one-sided conversations weren't aggressive, instead, I found myself pleading with them. Yes . . . quite a pathetic scene, I know.

The fish must have taken my pleading as a sign of weakness and swam off to find an angler that offered them a real challenge, because by the time I neared the tree, their rises had all but vanished. Had I spooked them all? Or had the 'invisible hatch' gone down? Or, perhaps I was now too far away from the inflowing slough? I was yet to catch a fish on a nymph in a lake that summer. Unfortunately, it was proof of just how difficult the fishing had been. But perhaps I had also grown a little too fond of fishing my miniature Matuka patterns, which I was enjoying tying. They looked so good in the water, and had finally proven quite effective on Lake Benmore, so it was hard not to. In the shallow water that morning, I knew it would have been fouling in the weed too quickly, so instead, I had opted for an un-weighted black nymph.

With one of my last casts out towards the tree, I was almost surprised to feel the line suddenly snap tight in my fingers. There's not many fish species that reach maturity and continue feeding on tiny invertebrates the way trout do, and I suppose it was this that saw the birth of fly fishing so many hundreds of years ago. For me, this is the primary reason why I love casting flies for trout so much, catching big fish on tiny flies. This fish didn't jump like the two fish had the day before, but it definitely made quite a commotion on the surface at times. Searching for options, it tore up the shallows from left to right, directly in front of me. The age-old rule I guess . . . 'Don't jump into a shallow pool!'

A beautiful brown trout of a similar size to the ones I'd been spotting was the result. Covered in a myriad of black spots like a leopard, it was only when these fish moved that their camouflage let them down. 'Movement', of course being the primary concealment consideration when trying to hide. Five S's and an M as they say in the military, with the M for movement being the most important: shape, size, shine, silhouette, shadow, and movement.

Releasing this beautiful brown trout, I decided to call it quits on a high note, and drive to a few nearby rivers. Hopefully they weren't flowing too high, but if they were, I'd only scratched the surface of Lake Benmore's shoreline.

The first river I ventured to was one that I had fished late in the season ten years earlier. I had done quite well with rainbow trout on their spawn-run at that time, and I had been looking forward to returning to it. It wasn't far off dark when I finally arrived.

The water turned out to be a little high here too, but it was clear, and compared to the other rivers I'd been seeing under flood, this river might well have been the jewel in the South Island crown. I couldn't wait to wet a line the following morning and after another long day, I fell asleep as though bludgeoned.

ʕ ▲ ∝

In the morning light, the river looked quite different to ten years earlier. After the recent rains it was meandering its way across the relatively flat grassland in two or three streams, it seemed a far larger river to what I remembered. The sun was shining this morning and, although the wind was suspiciously absent, I rigged my six-weight under the assumption it would strengthen all too soon.

With the rainbow trout ten-years earlier, it had all been about indicator nymph fishing. So, hoping to cover both options, I rigged up with a Stimulator dry fly and a black, bead-headed nymph-dropper.

Eagerly stalking my way upstream through the largely dried-out spring flowers, it took no more than two pools before I spotted my first fish. Well, spooked my first fish, to be exact. I was fairly sure it had been a brown trout and there was no mistaking that it had been quite a nice fish, at about three to four-pounds, it was a good sign. I was clearly going to have to be a little more careful.

I covered another few pools without seeing very much, and then reached a long, relatively slow flowing pool. Like some of the other rivers I had fished that summer, this pool offering more water also meant more fish. Some of the fish here were dark in colour and quite an impressive size; almost to the point that I briefly thought they might be salmon. One thing was undeniable; the fish in this river were incredibly flighty; they had the uncanny ability to pick up my presence even when I was a considerable distance behind them, and not even in the water. They didn't appear to be overly voracious with their feeding either and throughout this day I went on to see no more than half a dozen rises. They certainly weren't very interested in my Stimulator dry fly and bead-headed nymph.

Like many of the rivers around Lake Benmore and the town of Twizel, the didymo in this particular stream was dreadful, easily the worst I had yet seen. Ten years earlier, the didymo had only been in the South Island waterways for a year or two, and hadn't yet plastered the bottom of most rivers, this one included. As I said, indicator nymph fishing had been my go-to technique; it had been deadly on the spawn-run rainbows! But with the 'rock-snot' now so thick, it wasn't a case of the nymph bouncing along the bottom and occasionally dragging the dry fly under if too shallow, it was a case of the nymph picking up too much of the gunk. It wouldn't always drag the dry fly under as a result, but it would take no more than two casts for the nymph to become coated and resemble nothing more than a chunk of the filthy crap floating downstream. Unless I wasted time repeatedly checking the nymph, I really was just wasting my time casting it. Of course this was all the more reason for the fish to be flighty. After what had been the first two months of the fishing season, there were well-trodden paths following the watercourses on this river; there were already more than enough reasons for the fish to be flighty. An old setline I found hanging from one of the willow branches was another.

By mid-afternoon, I'd had an absolute gutful of the didymo, and I did what I should have done first thing that morning – get rid of the nymph.

In an attempt to show the trout something different, I started out using an unorthodox emerging pattern, but after fishing this in just one pool, I changed to a blue Humpy, or as I like to call them, a blue-arsed blowfly.

I slowly worked my way along the pool I was on. Flowing at a perfect angle and lined with willows on the opposite bank, it was tailor-made for casting a dry fly, and incredibly, the afternoon breeze was just ten to fifteen knots; not thirty to forty. Even more extraordinary was the fact that it was blowing upstream for once. There was also a hedgerow of bushes along my side of the river, low enough to avoid my back-cast, but high enough for me to blend into and hopefully not be seen by the fish. It was on a cast across the pool that my blowfly imitation finally got the nod of approval from a fish. It didn't come about from the perfect rise I had been hoping for, though . . .

Taking a few steps further upstream as the fly swung out of its natural drift at the end of the run, my attention focused upstream, it was at that moment, just as the fly turned upstream at the end of its drift, that the brief moment of life-like movement triggered a solid four-pound brown to scoff it down. It obviously wasn't willing to let it get away! Just as quickly, this wild brown trout realised its mistake, and instantly flew skyward with fright.

With my rod pointing up over my right shoulder as I negotiated my footing on the slimy rocks, one of my stripping loops had somehow managed to get wrapped around my leg. I found myself helplessly stumbling forwards, tethered to the fish, as it charged downstream behind me, jumping at will. I had only just cleared the line, gained some kind of composure and turned around to face my quarry on more even terms, when everything came unstuck.

I retrieved the line, and was devastated to see the telltale curl of a failed knot at the end of my tippet. To be let down in such a manner, after such a long and trying day, was infuriating. Nevertheless, every cloud has a silver lining and I was excited to see that, to a degree, my plan had worked. The fish might not have risen to the fly in textbook fashion, but despite the lack of an actual hatch, this incident had proven that I could persuade them to the surface. It also suggested that it might pay to momentarily leave dry flies in the water after they've broken their natural downstream drift. I could clearly imagine the fish hesitantly following the fly downstream, suspiciously looking up at it the entire way, and then nailing it the second it skated sideways out of the current. This wouldn't be the only time this happened that summer.

At the head of the very next pool, my dry fly approach proved effective once more. Only this time, the fish rose to it mid-drift, its take clear to see. A brief moment was required for me to register what was happening, but thankfully I snapped back to my senses, just in time to strike.

Pinning this beautiful brown in the very tip of its top jaw, it wasted no time exploding from the head of the pool and bounding its way downstream in a series of jumps. I didn't make a mess of this encounter thankfully, and it wasn't long before I had it safely unhooked and swimming free.

I was enjoying the pace of flow in this stretch of water, and I decided I would hike upstream to it directly, the following morning.

One thing was sadly undeniable from this day of fishing – my indicator nymph fishing days on these didymo-affected rivers were done.

ꞌꞧ ᴀ ∝

The wind had remained fairly light through the previous day and, in retrospect, I probably should have fished my four-weight outfit instead of the six. However, as had happened a few days earlier after being blessed with a windless day, it had returned with vigour come morning. The sky was also overcast, and it was past nine o'clock by the time I'd had breakfast and found the motivation to get out on the river.

It definitely wasn't a day for Polaroiding, but having found the fish so flighty the day before, I fished ahead of myself, casting to locations that looked promising, long before I got too close. With my leader and tippet well over twenty feet, I presented the fly in a manner that would keep the fly line as far away from the fish as possible, often letting the wind blow the leader and fly the remaining distance.

Sitting at the tail end of pools, or in little backwaters at the head of pools, I saw a number of fish throughout that morning, all trying to conserve their energy it seemed. It had me wondering if the fish were flighty due to their instinct to get upstream and spawn in a month or two; were they already on high alert and cautious with their feeding? Brown trout usually spawn in what could be classified as late summer, and rainbow trout a month or so after that, in early winter. Due to the two fish I encountered in relatively quick succession the evening before, a part of me was expecting fireworks this day, but instead, I fished for two or three hours before anything showed interest in the blue-arsed-blowfly.

Just like the two fish the afternoon before, this fish picked up the fly in a riffle that was flowing quite fast. The long, slow flowing pools that were quite prevalent, looked ideal for dry fly fishing, but perhaps gave these flighty fish too much time to peruse the fly. The take snapped me back to my senses!

They say you need to wait a long time before striking when dry fly fishing in New Zealand! Personally, I don't know whether this is a valid argument or not, I would have thought every rise is unique and dependent on conditions, but I guess an adequate amount of time is definitely needed for a big fish when it's feeding slowly, in calm conditions, on small and easily disturbed insects like midges and sandflies; a phenomenon that is quite common it seemed. With so much distance between fish that were proving quite a challenge on this river, I think the delay in my strike was more a case of me losing my concentration rather than any form of personal angling prowess.

This fish gently rose up and deliberately took the fly, so discretely, that had I not been watching, it could have easily gone unnoticed. I did get around to striking and, thankfully, the hook found its mark in the top jaw of a beautiful hen.

She would have easily gone four-pounds, and she wasted no time taking off on a solid run; downstream towards rapids that would have proven problematic, had I not kept her short of them. She responded with an indignant jump, clearing the water by well over a metre. Slowly but surely, I worked her back upstream, but just like the fish had the afternoon before, a few jumps were held in reserve when the shallows stressed her further. Of all the pools I had fished that morning, the shingle bank I brought this fish to was perhaps the most user friendly of them all. It was then just a simple case of hook out in the shallows and, 'thanks for coming'.

By mid-afternoon, a steady northwesterly wind had swept in a threatening cloud formation from the Alps. They were the kind of dark, grumbling, thunder-filled summer clouds that had me thinking, hmm, I wonder if I should really be out here waving this nine-foot fly rod around? The wind built and built, until I decided enough was enough.

One dry fly hook-up counts for three or four on a wet fly to me, but with the wind now knifing downstream, and the end of the day looming, I figured it was as good a time as any to try swinging a streamer on my way back to camp.

Baitfish imitations are often at their most lethal late in the day, but the trout didn't suddenly start committing suicide that evening. The largely forgotten didymo suddenly became problematic again too. Even if kept off the bottom, the streamer still picked up the didymo from within the water column; it was a testing end to a trying day.

My first take came in quite fast water, again. The fish broke the surface, but the hook didn't hold. I fished on until raindrops started falling, and my lightning rod status began weighing heavier on my mind – it was well beyond time to call it quits for the day!

ʄ ∆ ∝

After the stormy evening, I was surprised to wake up to a beautiful sunny day. There was still a bit of breeze, but it was manageable. Two brand-new-looking four-wheel-drives drove past heading upstream while I was having breakfast that morning. I hadn't seen anybody over the previous two days, and I wondered if perhaps they knew something I didn't, maybe a little bit of local rain would get the fish feeding.

Seeing that it had proven effective a few times already, I persevered with the blowfly pattern, fishing upstream, covering water I had fished on the first day. With twenty-seven degrees Celsius predicted for the day, there were already a few flies around, it seemed like a good option. There had been plenty of caddis moths out during the night here, but other than the flies, insect activity during the day was virtually non-existent. Throughout the entire previous day, other than the one that took my fly, I hadn't seen a single fish rise.

As my third and final day fishing here progressed, I didn't see any fish feeding off the surface that day either – none other than two fish that rose to my fly – two fish which I felt momentarily, but failed to hook. My concentration was to blame once again.

The manner in which these two fish took the fly couldn't have been more different.

The first was in the pool where I had encountered a large number of fish on day one, and second-guessed some of them to be salmon. Having fished halfway through this pool, I was in the shallows on the opposite bank. The water was flowing quite fast and directly ahead of me, I spotted a fish of about three-pounds, weaving to-and-fro in an upstream direction as though searching for something to eat. Its camouflage was impeccable, but its movement had given it away. Having approached from directly behind the fish, I was forced to cast straight over it, as I dared not move. I knew the fly line would spook it, so I cut the cast short, and allowed the lengthy leader to fall over the top of the fish instead. Even this would have spooked some of the larger fish I suspect, but in this case, the fish's response indicated that it was aware of the fly, and willing to eat it. Despite the sunny weather, I hadn't seen a single fish rise all day, and standing in such close proximity to this little fish, with such a short cast, pretty much straight over it no less, I was almost shocked by its boldness – and I missed it. Even though it was only a three-pound fish, they were hard to come by, and after what had been another trying morning; I had a few not so quiet words with myself.

The other take was in a relatively deep, long, and slow flowing pool. It was the kind of pool where fish could get a good look at the fly and, after my experience in such pools on this river, I wasn't expecting any kind of success.

With a long cast across current and slightly upstream, I was forced to mend the line in order to keep a natural drift; even so, avoiding a large belly in the line was impossible. Despite the fly being a good twenty metres away as it drifted, I clearly saw quite a large fish take it. I struck within reasonable time and, conscious of the belly in my line, I ran in the opposite direction, doing my best to set the hook and keep in contact with the fish. It wasn't enough, unfortunately, and the fish easily ridded itself of the fly. Although I was almost ready to concede defeat by this stage, I glumly sorted out my line and continued plodding upstream.

With clear skies and visibility good that day, I went on to watch another three fish take long suspicious looks at my blowfly imitation: one in fairly deep water, one in the shallows against the bank, and another in the shallows at the tail end of a pool – all of them were too wise to be fooled into eating it.

Adversely to the introduced and invasive didymo, many rivers in New Zealand are home to a tiny native snail simply known as the New Zealand mud snail. This river I was fishing was one of them, and they were there in good numbers. Well, perhaps not good numbers. Not much larger than a grain of sand, the New Zealand mud snail has taken hold in North America since its first detection in 2001. Incredibly, it has a widespread invasive distribution across the globe, dating as far back as 1859 when it is believed to have reached Europe and the UK. It's even said to have reached rivers in Iraq, in 2008. The snail might not be much larger than a grain of sand, but under conditions that allow it to flourish, it can be extremely harmful to river and lake health. Reproducing asexually, it can produce offspring alone, in other words, it can clone itself – and quite rapidly too – one snail can result in well over thirty million snails in just one year. As I've already made clear, aquatic grasses and weed growth is the foundation of any ecosystem, and it's on this that these millions of snails feed, consequently outcompeting other native snails and various invertebrates; upon which higher order species such as fish feed. Most likely introduced to North America via anglers returning from fishing in New Zealand, it poses grave problems to waterways in the region. Unfortunately for New Zealand (and the northern hemisphere were the native range of didymo is rapidly spreading), this NZ native snail doesn't appear to eat the disgusting stuff – who could blame it?

During that last day on this challenging river in the Central South Island, on two separate occasions I encountered quite large individual trout in the shallows, their heads down and tails sticking out of the water as though flying a flag; I was certain that they were scrounging for these tiny snails. Was this their best strategy to keep well fed, or was food scarce and they were making the best of a bad thing?

With the second of these two fish I saw feeding like this ('tailing'), I changed my dry fly to the little Matuka; surely it would rather feed on small fish over snails, I reasoned. The fly landed a few metres beyond the fish and a similar distance to its side. With my heart in my mouth, I watched the bow waves as it confidently veered towards the fly to investigate. As appeared to be the story of the day, though, it was far too intelligent to indulge in a feed of feather and fur.

The time had come to leave this heavily trodden, didymo infested, river behind. Hopefully the decent weather would hold, and I could find some water further off everyone's radar.

I drove into the rapidly expanding town of Twizel, without a doubt the fishing epicentre of the Central South Island, if not the entire South Island some might say. Taking the limelight here are the massive rainbow trout in the hydro canals that fatten themselves on food falling through aquaculture pens. There are also many natural rivers and lakes in the area that are very popular. Twizel, for me, was a location to stock up on supplies and check the weather reports, before putting myself as far away from these heavily fished waters as I could.

Apart from the didymo, the local rivers in the area did look good, and I ended up having a dusk session on the Ohau River, one of the main rivers filling Benmore Dam. Before sundown, I only managed one missed take, on my little Matuka. Considering the time of day (the 'hunting hour'), on water that looked as good as it did, I had been expecting a lot more. I wasn't to be disheartened – the missed take was enough to inspire me to have a look further upstream the following morning.

f₃ ▲ ∝

Apart from the Didymo, which again saw me slipping all over the place, the river looked even better by day.

The bump I had detected on the fly the evening before had left me guessing: was that a small fish hitting the fly hard, or was it a big fish taking a tentative nip at the fly, was it a brown trout, was it a rainbow, or was it a salmon escapee from the fish farms on the canal? The outcome of my morning session suggested that I probably hadn't missed the fish of a lifetime.

Three little scrappers fell to the Matuka: two rainbows and a brown –I could only presume that heavy fishing pressure meant the larger fish were wise to my game.

Later that afternoon, I trooped out to the largest part of Lake Benmore. Being a Friday, I thought it would be a good place to get away from the weekend crowds. How wrong I was!

I quickly discovered the dirt road following the steep western shoreline doesn't have many lakeshore pullouts, and where there was, there were caravans, tents, campervans, boats, kitchen sinks . . . you name it...

I kept trucking on, thinking they would eventually stop, but they didn't. I was miles off the tarred road when I eventually found a space that was free. There were groups camping a few hundred metres away on either side of my clearing, but with a few old poplar trees standing nearby, and grass manicured by sheep and rabbits to golf green perfection, it was quite a nice spot to spend the night.

To make matters even better, and much to my surprise, when I went out for a fish that evening, I quickly spotted a few trout. In relatively Didymo-free gravel-lined bays, the occasional trout could be seen quite close to shore; working the shallows in search of nymphs I suspected. Some were also taking dries, and I was quickly fooled into changing my leader to target them. As though trying to break my spirit, the wind blew from all directions over the next few hours, and eventually I went back to the tried and tested Matuka. My evening meals of pasta, baked beans, and sardines were proving monotonous, and in the back of my mind I was hoping I could pick up one of these pan-sized trout for dinner. Deciding on which stretch of shore to fish in the variable wind was just as frustrating with the wet fly, but eventually it settled on the one direction, and I got onto a nice straight stretch of easily waded gravel and rock. After covering about thirty metres, with darkness setting in and showers of rain threatening, I was at the point of making one last cast, when an unfortunate brown made the untimely mistake of eating the little fish imitation. More than willing to show its colours, this three-pound fish paraded proudly. I didn't dare rush it to the bank, but when the time came, I wasted no time getting it on dry ground either, its chances of escape reduced to nought.

Walking back along the shoreline in the fading light, the fish in one hand and rod in the other, I was making my way around some willows in knee-deep water with random thoughts passing through my head at the end of the day; when, from a distance, I spotted a massive trout, casually cruising straight at me. My initial thought was that it was an eel, and a damn big one! That was until we ran headlong straight into each other.

It exploded out of the shallows towards deeper water, leaving me shakily standing my ground, stunned, and with mouth agape. This was by far the biggest trout I had yet seen that summer, easily over twelve-pounds. There was no reason why a fish couldn't have reached such magnitudes in Lake Benmore, it's the largest man-made lake in New Zealand and I would assume there's an adequate amount of food for them. Even so, I suspect this fish had reached this size in the dam's headwater canals, gorging itself on the aquaculture feed slipping through the fish-farm pens. It had most likely exited the canals and lower Ohau River into the lake. Fishing the canals is incredibly popular, but with such beautiful natural waterways in New Zealand (for now), I fail to see the attraction of fishing man-made canals, even if the fish are ridiculously big. Pursuing them in a lake (albeit a man-made one) was appealing, and as I sat by the lake eating the fish I had kept, I contemplated the possibility of fishing the flats into the dark the following evening. But with the number of people already on the lake that Friday afternoon, I suspected there would be even more arriving the following day. I was fairly sure I would be leaving come morning. Besides, in such a heavily fished area, a fish like this, although not uncatchable, it was the piscatorial version of Einstein, it would take quite a bit of luck and skill to catch such a fish, not to mention time. At least that's what I was telling myself.

ᶠ₁ ᴀ ∝

I woke to a tranquil lake, and although I planned to leave, I was still thinking I might have a quick fish across the flats in front of where I'd camped, for all I knew, the massive trout might still be out there; vulnerable due to a lack of sleep after hunting on the flats all night. I ate breakfast contemplating the possibility, but by the time I'd finished, the serenity across the lake had been torn to shreds by half a dozen ski boats, some of them launching right in front of me as I ate. I needed no further justification – it was time to leave!

Unbeknown to me, it was the Waitangi Day long weekend, a public holiday falling on the sixth of February, commemorating the signing of a treaty between the Maoris and British in Waitangi Bay, on the same day in 1840. At the initial signing there in the Bay of Islands off the north of the North Island, there were forty Maori chiefs who signed the document, however, over the next seven months, copies were carried around the country so other chiefs could also sign it, thus further endorsing rule over New Zealand to the British. That complete sovereignty was fully recognised three months later on the twenty-first of May 1840.

After breakfast on Lake Benmore that morning, with conditions calm and the ski boats out in full force, I was in dire need of relocation, and quickly. But where to go, surely there would be people everywhere, particularly with such a good weather forecast?

I decided to head to lake Tekapo and the town of the same name on its shores. With the number of rivers in the region, and the lake itself, I was relatively confident I could escape the crowds and still get onto some reasonable water.

Much like any small town in New Zealand and Australia, with the remotest hint of character, I was disappointed to see that during my ten-year absence, the Tekapo council had also decided to 'cash in' with an urban sprawl sell-off (or sellout depending on how you view things). The surrounding lake shoreline had gone under the hammer too. There were houses popping up like mole heads, new subdivisions, spreading as quickly as the plague, and just like Australia, the blocks of land (sections as the Kiwis call them), were getting smaller and smaller; 'postage stamp real-estate syndrome' – there wouldn't have been space for a lawn in which moles could have lived!

What exactly defines the nature of the beast I wonder (and it is a beast, it's as ugly as they come), do councils and developers think people want more affordable holiday homes, or is there a correlation to more profit when people are jammed in on top of each other? I wonder about the people who; decades ago, first bought property in these small villages; did they do so because they wanted homes, and/or holiday homes in over-developed tacky tourist destinations? I suspect the vast majority wanted a reasonable sized home in a comfortable rural village environment, a place with a yard for the children, or their grandchildren, to play in. Even if there was a percentage that did want a holiday home, I'm guessing that they also wanted it to be in a nice country town, not one full of tourist buses and a sprawling network of houses that stand empty for the majority of the year.

So, to all the developers and money-hungry councils of New Zealand, and the world for that matter, apart from lining your pockets with cash, what may I ask is the attraction with building on top of everything that is naturally beautiful? Or worse still, selling it to foreigners, so they can build on top of it? Nothing! That's right, the simple answer to a simple question is nothing, the ONLY attraction to building on top of beautiful natural scenery, is to satisfy overindulgent selfish people and to make money for developers and local councils (whose council members, in one way or another, are invariably in it for themselves). Creating jobs is NO excuse, if the council didn't allow these developments, these jobs would go to already overdeveloped areas – so PLEASE, stop creating new ones!

What's more important, money for a select few, or a beautiful landscape kept untouched for centuries to come? The children of 2090 aren't going to care how much money you died with – no one will.

With the uncontrolled excessive growth of the tourism industry in New Zealand, and the nation's expanding population, I struggled to get away from everyone here at Lake Tekapo, especially from the onslaught of Chinese tourists on holidays for the Chinese New Year.

Whether it's Germany, China, the UK, or even the USA, it amazes me that parts of the world are now so heavily populated that their national holidays at home result in other parts of the planet becoming crowded – when and where does it stop?

Call me a right-wing fascist, but if couples had a maximum of two children per couple (one for one), or perhaps three at the upper limit, I suspect our planet would be better off for it. The planet would be better off for it in my lifetime even! Of course the problem is that natural population growth in much of the Western World has slowed, it's in the developing world (Southeast Asia, Central Asia, India, the Middle-East, Africa, and elsewhere) that population growth is still too high for its means. It's too high for our planet's means! These areas often see a great deal of humanitarian issues as a result, and it also sees immigration demands (whether legal, or illegal) placed on parts of the West (primarily: Europe, North America, New Zealand, Australia). What I wonder for us in the West is this: when will our Western media discuss why birthrates are so high in these underdeveloped parts of the world, nations with socioeconomic inequity, nations torn apart by war, nations rife with corruption, and with gender inequality? Generalisations, I hear you say? Yes, they are, but there's no doubting birthrates are higher and population density is higher in these corners of the globe – that's a simple fact!

What I wonder, is this: when will our media, and the world come together and genuinely discuss the fact that women often have no choice in the matter of conception and childbirth in so many of these cultures? Women who are often hidden away, and deprived of an education and opportunity purely due to their gender! When will the media and the world acknowledge the fact that these women (even prior to being burdened with too many children to realistically support) are far less likely to have the opportunity to join the hordes of men looking for a new life, with dreams of more money and assumed prosperity, in the West? Supposed 'aid' companies benefit from overpopulation! Humanitarian crises are a Godsend to them, as are these women being forced to raise a ridiculous number of children, basically alone. That's another fact! After all, it means more malnourished children for our media to splash across our televisions at dinnertime – it means more donations – more MONEY!!!

These disasters bring more viewers, readers, and listeners to our media outlets, which in turn, also deliver higher profits to these billion-dollar companies (companies that are often equally corrupt!). What 'aid' companies are out there actually tackling the underlying problem of overpopulation? Sure, keeping the masses of destitute people alive through drought and war is admirable, but these masses discarded by governments that couldn't care less wouldn't be a MASS, if education and social awareness kept populations at a manageable and sustainable number in the first place. How are our Western governments trying to deal with the issue, if at all they are?

Education is key! If you've read my West Africa book, you might have been as surprised as I was by the encounters I had with young men, far younger than I, who maturely told me they weren't going to have more than two children. "I can't afford it," they said. In a world where more children, more cattle, and new, shinier 'things', equals prestige and respect, I was taken by surprise by these comments. But even more so, I was impressed! Impressed by their awareness, their common sense and their maturity, their educated and conscious outlook on life. Without realising it, it probably made them more globally aware than the corrupt, black Mercedes driving 'big man' leading their country. Or preying on it, again, it depends on how you look at things.

Awareness, common sense, education, knowledge; whether it's a kiwi dairy farmer sucking a river dry and filling the water table with nitrogen because that's what everyone else is doing, or whether it's ageing Australian politicians suggesting we build more dams on already struggling rivers because that's the kind of action that secured votes a hundred years ago, or, if it's a woman mustering cattle on horseback after being brought up on the land, or, if it's these young men in Sierra Leone with good parents, teachers, and community actively showing them that there's more than one way to live their lives, people's ACTIONS are always based on EXPOSURE! Instead of coming in and feeding the masses and filming the flies in the mouths of babies born in humanitarian disaster zones, perhaps it's up to us in the West to help show these nations and cultures with unsustainable birthrates that there is another way – that our planet NEEDS there to be another way!

I've discussed the threat overpopulation poses to our planet quite extensively in my two African books, which, despite me thinking they're the most interesting and diverse of my books, don't sell anywhere near as well as my books from other parts of the world. I could write multiple books on what might help to limit population growth in these overpopulated, relatively uneducated, and almost always corrupt parts of the world, but for now we're in New Zealand, looking to avoid the crowds, and simply find some fish, perhaps our Western governments and Western media will get around to addressing the underdeveloped world's family planning issues (or lack of) another time. If you can find an 'aid' company that genuinely does, I'd love to hear about it. Yes, religious beliefs are likely to get in the way I know, but can't an attempt at least be made to educate people on their options?

Here's an idea that just came to me: 'doctors without borders', good for you, you do an admirable job in some rugged scenarios and have sadly paid the price at times, but from my research it would seem that there's never much focus in your mission statements about family planning. In other words, getting there *before* things become unmanageable. Family planning, or at the very least basic female human rights, should be at the forefront of your propaganda regime. So how about Vasectomies Without Borders? Look closely at that idea, it's not as crazy as you might think, with effective education programs the men might even think it's a good idea. In the long run though, it would mean less patients for doctors without borders, and it might mean less donations and less money, but who benefits? The people, that's who, and most definitely the women! That's the goal is it not, help the people in need?

Anyway, I digress again; let's get back to the fishing . . .

Poking around the shores of Lake Tekapo, I eventually managed to avoid the pockets of people flocking together, and I found a stretch of shoreline all to myself. There was nobody for miles, boy did it smell good!

I first ventured out on a long river-stone spit; it stretched out into the brilliant blue water as though it were a man-made harbour.

Quickly spotting what I thought to be a brown trout in the first twenty metres, it adamantly rejected my Matuka and unflappably continued cruising the shoreline.

I then took advantage of the offshore breeze and open spaces, hurling my entire fly line out into deep water on long casts, working my way along the spit to its very end. I did see another fish at about the halfway point, but it seemed nothing saw my fly. Or at the very least, nothing saw it as a possible meal.

The wind was frequently changing direction; giving me the run-around like it so often does in New Zealand, before I eventually got onto a long shingle beach. Setting out to walk its length, I would then fish my way back with the wind behind me.

With the sun low in the sky, I traversed the beach from a distance, keeping my shadow off the water. I'd only progressed perhaps thirty metres when I spotted a behemoth-sized trout in the wave-wash, no more than a metre from shore. This thing was huge, easily as big as the fish I had spotted the night before, and without doubt, another very smart customer. It was so big, that for a brief moment, my usual, 'is it a salmon?' speculation passed through my mind. I watched it offhandedly prowling along the drop-off and then doubled around ahead of it. Get in a suitable position to make a cast, I told myself, let it come to you.

Now this fish was likely to have been well over ten-years old, it had most likely seen more than its fair share of anglers fishing off its beach, not to mention being bombarded by the boats that troll the lake. As such, halfway through my first retrieve, I wasn't too surprised when it disappeared like a puff of smoke.

Earlier that day, out on the spit, with the clean weed-free shoreline and sediment looking somewhat sterile, I had dug amongst the gravel to see if I could find some nymphs and work out what the fish might be feeding on. My excavations had revealed very little, but judging by the panic-stricken exodus this massive fish had made, even my size six Matuka was too big. Unlike the sea-run trout I encountered in my Patagonia book and film, there's no way you can hurl massive streamers at these fish in New Zealand. It's almost like these big trout in New Zealand feed on such small prey as a means of self-preservation, a kind of defence mechanism – it's definitely an effective adaptation for them.

I couldn't pull a rabbit out of the hat on dark that evening, but regardless of my inability to snare a fish, I felt privileged to have seen such a beautiful fish – a massive thing!

f₇ ▲ ∝

Another sunny day greeted me and again it was perfect water-skiing conditions on the lake. Thankfully there were just two boats trolling off my stretch of shore. There was still the occasional boat and Jet Ski that roared past at full throttle; it really was a dastardly shame that these windless sunny days had fallen on a long weekend. There I was choking on motorboat fumes, casting nymphs on a busy lake simply because I didn't want to risk hiking to backcountry rivers only to find people already there.

Yes, New Zealand's 'clean-and-green' marketing ploy is questionable at times – the number of light aircraft and helicopters flying towards the Alps suggested the airspace over Mount Cook would have given London's Heathrow Airport a run for its money . . .

I fished some flooded shallows for an hour or so with a nymph, but apart from an unidentifiable juvenile trout or salmon that I briefly hooked, I saw very little indeed. Having kept an eye on the two boats trolling, it looked like they weren't experiencing a whole lot of success either.

Continuing along the shoreline to the beginning of the spit, again I saw a trout of about three-pounds feeding in the shallows. Unfortunately, it showed as little interest in the nymph as the fish had to my Matuka the day before. Was it the same fish, it was a similar size and in the same area?

With the entire lake so incredibly calm, there were slicks of scum on the surface in places, the kind of wind lane slicks where you might find trout feeding off the surface. The insects were there for the taking, I could see them, but incredibly, I didn't see a worthy rise all day.

It was only as the sun was creeping behind the mountains to the west, and I was a good five kilometres or more further along the lake in that direction, that I finally hooked a fish.

It had been an incredibly long day, quite hot even, and as I waded across some shallows towards the mouth of an inflowing stream fishing a nymph in slow motion, I knew it was my time. Trout would be moving in for an evening meal and I knew it.

With a cast across the shallows to my left, the line drew tight at the extremity of the cast. I could make out a few melon-sized rocks in the area, and it took me a moment to realise it was a fish and not the bottom. I thought I deserved a fish by this stage but, incredibly, it took just seconds for this fish to wrap my tippet around one of these rocks and earn its freedom. Equally unbelievable was the fact that this was the first 'bust-off' I'd had in six-weeks – it was testimony to how hard the fishing had been.

I persisted near this inflowing stream for another half dozen casts, when a poorly conditioned rainbow trout finally helped me get on the scoreboard. It wasn't a beautiful wild brown trout like I had hoped, but after two days of fishing, this axe handle of a fish at least helped me get on the books.

It was also a good point in the day to say enough was enough, and I turned back, planning to hit the road and truck on into the evening towards some rivers. With the long weekend finished, I was hoping the crowds might have dispersed.

As always seems to be the case in much of New Zealand, the majority of the land along these tributaries belonged to a couple of stations. In this case they were running cattle and red deer. It was dark by the time I reached a clearing near one of the rivers, and as I jumped out to fetch some water, I met a mountain-bike rider that had been camped there over the weekend. "Was it busy here over the long weekend?" I asked him.

"Oh hell yeah! There was everything from four-wheel-drives to horse floats jammed in here!"

I could only hope that there hadn't been many anglers making up the numbers. I wasn't going to kid myself though, and unfortunately, I already had low expectations for the fishing ahead. Even that evening, a number of four-wheel-drives crossed the river and continued upstream on the braided rivers.

Around ten o'clock, another four-wheel-drive stopped at the river crossing, and in the dark, the driver started throwing pebbles into the river to see how deep it was. Not too sure how that works, particularly in the dark, but I'm fairly sure it was the intention. It was a Chinese family and it turned out they were trying to reach Queenstown. Considering they were thirty kilometres down a dirt road and heading west, I suspect their GPS may have had a few issues. Maybe, just maybe, they were a little too dependent on it. Pointing them in the right direction, they turned around and didn't continue driving into the middle of the Alps.

ʳ₃ ▲ ∝

The weather forecast was predicting rain for the afternoon of my first day here, so I decided to fish upstream on the smaller of the two rivers where I had parked. I would explore the larger river the following day.

Not only were these rivers likely to have been flogged over the long weekend, I also suspected that the larger river might be used by a lot of guides in the region, both by helicopter and four-wheel-drives. I was banking on the slight chance that the smaller river had slipped under everyone's radar. Or was that just wishful thinking?

I had only gone perhaps twenty metres upstream when I spotted a trout, quite a decent one too, easily four-pounds, if not bigger. The current was strong and this fish was sitting just off the side of the main flow, but still in quite fast water. Unless it was on the move, it was quite a strange position to be holding. Suspecting much of the river to be flowing fast like this, I had tied up a fresh batch of small Matukas the night before, but had added extra weight. I gave this fish a wide birth and fished back down through the run, swinging one of these heavier flies. As I suspected might be the case, this fish had been well aware of me gawking at it – the very sight of me putting it off its food.

Continuing upstream, it wasn't long before I was following a small side-stream, which hugged the right-hand side of the valley. In the gentler flow, it was at the tail end of a pool that I found my next fish. Dark in colour, had it not been sitting in such an obvious position for a trout, I might have easily mistaken it for a rock or log, and walked straight past.

I did walk past, but from a safe distance. I was certain my little minnow pattern was the perfect breakfast for this fish to start the day with – or so I hoped.

I debated fishing the pool from the very top, but thought if I hooked a small fish it would spook the larger one, so I went in halfway, and nervously fished down towards my primary quarry. I made perhaps two or three casts. Each cast would have seen my fly swim out of deep water into the shallows, right in front of the fish. A fish that was easily close to the magical ten-pound mark.

The savage take that I was hoping for was as elusive as a rural water tariff. As I passed the position where the fish had been, it was nowhere to be seen. As I said, flogged! In the water's defence, perhaps the dry fly approach wouldn't have unsettled it quite so much – or is that more wishful thinking I wonder?

Turning around and continuing on my upstream scout, the water flow slowed to the point that I decided to re-rig with a large Royal Wolf and nymph-dropper. It was at perhaps the second pool I fished with this rig, when it suddenly proved effective.

To my surprise, it wasn't in one of the long perfect looking pools where I found success. Instead, it was an awkward, doglegged pool, with a short window of opportunity, where I finally hooked the fish I was searching for.

On my third cast, just below the dogleg where the water rushed into the pool, a flash of silver caught me by surprise. A solid rainbow trout! It darted out from against the bank and grabbed the dry fly. There was no mistaking the take, or the hook-up. I was so confident; I even chuckled to myself at this fish's brazen disregard for its own safety.

"Ha-ha. Hello there," I said out loud.

I was suddenly in a state of disbelief, looking downstream I could still see my van, and there I was, playing tug-of-war with a long-jawed silver rainbow of about three-pounds.

This fish could have easily blasted downstream out of the pool and had me in a world of strife, but instead it defiantly danced around its home pool as though spitefully refusing an eviction notice. I had no intention of displacing it entirely, and once I'd successfully subdued its antics and removed the hook, it was sent straight back from whence it had come.

Interestingly, this fish looked a lot like the rainbow I had caught in the lake the evening before. Virtually pure silver in colour, it almost looked like a cross between a rainbow and a chinook salmon. It also looked a little under-conditioned, thin, and lacking the vibrant colours of the rainbows I had been encountering elsewhere.

I encountered another two big fish that afternoon. Both of them sitting in still water right on the edge of the river, and both of them trying to hide under overhanging foliage, reticently seeking concealment as though caught stark-naked. None of these bigger fish seemed to be feeding; it was as though they were sleeping, nursing a hangover after a big night. Or perhaps getting over a big long weekend, I wondered. Were they shaking off a catch and release encounter? Or, maybe they were just trying to shake off all the attention they'd been getting. Then again – older and wiser – maybe they fed at nighttime and hid during the day.

Even though the river started to thin out the further I went, and I even stopped spotting fish, I hiked on regardless; the scenery was too spectacular not to. The mountains progressively towered over me the further I went, their snow-caps growing in size as though threatening to come crashing down. Eventually I had to turn back . . .

I found the big dark coloured fish back in its preferred spot in the lower end of the same pool, and now, still with the dry fly and nymph-dropper, I stalked into a casting position from downstream.

Back-casting from against some bushes on the opposite bank, I tried my luck again.

I made just four casts, and probably should have changed flies in order to work out what it was feeding on, or to simply tempt it into taking something different. But in all honesty, after seeing the sleepy almost shell-shocked nature of the fish that day, I suspect I could have thrown a handful of worms at it and still got no response. If I sound pessimistic, it's probably because I was.

The following day I would hike upstream on the larger of the two rivers. I had even higher hopes of finding success there, and I should have been excited about the possibilities. Unfortunately, though, the foremost thought on my mind wasn't the fishing, it was a question of how many people I would find there?

ʕ ▲ ∝

The sun was shining as I cut out across the expansive valley floor of the larger river, and eventually I reached the main channel. Like most, if not all of these braided glacier-fed rivers of New Zealand, it was like a watercourse of dirty milk. This doesn't necessarily mean there were no fish, but I certainly wouldn't be spotting them.

As I continued upstream along the bank, scanning the slightly clearer margins on the very edge, I was hoping to find snow and spring fed tributaries coming off the mountainous valley walls. If these streams existed at all, they would be flowing clear and, if large enough, I knew the trout would prefer them.

The first clear tributary I came to was extremely small, but where it reached the main river channel it created a clearer mixing point – a favourable spot to be keeping your gills clear of silt, and if you were the alpha fish on this stretch of river, a favourable locale to be spotting an easy meal.

In typical fashion, it wasn't going to be easy getting a clean drift with my flies but, not expecting too much, I had a go anyway. The blue Humpy and nymph drifted the length of the clearer water reasonably well, but just as the current got too strong and the dry was beginning to submerge, a rainbow swooped out of the silt cloud like a spitfire descending on a stricken bomber. A similar size to the previous day's capture, this fish appeared to be on a one-way train to annihilating the dry fly, but realising its mistake at the last minute, it aborted its headlong charge and slipped back beneath the safety of the discoloured water. "Well, they're here," I said to myself, nonplussed.

I ended up finding a larger spring-fed stream even before I reached it. I had decided to beeline straight across an expansive stretch of valley floor which, from a distance, didn't appear to have any river braids flowing across it at all. However, spying the number of smaller valleys chiselled into the side of the mountain looming over this side of the river, I knew otherwise; given time, I'd have to bisect a stream eventually.

All this reading of the terrain aside, it was the materialisation of a four-wheel-drive sitting like a wart on the valley floor, which eventually let me know I was on the right path. As I continued hiking, two men also materialised near the vehicle. I held hope that they were casting chunks of metal into the soup for salmon. But, unfortunately, I realised I was kidding myself; I knew it was likely to be a guide and client chasing trout.

I kept trekking on the same route. I figured that I had just as much right to be out there as anyone. Hell, I'd walked there!

Hitting the tributary on a beautiful pool perhaps half a kilometre upstream from them, I quickly spotted a dark coloured fish, conspicuously sitting over a patch of sand. The slower water on the inside bend at the head of the pool might have been helping it conserve energy and deliver food, but it wasn't doing its concealment any favours.

However, this fish might have been smarter than I gave it credit for as, once again, it was in a location that made it virtually impossible to present flies to with the all-important natural drift. Fishing the long leader as I do, it can help to allow the flies to work out their own natural drift, but in doing so, it also means that you end up with a lot of slack line. If by chance you do manage to fool the fish, it's often even harder to effectively set the hook – much like the problem I experienced a week earlier on the didymo riddled river where I'd missed the fish on my last day.

I made three fruitless casts at this fish, before tiptoeing out of the pool and leaving it to its own devices. Perhaps the guys following in my footsteps would have better luck with it.

The next fish I found was behaving in a similar manner to the three big fish I had seen the day before. In no more than knee-deep water, it was sitting barely a foot from dry ground. Much like the fish the day before, it also appeared not to be feeding; it sat motionless, almost as if it were asleep. Did they wait out the brightest part of the day, take a siesta and feed later, I wondered? Too bad if this were the case, I was definitely going to try coaxing it into a meal.

I crept out midstream from behind the fish, maneuvering into a position where I could avoid casting over the top of it, presenting the fly above it on an angle instead. The strengthening wind drifting up the valley would also be easier dealt with from midstream. Considering how shallow the water was, I did away with the nymph-dropper, but stuck with the blowfly imitation.

My first cast drifted just to the side of the fish and was ignored, but on my second cast, with the dry fly sitting upright and clearly visible, it floated straight over the top of it. I couldn't believe what happened next!

As though waking up and groggily rolling out of bed after a big night, this dark-coloured fish swivelled around, and I clearly saw its beaked snout open. Oh so languidly, it made a half-hearted lunge at the fly. I could have sworn I saw the fly drift straight through the gap between its jaws. But much like your hung-over mate who won't get off the couch and go to the store for milk, this fish wasn't about to chase it downstream.

I couldn't understand what the situation was with the larger fish in these two rivers, none of them seemed to be feeding; were they all nursing sore jaws after an onslaught of long weekend anglers, or was it still too cold for them perhaps? Surely not! One thing was certain – they weren't making my life easy!

I spotted a few more fish as I made my way upstream, and it wasn't long before the two men with the four-wheel-drive drove around me and pushed further ahead. I planned to turn around within the hour, so I wasn't too concerned about them covering water ahead of me. It was over ten kilometres back to my camp!

I fished just two more pools, and with another fish showing no interest in my fly in the last of these, I dejectedly decided that enough was enough. In the distance, I could see that the men in the four-wheel-drive had already done the same. The afternoon breeze had clocked around by this stage, and was coming off the Alps at quite a pace; I planned to make the most of my walk back by swinging a Matuka through likely looking pools along the way. Some might say this isn't the kind of tactic a purist fly angler would adopt, but there were plenty of bullies and fingerlings in the shallows, that were sure to be on the menu at some stage – particularly late in the day, as it was.

I actually felt like I might now have the upper hand, but with the fish continuing in their defiance, it clearly wasn't the case. I guess they had only seen me a few hours earlier – they weren't stupid – or were they?

Reaching the pool where I had spotted my first fish, it was now nowhere to be seen. Nonetheless, on my second cast, I found it . . .

It was an aggressive take, and expecting a long hard run, I tentatively backed off my drag. The downstream freight train run never eventuated, but it did perform four or five consecutive jumps, virtually on the spot. Thankfully the hook held. After such a long time on the water that day, I didn't want to blow my one and only chance. Eventually securing it by hand in the shallows, I was surprised to discover it was a rainbow. It was in a similar condition to the rainbow I'd caught the day before, and on Lake Tekapo. Weighing perhaps four-pounds, this fish was the largest, but it still appeared to be relatively lean, lacking the vivid colours of a well-conditioned rainbow. All the same, it felt good to have at least picked up one fish per day while in the area.

I fished right through to where this clear stream reached the silted river, but I didn't see another fish.

On the remainder of the long walk back to camp, dodging thousands of dollars' worth of stock fences washed into the river, I decided I would travel to another river the following day. I was hoping I might find some brown trout, as until then, they had appeared relatively scarce in the majority of rivers I had fished. It was dark by the time I got back to my camp, and after a late evening meal and some journaling until after midnight, I fell asleep, dog-tired, but excited about getting to some new water the following day.

ʿ؛ ᴧ ∝

After a day at the wheel, it was late by the time I reached the upstream spot on the river from which I planned to spend two days hiking out, and fishing. I would hike upstream the following day, and downstream the next downstream. There was, however, still light enough left in the day to find out what the river had on offer; the sun seemingly balanced on the rim of the valley's western wall, soon to fall out of sight until the new day.

With the weighted Matuka still on my six-weight from the previous day, I swung it out of the current at the head of a pool, just below where I had parked beside a little tributary. I received a tap to the fly on my second and third cast. Positive signs, but as always, these were the kind of inquiries that left me guessing: had that been a large trout tentatively snapping at the fly, or had it been one of a number of juvenile trout, or even the fly swinging through a school of salmon, their focus on breeding and nothing else? Incredibly, I then fished downstream through perfect looking water for a kilometre or more, and couldn't find a fish for the life of me. Even so, it was spectacular countryside, the water as clear as polished glass, free of didymo, and it seemed there were fish there to be caught, if I could find them — the following day couldn't come fast enough . . .

ƒ ∆ ∝

It was a bit of a grey and gloomy day as I walked down to the edge of the river, there was a breeze blowing, but it was yet to get unreasonably strong. I took a look at a couple of rocks I had put in the shallows to gauge what the river level did overnight, and it appeared it had possibly dropped a touch.

I tiptoed upstream along a smaller, outside braid of the river, hoping it might offer similar brook styled qualities that the rainbows had preferred on the previous two days. I was still out on the river flats and quite a way from the green foliage lining the base of the mountains, when I spotted my first fish.

Being an overcast day with wind rippling the surface, it was by no means an easy day for spotting fish. Despite the added challenges, there was no doubting that the dark shadow I had spotted was a fish. Sitting in a narrow stretch of water not flowing too fast, but fast enough to deliver it food, it was right where a trout should be. Judging by its position relatively close to the bottom, in water around waist-deep, I presumed it to be feeding on nymphs.

I did away with the wet fly from the evening before, tied on a blue Humpy and attached a brown bead-headed nymph-dropper. Even though it was overcast and somewhat cool, I had already noticed an abundance of flies on the river stones and shingle that morning. Before my grandmother's vision began to fail her, she hadn't lived in

Canterbury with a flyswatter close at hand for nothing – I suspected that imitating the flies would be a safe bet.

Aware of the wind coming down the valley and the fact that my leader would be blown downstream from the fly line while casting, I knew I needed to cast quite a good distance upstream from the fish. I crept in . . . knelt down . . . and made the cast.

The black-and-white fly was almost easier to spot on the grey water than if the river were bathed in sunshine. I picked it up quickly and watched it bearing down on the fish, excitement and anticipation coursing through my veins as I waited for the nymph to be taken, and the dry fly pulled under. This, however, wasn't how proceedings unfolded.

My blowfly pattern zeroed in on the dull coloured fish shape, and I watched in disbelief as the smudge of darkness materialised into a fish rising to the surface. Moving in slow motion as though swimming through jelly, its pointed snout cleared the water as it rolled on the surface, leaving the jelly bowl undisturbed and my dry fly suddenly nowhere to be seen.

I struck just as gently, but with a firmness that ensured there was no mistaking a clean hook-up.

"Well, I didn't expect that," I said to myself; standing up with my four-weight rod held high, but bent low.

Rapids in the lower end of the pool threatened at just a short distance, but with my knots pushed to the limit, I persuaded the fish to stay above them. There was little I could do to prevent it from jumping, however, and as though throwing a tantrum after being denied downstream passage, it quickly turned to this tactic; launching into three consecutive jumps. But there was no shaking the hook; this fish had been so focussed on its morning meal that I ended up having to remove the fly from the back of its throat – the kind of deliberate and confident take that every fly angler dreams of.

Releasing this fish, I continued upstream. I hadn't gone much further, when I spotted a fish take a natural of some kind off the surface. This fish was sitting halfway along one of those gravel barrages that leak multiple rivulets like a line of checkouts at the supermarket, which one will serve you best, you're left wondering.

I fed my fly down a few of the rivulets, but I never did see that fish again. It's often the way.

Seeing that the dry fly had been given the nod of approval over the nymph with the previous fish, I did away with the problematic dropper. I was more than happy to put all my eggs in the one basket, and rely on the dry fly alone.

Eventually I ended up against trees, at the base of the mountains. Here I found a string of tranquil pools, bubbling their way through scenic tussock grass countryside, so beautiful that it should be a crime to destroy. A trout of about three-pounds was busily patrolling the lower end of the first pool, but just as a plan of attack was hatching in my head, I spotted another, possibly larger fish, just a little further up the pool. Decisions, decisions . . .

Both these fish were quite mobile, moving about the pool freely, and clearly well aware of each other's presence. Crawling along the bank as though pleading with them, I offered a number of different flies to each of these fish, but they wanted little to do with what I had on offer, or with me. It's interesting in life how having too many options can sometimes result in a betrayal of one's self.

There was no doubting that these fish had seen more than their share of flies over the years. There was a two-lane highway through the grass along the bank of these pools; one for the guide, and one for the client I presumed. Clearly flogged on a regular basis, I wasn't too bothered about leaving these otherwise beautiful pools behind.

Eventually I got back onto the riverbed proper, and much to my surprise, I quickly spotted another fish. At about four to five-pounds, this was a similar sized fish to the one I'd caught and released earlier that day, perhaps even a touch bigger. Sitting right at the base of a metre-high bank in a narrow slot of quite fast flowing water, it was miraculously somehow able to limit its effort while still holding its ground. Like the previous fish I had caught that day, it was sitting in a channel with uniform flow, something that had been such a rarity on the rivers I'd been fishing until then. Other than the fact that the stream was quite narrow and the wind still blowing downstream, it made for a relatively easy presentation.

I moved into position, just behind the fish and off its left flank. I made the cast upstream on an acute angle, letting a good amount of fly line land on the gravel bank in front of me so as to keep it clear of the fish. The fly landed adequately and fast stripping was required to keep up with it. Much to my surprise, again, the fish went up for the fly, quite quickly this time, and I struck. I felt the fly make contact with the fish's mouth . . . but oh so briefly.

"Ah, damn it!" I said out loud.

I decided it was time for some lunch, so I sat down pretty much on the spot and ate, able to keep an eye on the fish, and hopefully let it settle.

The entire time I sat there, eating my triple slice peanut butter and strawberry jam sandwich, I didn't see the fish move once. I decided to show it something different, and changed to a Royal Wolf dry fly.

Again the fish made a fast lunge for the fly as it zipped past. I instinctively struck, only this time I got nothing but air. I cast again, and the exact same thing happened. It was time to question what was happening. Was it hesitating at the last second and aborting the rise, or was I pulling the fly out of its mouth and not giving it enough time? To be honest, I had no idea!

I decided to go back to the blowfly pattern and add a nymph-dropper. I was certain it would pick up the nymph in this kind of water; after all, it wasn't rising to anything other than the dries I was throwing at it, perhaps it was actually picking up nymphs.

I made the cast, but the nymph briefly got hung up on the bank. It sorted itself out eventually, and fell in the water, but I could see that the dry fly was slightly submerged. I mended the line and stripped frantically; my eyes glued to the white indicator wings of the blow fly imitation as I vehemently willed it to get pulled under the surface. Surprisingly, the outcome was quite the contrary . . .

Seemingly aggravated by repetitively missing its prey, the trout pivoted on the spot as though dancing around a boxing opponent, and with a lightning fast left jab, it pounced on the dry fly, milliseconds after it had passed. All hell broke loose!

Tumbling upstream across the surface, the rainbow exploded from its narrow channel. Sensing it was boxed into a corner, it quickly aborted that angle of retreat, spun on the spot again, and powered downstream in the fast water – I jumped the ropes and frantically ran after it.

On its brief upstream run to the head of the channel, I had seen another fish come out from the undercut bank, perhaps even larger. That was the last thing on my mind, though. By the end of this downstream chase with my rod held high in order to keep clear of the remaining flood debris, I had negotiated multiple pools and rapids, and was well over fifty metres downstream. It was a run that deserved the fish its freedom, but somehow, luck was on my side.

In the slower water at the lower end of one of these pools, well and truly out of breath, I managed to get things partially under control. Thankfully, the fish was more winded than me and lacked the steam to reach the next set of rapids. The nymph had caught on some debris or some such on this downstream charge, and was long gone; luckily it hadn't resulted in pulling the dry fly free from the fish. I was glad to be done with it. On both occasions that day, and a number of other times already that summer, the fish appeared to be more partial to the dry fly. I suspected that wasn't always going to be the case over the remainder of the summer, but like most fly anglers, I was more than happy to have the fish rising.

Swimming strongly from my hands, this beautiful rainbow of about five-pounds quickly disappeared back into its surrounds. I was buzzing! Finally I had found fish that were relatively aggressive, and were willing to take what I was throwing at them.

I fished upstream for another five kilometres that day, and by late afternoon I was on the other side of the valley, against trees on another spring creek. The vegetation backing the stream could only be described as rainforest, and even with late afternoon shadows being drawn across the entire valley, I still managed to spot a few fish. They were by no means prolific and as the water thinned out the higher I went, luring them into taking a fly proved to be even more challenging.

I felt like I had given the river thorough scrutiny that day, so much so, that I decided I would fish downstream the following day and that would be enough for me on this river. The fish were spectacular but there weren't huge numbers of them – there was no point fishing them too heavily.

$$f_{\jmath} \; \blacktriangle \; \propto$$

Having driven closer to the adjacent river valley the night before, I woke at seven-thirty, eager to get an early start, and if I'm totally honest, to get on the water first. I was hoping that my parked car would deter others from following me.

As I set out across the valley floor, conditions were perfect; suspiciously glancing around me, I wondered if I might actually get a day with no wind? Beautiful clear water, spectacular countryside, superbly conditioned fish, and no wind? Surely not . . .

I came across a little tributary stream falling off the nearby mountain, and decided to take a walk downstream to see what I could see. I was disappointed to find didymo present here, and while contemplating this at the head of a long pool, forgetting that I was actually looking for fish, I spooked quite a big one below an inflowing braid on the opposite bank. The further downstream I went, the pools became longer and shallower; I didn't come across another fish, so back upstream I went.

Reaching the pool where I had spooked the fish, I couldn't see it for the life of me. I was on the verge of continuing upstream when, just below the same narrow rapid entering the main stream, I saw it rise. Although this split branch of the stream was narrow, the remainder of the pool was perhaps four metres wide, a narrow chute flowing downstream against the opposite bank beneath the rapid confluence, but then most of it coming back at me, in a gentle eddy. In typical fashion, the fish was sitting right at the top of it all, perfectly positioned to receive prey from the streams and the back eddy, but in an extremely difficult position for me to get a dry fly to it, in a natural manner. I stood there considering my options for quite some time: do I cast across the back eddy on a slight angle and allow the long leader to do its work before whipping it out, or do I sneak upstream on the opposite bank, and feed the fly down to it? Both options meant the fly would only drift naturally for a short period of time.

A southwesterly wind was rolling off the mountains by this stage, and I chose the latter option. Tussock grass and other vegetation quickly proved this approach to be the most challenging; it wasn't long before I was winding in and doubling back around to attempt the cast across the back eddy, and into the wind. Hopefully my long leader would sort itself out.

One difficulty that comes with fishing a long leader is that it's easy to lose sight of where your fly lands. With all the bubbles on the surface from the rapid here, this was one of those occasions. It was the movement of the fish that ended up giving me an idea of where the fly was. I couldn't make out if the fish had actually taken the fly, or just moved to investigate, but better to be safe than sorry – I struck anyway.

Confirming that this fish hadn't been entirely fooled by the blowfly imitation, my fly and line flew straight back over my head.

Considering the stream was likely to get smaller the further upstream I went; it was difficult to consider that the better water was yet to come. But it was!

The interesting thing about these little brooks was that it appeared the fish were only willing to live in the pools. There were some lovely looking streams in between, but there were no fish in them. Invariably, they were at the head of the pools and it was only the 'penthouse pools' that held fish, the best of the best, the deeper pools, those offering some kind of structure for cover, and providing habitat for their prey. I hiked up past two lesser pools before coming to what was definitely a penthouse pool, it was hot property, but thankfully, trout have wiser, less greedy heads on their shoulders; they'd left their beautiful home in its natural state. Take a look at the animal kingdom, we humans are the only ones that are likely to wreck it for them – and yet we think we're the smartest of them all – that's definitely debatable from where I'm sitting . . .

This deep circular pool lay cradled in a bowl of granite bedrock; with wide rapids at the top and bottom of it, it looked perfect. If not for the water temperature, it wouldn't have been out of place at a tropical resort. Amidst the weed at the bottom I knew there had to be a fish, and immediately confirming my suspicions, a trout suddenly nailed something off the surface, just below the intake rapid. If ever I'd seen one, this was a sure thing!

I figured a fish in hand was better than two in the weed, so, crawling through tussock grass next to the intake stream, I moved into casting range. While doing so, this fish took another natural in the exact same spot, just below the rapid. It was exciting stuff! So confident of my success, I even set up my video camera on a tripod ready to film the successful capture – would I jinx myself . . . ?

On my first cast, the fly drifted down the shallow rapid and into the pool unmolested, straight past where I had seen the fish take the two naturals. Swinging on the lengthy leader, the fly continued drifting out across the turquoise coloured pool, as obvious as an iceberg. Or so I thought. It drifted perhaps halfway across this deep pool, when a trout confidently rose to the surface and swallowed it.

"There we go," I said, striking and standing up in the one motion. The tranquil pool instantly shaken to life by a leaping rainbow. I saw a few fish moving in the depths during the fight here, but otherwise, the hooked fish's larksome performance in the air had my undivided attention. Much like the day before, so confidant was this fish's take, I would later find the fly at the back of its throat. There was no shaking a hook pinned to its gullet, and with the fish safely in my hands, I was heartened by the success I had again found so early in the day. Maybe I can get three decent fish in one day, I pondered while watching this fish swim back into the depths, seemingly as fit as ever.

Leaving behind what I thought to be the penthouse pool of all pools, I scanned my way along a couple of shallow runs to no avail. With gin clear water and a smattering of weed and rock on the bottom, they looked beautiful, but were simply too small and shallow to house these large rainbows, fish which seemed to be averaging around four to five-pounds. Did they get into the smaller stretches at nighttime to feed, I wonder?

Like stumbling across a hidden treasure, just when I thought I was running out of water, I reached the pick of all the pools. This wasn't just the penthouse; this was the entire top two floors.

Stretching for at least forty metres, this pool had a high bank along the side closest to the mountain, and a shallow gravel bank on the other. It was from a safe distance on this gravel bank that I was drooling at the pool, picturing all the fit, well fed, physically dominant trout looking down at the 'lesser' trout below.

Being at least chest deep on the deeper side of this pool, there was a healthy crop of aquatic weed running along the base of the bank.

It was no easy task spotting fish on my way upstream along the shallow bank, but when I crossed over above the rapid at the head of the pool, I looked back downstream; there just had to be a fish there somewhere. The wind was howling by this stage, large dust clouds barreling their way down the valley floor, running riot beyond the shelter of the mountains. The wind made it virtually impossible to cast upstream, or across the stream, however, this water was the perfect candidate to employ my tactic of what I've referred to in previous books as 'walking the dog'.

The top of the high bank was groomed to perfection; there was nothing but a bouquet of yellow flowering weeds on the very edge of the cliff to blemish it. I would be extremely exposed walking along the edge of the bank, but if the fish were there, it seemed that one good drift was all it took with these rainbows – they were hungry and aggressive.

Walking the dog meant casting the fly downstream with the wind, and creeping behind it as it drifted downstream in the gentle current; and rippling the surface, the not so gentle wind. If done correctly, it presents the fly to the fish as naturally as is humanly possible. The added bonus is that it can be done from quite a distance, the fly reaching the fish long before my presence is likely to startle them. The only downfall is when, like in this situation, you haven't spotted a fish, and you're left to guess where the fish are: against the bank, midstream, or on the opposite bank. Always one to prospect the foreground first, I'll walk the fly through a pool multiple times if it looks good enough, and usually in that order.

On this occasion, I was perhaps halfway along the bank, the fly a good fifteen metres ahead of me, strung-out like a fraudulent enticement, a bribe drifting above bankside weeds, where the goons lurked below. And then . . . suddenly . . . but right on cue considering the modern-day state of self-indulgence, a fish rose from the depths and greedily inhaled the fly. I had known it was only a matter of time, it was a sunny day and in typical NZ fashion there were plenty of flies around, the strong winds of capitalism blowing them to the water, keeping the insatiable fat-cat goons below well fed. I had this one on a string for once, but before the day was out, as always seems to be the case, one of his mates would commit the crime and slip away without paying the time – we would all be dead and gone before anyone realised what had been done.

Living in the moment, what I didn't know was what this fish would do next. Perhaps it was a good soul . . .

Launching into an opening run straight at me was its preferred tactic. Spirit and confidence! A willingness to fight in the open! No hiding behind words and lies! No mistrust of others' beliefs! No money passing hands! No false agendas for power and monetary gain! A uniform pulled on and the bravery to stand up and fight in the open! A fight for survival, for equality and freedom no less. I liked this fish's style!

Despite my appreciation of its morals, this fish's headlong charge saw me backpedalling at a great rate of knots. Thankfully, the end wasn't nigh, my back not yet against the wall . . .

Catching up to the fish, it felt the full weight of its actions, and the sting of the hook in its mouth, a second time; inspiring it to flee the chambers of supposed egalitarianism, and exile itself with a long downstream run. I had confidently gone out with a four-weight outfit that morning and there was a considerable bend in it. Considering my position high on the bank, this fish surprised me; it was full of fight, or so it appeared, yet, in an apparent fear of the public eye, it only got its head up for the one jump; sullen guilt, or modesty, I wondered. Suggesting the latter, it put on a dignified working-class fight, choosing to keep its head down and test the strength of my knots. I respected that too.

Where and how to secure it from high on the bank was my next challenge, but by the end of the fight I had managed to get down onto a narrow platform of clay; from there I was precariously able to apply the finishing touches. I removed the hook from this beautiful, dark coloured rainbow, and quickly sent it on its way, hopeful that it might keep its morning experiences quiet. I was confident there must be other candidates in the depths of this pool and by day's end I intended on tracking them down.

As I continued upstream, it quickly became obvious that this was the last of the suitable pools in the stream. I hiked on regardless, eager to have a look around one of the spurs bracing the mountain against the winds of time, forever hopeful of finding another stream hidden around the corner.

On and on across open ground I hiked and by the time I exposed myself around the base of this buttress, the wind stopped me in my tracks. Dust clouds were blasting down the valley of another major river here. I dared not venture out into the maelstrom to fill a bottle of water, let alone find a stream. Besides, it was well into the afternoon by this stage and I was confident I could raise another fish or two from the three pools I had already spotted and caught fish in.

Surprisingly, the most likely pool was the one where I had just caught the last fish. After all, I had only really fished half of it. However, the fish I caught there had gallivanted all over the pool and then been released back into it . . . only time would tell.

By the time I got back to it, adding to the challenge ahead of me, the pool wasn't escaping the afternoon wind either. Severe chop quickly created all kinds of problems for the dry fly to stay afloat. I walked the fly the entire length of the pool from the high bank twice, but didn't encounter a thing this time. Having given up and wound in, I was halfway back along the pool, when out of the corner of my eye; I thought I saw a rise amidst the chop, just off the opposite bank. Rather than sitting amidst the shelter of the weed and deeper water, I hadn't stopped to think that a fish might choose to sit in such shallow water and chop. I guess the wind and chop might have been delivering more in the way of surface prey than my eye could see. The rise I had detected suggested there was definitely some form of food on the surface out there – blue arsed blowflies perhaps!

I momentarily debated whether or not I should walk around and cover the fish from the opposite bank, but quickly decided to fish it from the high bank I was on. Now that I knew where the fish was, I probably could have drifted a fly onto it from either bank, but just in case it moved, I decided not to waste time. What could go wrong – it was going to be a piece of cake . . . ?

Casting the fly across the pool and across the wind was no easy task with a four-weight and so as to not hook myself in the back of the head, I got the job done with a backhand cast, and started walking the fly onto the fish. As sure as the sunrise, it scoffed it down. I was onto my third fish for the day. Everything was going nicely . . . until . . . I realised a few loose loops of line were rudely wrapped around the one and only piece of vegetation along the majority of the bank – the yellow flowering weed bouquet. The fish of course was like a bull at the gate. Like any hooked fish, all it wanted to do was run. But with the line stuck, I was forced to hang on – locked in battle on two fronts.

Using my rod hand fingers to halt the fish's downstream charge, I took hold of the remaining line with my stripping hand, and yanked at the weeds. It tore free, but I wasn't in the clear yet. Some of the weeds were stuck in the line and I was forced to desperately hang on longer, trying to get rid of it so as to not rip the rod-guides off if I let the fish run. In the end I had been forced to halt the fish's run for too long; the knot to the fly couldn't handle the strain any longer, and it broke.

Gloomily, I stood there in the wind, thoroughly disappointed to have lost a fish in such a manner, and regretful that I'd left a fly stuck in its throat. I tied on another fly for the last two pools, and rather unhappy with myself, I moved on.

Approaching the tropical hotel pool from the opposite bank of the broad rapid entering it, I crawled in closer on my hands and knees. In the current free corner rimmed with aquatic weeds, my plan was to feed the fly out on the wind. I wouldn't even make a cast.

The fresh fly was nearing the other side of the pool, and also nearing the limit of my leader, when a rainbow honed in on it. But then . . . impossibly so . . . it missed the fly by millimetres. I suspected that this fish had missed the fly intentionally. Like the second fish I had managed to catch the afternoon before, maybe it was trying to submerge the fly, and then come back to eat it. Or maybe it was being rushed due to competition presented by another fish; this was a theory that came to me after seeing the second fish just moments after hooking up the previous afternoon.

Changing the fly to a Royal Wolf, I decided to show it something different, not vastly different, but different nonetheless.

This pattern proved no more effective than the first. Like a wayward heat-seeking missile, the same fish, or perhaps another, committed to little more than identical sideswiping missed takes, on two casts. Incredibly, a tiny Adams dry fly produced the same kind of behaviour. How could the fish be so uncertain, or so off target?

The trout were sitting down there laughing at me as I struck and missed time and time again, they laughed at my wasted effort and wasted dreams – the goons were on holiday in their penthouse pool – 'we've got that fool on the ropes,' they were saying.

I knew I should let them swipe at the fly and then leave it, but it was so hard to stop myself from striking. In the end I realised I was doing little more than educating them on what not to eat, and decided it was time to move on to the next pool.

This was the pool where I had first encountered a fish, an eternity ago, early that morning.

Now with less light and considerably more wind, it was even harder to find this fish. I chose to hike down to the lower end of the pool, and blindly fish my way back up. In the end, however, my efforts probably resulted in educating this fish too, no doubt adding valuable entries to its 'Surviving Humans Handbook'.

This was it for me on these rivers and streams. Finally the fish had come out to play; I hadn't had it all my own way with them, but it felt good to finally be rewarded for my long days on the water.

I was nearing the end of my time in the southern part of the Central South Island by this stage, but before heading further north in the region, there were still a few rivers around Lake Benmore that I was interested in having a look at . . .

᚛ ▲ ∝

It was late in the day before I arrived in the Lake Benmore area and, for simplicity sake, I went back to camp the night in the same spot where I had previously been so challenged fishing the floodplains. With a few hours still left in the day, it would be the perfect time to get out for an evening session.

There hadn't really been much rain over the previous week or two (even if there was a light dusting of snow on the mountains from earlier that day), but the lake was even higher than my previous visit, the flooded regions considerably more sodden. Seeing that Lake Benmore is a hydroelectricity dam system, the water might have been high for any number of reasons.

The tussock filled slough where the fish had driven me crazy now appeared to hold no fish at all, or at least I couldn't see them with the extra water. I climbed my way through the flooded willows and got out on the corner of the lake where I knew it would be firm enough underfoot. This area was also where the slough drained into the lake and had been a popular hunting ground for the fish days earlier – I didn't see any reason why it would be different this afternoon.

As I had hoped, the fish were there, feeding on tiny surface prey, again so small to be virtually invisible. Geez, do they ever let up?

As I'd been edging around the slough and beating through the bush, I had noticed a small hatch of caddis moths. They had been remarkably small; so seeing that I couldn't identify what these fish were feeding on, I decided to try one of my smallest elk hair caddis patterns. With a bit of luck there'd be a fish out there that wasn't too particular.

There were two or three fish feeding quite ravenously and with daylight slowly fading, I should have had every right to feel quietly confident. Quite close to my fly, a couple of 'naturals' were sipped down in quick succession. And then, with another delicate sip sounding like a gentle kiss, my fly was finally taken; a take that was detected by this barely audible noise, and instinct alone. In general, it often pays not to rush the strike when dry fly fishing. Nowhere is this more important than in New Zealand, where the surface prey is often so small you really do have to bide your time, and let the fish get the job done first. Of course, there's a fine line between hooking the fish and having it spit the fly back out, but when left to their own devices, these delicate sips often suck the fly a lot further down their gullet than one might think. Even so, over the days ahead that summer, it was almost a guarantee that I would end up being too quick on some occasions, and too slow on others. If every encounter ran like clockwork, it just wouldn't be fishing would it?

Regardless of whether or not the delay in my strike helped me hook this fish, the fly was embedded in the roof of its mouth, and it was never going to be shaken free. There really is no feeling quite like it! Your fly discretely disappears in oil-calm stillness; you strike, your rod bends to the weight of a worthy opponent, and almost simultaneously, the tranquillity is torn to shreds by a frantically leaping trout.

It felt great to have hooked a brown trout again, and being right on dinnertime, unfortunately for this fish, its day couldn't have got any worse. I had only killed and cooked a couple of fish until then. This guy was three to four-pounds, not too small and not too big – perfect for my fry pan and a fresh evening meal.

$$f_{\flat} \quad \blacktriangle \quad \propto$$

Oblivious to my presence the following morning, there was a brown trout rising out in the open, directly to the front of my camp. Not one to walk away from a gifted opportunity, I grabbed my rod, and with a pair of board-shorts on and bare feet, I snuck through the willows onto the shallows. With early morning light freckling through the overhanging willows, there was little room to cast, but with no more than a metre and a half of fly line out, I got the tiny caddis pattern in the cruising trout's path. Another two unidentified naturals were sipped down, but it didn't stop there; my fly was next in line, and with unquestioning trust, the fish kissed the surface. As easy as that, my fly disappeared.

If only it was always that easy. I'd barely got dressed, hadn't even thought about breakfast, and I was already hooked into a fish. A touch smaller than the fish the evening before, we were locked in battle in an opening beneath the willows no bigger than a living room; a close quarters battle at its best. Limiting this worthy opponent to a short leash, I managed to keep it out of the surrounding timber, and quickly had it in hand. Removing the fly and releasing it just as quickly, I suspect it was less happy about the way its day had started than I.

I didn't bother fishing anymore of the lake that morning; I had plans to investigate some of the other lakes in the dam system and a couple of its tributaries.

Unfortunately, the first tributary turned out to be a didymo filled disaster. Parking near a bridge I spotted a few small trout from, I fished no more than three hundred metres upstream before I lost interest entirely. Had it not been for the agriculture lining both banks, complete with irrigation booms working overtime, it could have been a beautiful river. Along with the didymo, the extraordinary amount of green slime here was also a likely indication of excessive nitrification. Poor bank stability, excessive stocking density, excessive feces, excessive fertiliser, excessive irrigation, reduced water; they were all obvious problems. It's as simple as that – for water quality and the health of natural ecosystems – they are almost *always* OBVIOUS problems.

I bumped into a couple of men fishing upstream from the same point that I did. Out of courtesy, I told them that I hadn't fished very far.

"How'd you go?" They asked.

"I didn't see anything," I told them. "I lost interest quite quickly."

"There's some quite good trout here," they said. "But they're very easily spooked."

I just nodded. It was all too much of a natural disaster for me. It was the most uninspiring water I'd seen that summer, far from the kind of river you dream of fishing in New Zealand. Sadly, those kinds of pristine Kiwi rivers were becoming progressively scarcer.

I drove back up the valley to take a closer look at the other two lakes in the series of dams. Woefully, both these lakes turned out to be lined with caravans, available for people to use on an honesty payment system. Lining the lakes like washed up flotsam, the eyesore created by these caravans effectively ruined the lakes as far as I was concerned, it looked like some kind of gypsy convention; I wasn't remotely interested in staying anywhere near them. I certainly wasn't going to squeeze in between them to fish. Caravans like this aren't an uncommon occurrence on lake and river frontage in New Zealand. They're not camping grounds as such, but instead, lines of old caravans, usually well past their use-by-date, standing like ranks of rusty tin soldiers. Personally I think these caravans, and to a certain extent the cabins (known in New Zealand as batches), really can destroy otherwise beautiful places. Sure, recreational accommodation is something people demand, and to a certain extent I can live with the batches, but these strips of old caravans . . . they're a monstrosity! What on earth happened to pitching a tent, camping, and leaving nothing but footprints as you take your rubbish out with you – a peaceful stay in the wilderness?

Of course in today's day and age, people are turning to the even cushier holiday housing developments over tents and caravans. With the foolish over-development of Ireland, Spain, and Portugal being the exception, Europe is perhaps the only place in the world that has escaped this phenomenon in the past two decades. Why? Simply because over thousands of years, they've developed their countries to the point that there's very little land left. Forward thinking nations such as the UK respect this and generally have quite stringent zoning and planning regulations. Rural landowners can't just chop up their farm and sell it, because the rural landscape is valued at a cultural heritage level, it's a national asset. Sure, taxpayers might end up subsidising farmers in order for them to stay afloat at times, but if the farming is sustainable and not impacting negatively on the environment, is this not money well spent, after all, what's a nation without a rural landscape?

The sad example of a nation's government not considering this, is Ireland! After the past fifteen years, Ireland's landscape on the west coast (and elsewhere I suspect) looks as though someone sprinkled white Monopoly houses along its length. The Spanish, since also getting cashed up on their acceptance into the European Union, have perhaps been even worse with their corrupt overdevelopment. Portugal, Ireland/Italy, Greece, Spain – known in the Australian press as the PIGS of the EU – they were a greedy bunch during that period.

When chatting to North Americans, apart from many other terms I could use to describe this kind of greed, selfishness and simple stupidity, I refer to this over-development of beautiful natural assets as 'Lake Tahoe Syndrome'. More often than not, they know exactly what I'm talking about.

Europeans, Southeast Asians and North Americans flock to New Zealand for its natural beauty! Surely the less urbanized nations of New Zealand and Australia can learn from these generally over-populated and over-developed parts of the world, and assuming we can put a stop to profit driven greed, perhaps we can enjoy true WILDERNESS for many generations to come. Unfortunately, we probably can't all afford to live at the beach, or on lakes and rivers, or in the mountains, but what would we prefer, being able to live there jammed in amongst tiny postage stamp housing blocks like those currently eating into Australia and New Zealand, or would we rather be able to visit these places with development left to a minimum? Looking at places like the Gold Coast in Australia, I struggle to see how that kind of Miami styled high-rise growth can be classified as success and progress – all I see is destruction.

Sadly, the high-rise and urban sprawl phenomenon looks like it's going to eat its way into Queensland's Sunshine Coast too, a region where I've always thought the politicians had learnt from the mistakes made on the Gold Coast. Surely there's other ways for councils to generate revenue than by selling off land and allowing everything to be covered in concrete and bricks. And surely there can be job prospects created in fields other than just construction. If there aren't enough construction jobs available, then perhaps move, or commute to the bigger cities; keep our tranquil smaller towns exactly that, small and peaceful; that's why most people live there in the first place.

Politically, New Zealand and Australia need to be more aware of this and, hopefully, in years to come there'll be a stronger representation (particularly in the big parties) for people who simply don't want every corner of our countries to be overdeveloped and overpopulated.

As for these rundown caravans littering the foreshore of lower Lake Benmore and its adjoining lakes, I couldn't figure out if they belonged to the stations, or if perhaps they were council owned and on council property. Either way, all I saw was a beautiful spot that had been destroyed. I was glad to put it behind me and move on.

Eager to explore another river and put a good number of miles between Lake Benmore and me, I drove for the rest of the afternoon.

On arrival, I quickly discovered there were also a number of lakes dotted along this river, all of which were regulated for 'fly fishing only'. I suspected them to be heavily fished as a result, but I was still interested in having a look. With the evening getting dark, it was on the shores of one of these small lakes that I found myself.

On first impressions it appeared to be quite a shallow lake and I found myself questioning whether or not there were fish there at all. That was until I heard a distinct slurp. Something had risen out there in the ripples whipped up by the westerly wind. They were there!

As the wind calmed into the evening, what I thought to be a caddis hatch had a number of trout rising beside some bushes halfway around the lake. With my eyesight starting to fail me as darkness set in, I briefly hooked one of these fish, only for it to punctually dislodge the hook. It was time to hit the hay – they could wait until morning.

f₃ ▲ ∝

A flock of sheep being herded towards some nearby shearing sheds greeted me as I stepped out of the van. The westerly wind was still fresh, but the previous evening's rise had me eager to get on the water. What would I find?

I had a few casts in the shallows at the sheltered end of the lake, as I made my way around towards the bushes. If there were fish rising, they were hard to spot on the wind-rippled surface. Getting side on to the wind and ripples at the beginning of the bushes, I was in the process of swinging a blue Humpy around the corner, keenly focusing on the fly – when out of nowhere – a man scared the living daylights out of me.

Having quietly approached from behind me, he made his presence known with a gruff, "Hello," at a range of no more than a few metres.

I jumped clean out of my skin!

"Geez! You scared the crap out of me!" I said.

"Have you got permission from the owner to fish here?" he asked, wasting no time getting to the point.

"There's signs on the road saying 'fly fishing only' on the lakes, judging by that I presumed fishing here was allowed."

"No, not here, this is private property."

Right at that moment, with my fly drifting out of sight behind me, it suddenly started pulling line through my rod hand fingers, and I struck!

"Whoa! Fish on!" I said grinning sheepishly. "I'm about to get kicked out and I finally hook one."

"Yep, that's right," my new acquaintance said.

"Who's the property owner?" I asked while going about fighting the fish, "Is that you?"

"No, I just lease the property. But the owner wants to do something with fishing in this lake."

"More money hey? When is enough, enough," I asked as the fish neared my feet? "Where's the property owner?"

"I don't know," he said, looking down as a nice rainbow fled the shallows for a second time. "He's some overseas businessman."

"And one bloke can't come in and have a fish on his lake huh? What a great world we live in."

"What now, do you need a net or something?" he asked, as I eventually reached down for a beautiful rainbow, with an unusually big head. "What is it, I don't know anything about fishing?"

"It's a rainbow trout! I unhook it by hand and let it go – no nets – nets damage fish!"

This man seemed like a reasonable bloke, and in a way, I had a feeling he didn't really want to shoo me away, but was just doing as he was told. At least that's what my faith in humanity was telling me.

"There's lots of lakes along the river you can fish," he said as we walked back along the lake.

"Yeah, but that's where everyone fishes," I said. "I was trying to get away from everyone, it's getting harder and harder to do that these days."

With my wings somewhat clipped, I drove down to the river. Even though it was a weekday, there were people everywhere.

The dirt road into this area snaked along the river. It quickly became obvious that it got fished heavily. The lakes along the floodplain looked like little more than weed filled duck ponds, the kind of thing all the German tourists pay money to swim in when they're at home. Although there was a good chance the fishing in these ponds may have been okay, I couldn't bring myself to park with the RVs and join everyone else fishing in 'beautiful New Zealand'. I turned to the river instead.

In places, I found people fishing here too, but eventually I got onto water in the upper reaches that demanded a bit of a walk. Braiding its way through open grassland on the doorstep of the Southern Alps, had it not been for the winks of sunlight off the surface of the water, it was so clear that I could have been mistaken for thinking there was no water there at all – it was a beautiful river.

Hiking out with rod in hand, I found a rapid where I could cross, and then headed upstream along the top of some high ground. With eagle-eyed views of the long, sand-coloured pools below, I didn't see much for quite some distance, but on reaching the head of one of these long pools, a dark patch in the middle of the river had my eyes glued to it. What is it, weed or rock? Surely there'll be a fish sitting near there.

It was at least fifty metres away, but with the clean shingle bottom, I knew I would be able to spot a fish easily. As I came parallel to this rock, it suddenly became obvious that I could spot fish far easier than I thought.

Just as I was thinking about edging down to the water's edge and presenting a fly, the dark coloured rock suddenly spun around and torpedoed its way downstream. It wasn't like I was walking along the rim of a cliff waving my arms about; I'd been traversing a slope and was a remarkable distance away. All the same, this fish had sensed my presence and disappeared like a runaway bride. It was a massive trout, easily over ten-pounds and clearly well accustomed to anglers trying to outwit it.

As I progressed further upstream, the average size of the pools decreased. I saw a few other fish here and there, but nothing in the same calibre as that first fish. All the fish were equally flighty it seemed, and surprisingly, it wasn't until I reached a pool right next to a car park that I finally found a fish willing to show some interest in my blowfly imitation – two fish in fact.

Again I managed to spot these fish from a distance, but I showed even more caution on this occasion, and crawled in towards their flank. From a seated position, I angled my cast upstream and above them. One of the fish peeled off and followed the fly a surprisingly long distance downstream; its eyes glued to it as though it were a shining light. As I craned my neck in order to keep an eye on the fly myself, I nervously waited for the rise.

Up towards the surface it went, and right at the last minute, just when I thought I was in business, it aborted the take with a spectacular water explosion.

The second fish showed itself on my next cast, and as though receiving telepathic counsel from its departed companion, it also remained ambivalent towards my fly.

Bathed in sunshine, it really was a beautiful river valley that day, but after another couple of hours continuing further upstream, I didn't manage to spot another fish. I decided to throw in the towel! Had it not been for the rainbow trout I'd caught that morning while being banished from private water; I wouldn't have caught a fish here.

With a few lakes on my radar, the time had come to edge further north into the Central South Island region.

It was dark by the time I arrived at the first of these lakes, and after a good night's sleep, I woke to perfectly calm conditions.

ʕ ∆ ∝

It was a large, generally circular lake and was actually a dam. Surrounded by agriculture, the stagnant recesses around its perimeter suggested excessive nitrogen runoff wasn't doing this water body any favours either. I may not have dared drink the water without boiling it, but the amount of fish life was surprisingly promising. Again, their target meal was tiny, midges or sandflies I suspected. The trout were making up for the lack of size with quantity.

I attached a tiny size eighteen or twenty Adams to a four-pound tippet on my four-weight outfit and waded out near what I thought to be one of the dam's inflowing creeks. It was dry at that stage . . .

The trout were feeding in flooded shallows here and not long after wading out, I spotted quite a big one. As always, they were on a strict diet, typically fussy about what was eaten and what wasn't.

I resorted to scaling my tippet back to just three-pounds, and eventually got one of the wily trout to take the little Adams. Three-pound line doesn't give your knots much leeway to a decent fish, however, and this fish popped the tippet with ease. It was well past noon by this stage, and I finally got back for breakfast.

I waded out across the shallows in the opposite direction that afternoon, drifting a blowfly pattern on a strengthening southeasterly breeze. There was still the occasional rise across the textured surface, but the fish were significantly quieter than in the calm conditions of dawn.

Green and toxic looking with agricultural effluent, I came to a small bay that wasn't about to make it onto the cover of New Zealand's travel brochures anytime soon. The breeze was directing chop down a small point into this bay and when I reached the green algae clogged corner, I spooked a really big brown trout that must have been managing to scrounge a meal amongst all the turmoil and slime. I doubted it was focussing on surface prey, suspecting instead that it was finding food getting washed into the bay on the bottom: nymphs, worms, snails, and possibly even small fish.

Getting out of the water, I changed flies to a nymph, and doubled around to fish down the point into the bay. Perhaps this fish would be back on the job in search of an evening meal by the time I reached it. Who knew what I might find along the way . . .

Very little as it turned out! Nevertheless, I was just within casting range of the wave-washed weeds and slime, when a cast to open water resulted in a brown trout of about three-pounds finally taking the nymph. It offered a bit of a lacklustre fight, and wasn't in great condition, but after a challenging morning, at least I'd managed to catch a fish. After releasing this fish, I retired to a nearby town for a sit-down with a much-needed coffee.

Later that evening I was back on the lake. In lee of the wind on its eastern shores, I found a willow tree lined clay bank. Perfectly aligned to the afternoon breeze, I suspected all kinds of prey would be getting blown out of the trees. The water was deeper off this bank and there was a dry stretch of dirt and rock stretching from the willows to the water's edge. It generally offered enough space in which to cast, but I quickly realised the fish were a lot closer than I expected.

I'd only just crept through the willows near where I planned to camp the night, when a big brown started harassing a school of juvenile bullies unsuccessfully trying to hide in the shallows. Crouching down, I watched it edge past from left to right like the High Street constabulary. Then, with its back to me, I crawled down into a seated casting position. I tied on a medium sized Royal Wolf for no particular reason, and cast it out just two metres from the shore, most of my leader lying on the dry ground in front of me. Sometime later, I spotted the fish edging back along the shoreline. The bullies fretted. Nervously, they clung to the assumed safety of the shoreline, huddled together like terrified school kids trying to eat their lunch near the principal's office. The big trout, the primary instigator, ignored them on this occasion. At a distance of two metres or more, I could see from its body language that my fly symbolised a possible meal. Was it a preferable meal, I wonder, or was it just easier than chasing the bullies?

Much to my surprise, it swam directly along the shoreline, straight up to the Royal Wolf, opened its mouth, and closed it over the fly. Or so I thought . . .

I struck! And surprising me even further, my line sailed straight back over my head. Despondently picking it all out of the willows, I couldn't believe what had happened, it wasn't like it had been hard to spot the rise; it had only been a few metres away. I was certain my timing had been spot on – obviously it wasn't!

Had I struck too soon, or had the fish covertly aborted the take? I was left guessing, but this fish and I would meet again.

There were a few other smaller trout along this stretch and deciding to try a different approach, I dropped an un-weighted nymph in their path. It might as well have been a twig blown on the wind; they weren't remotely interested in it.

Reverting back to a tiny Adams dry fly, and adopting cover provided by the willows at the top of the bank, I continued stalking along the shoreline.

Similar to the flats that morning, the trout were equally prolific along this steeper bank that evening and appeared to all be brown trout. Whether it was little bullies in the shallows, or unidentified surface fodder, the shallow water was unquestionably their preferred hunting ground. For a keen line-of-sight angler like myself, it was great fun. I could basically keep my feet dry, and with short bow-and-arrow casts of no more than a few metres, the little dry flies proved to be quite effective. Well, they were effective in fooling the fish into taking them, but at that point, my success in hooking them was questionable.

The second fish to get the better of me was a fat brown trout of about three-pounds. I'd spotted it sipping down dries while patrolling a lengthy beat along the bank, and without even stepping out of the cover of the willows, I fired a bow-and-arrow cast out to the water's edge. With its dimpled rises blossoming along the bank from right to left, it was obviously hungry, and I saw it coming. It was well over a metre off the bank by the time it levelled with my fly, but it veered in accordingly. In almost machine-like fashion, it then bared the white of its mouth straight at me, and took the fly. I struck with almost brazen certainty.

My fly, however, came flying straight back at me, disappearing into the willows over my shoulder, again. I was well aware of my mistake on this occasion.

This direct face-to-face encounter at such close quarters had been new to me, and I suspect I hadn't gauged the closure of its mouth quite like I might have with a side-on view – I'd been too eager to strike and had pulled the fly straight out of an open mouth. Instinct and eagerness can make a man do funny things, but as they say, live and learn.

With daylight diminishing, I tiptoed around the corner into a small inlet lined with weed. While hiding in the willows, which eventually prevented me from following the shoreline any further, I spotted a fish working the weed bed. It was a big one!

Swimming away from me, it disappeared around the willows and I capitalised on the opportunity – it would return – I knew it would!

Creeping forwards, I cast along the bank on an angle; placing the little Adams no more than a foot from dry ground. Hidden around the corner at the head of this inlet choked by willows, I could hear the occasional rise, whether it was the same fish, or others, I couldn't be sure. The water was perfectly sheltered from the wind and with the day drawing to a close, it had virtually come to a standstill. From my crouched position, even with the lack of light, my view beneath the surface behind the fly was like looking through a window. Having exhausted its choice for food around the willows, it was through this window that the same thick-bodied brown trout re-appeared. Patrolling over the weed bed, it veered towards my fly with seemingly supernatural instinct. How on earth did it know it was there? I guess instinct and eagerness make fish do extraordinary things too. With the fading light likely to have the fish more confident, but perhaps not see its prey so well (or me), the odds were in my favour – or so I thought . . .

The fish confidently drifted up to the grey coloured Adams, and engulfed it unhesitatingly. There was no mistaking the hook-up. The little four-weight rod loaded as I struck, and the fish erupted from the shallows in panic. It was a big fish, easily five-pounds or more. In the dull light, though, this fish even lost sight of where the lake was. It had taken the fly right at the very edge of the lake, and on feeling the hook, launched itself straight onto dry ground. Landing over half a metre up the bank amongst some fallen willow branches, it kicked and bucked like a rodeo bronco, bouncing its way back down the bank and into the water. This was enough to break my tippet, and much to the fish's good fortune (other than the bruises and fly left it its jaw) it managed to bounce its way back into the drink. I'm not sure if a clean fight and prompt release would have been less traumatic for the fish, but I was certain it would have been less traumatic for me!

Walking back in the dark pondering my day, I realised it hadn't been overly successful, but I wasn't going anywhere, and come morning, I was determined for a better personal performance.

ʕ ▲ ∝

Not long after dawn, with misty weather hanging in the air, I marched in the opposite direction from my camp, and was quickly presented with an opportunity to redeem myself.

At little more than three-pounds, the fish I had spotted wasn't overly big, but it was rising on a regular basis and couldn't be ignored. It quickly became obvious that this hungry little brown thought my fly couldn't be ignored either. It rose to the Adams without hesitation.

There was no messing around on this occasion, in its mouth it went; I struck, and the hook made sure it went no further. Despite the lack of sunshine, it was an eerily still morning that day. This fish broke the calm as though its life depended on it. Jumping into the air, it crashed back down and tore along the shallow bank; how it managed not to hit the bottom on its re-entry, I have no idea. After this initial outburst, the fight tapered off quite quickly, before a somewhat poorly conditioned brown trout was swiftly restrained and then released. I couldn't complain; I was on the scoreboard for the day with the first fish I had spotted, and on my very first cast. I'd had less successful weeks, let alone days.

The fish were abundant here and with the fog slowly burning off, it could only get better – of that I was sure!

Keeping a careful distance, I had only gone another five metres along this little bay, when I spotted another fish, albeit quite a good one.

Prowling the shallows like all the trout were here, it didn't appear to be feeding as regularly as the previous, no doubt hungrier, and perhaps less wise, younger fish. As it patrolled away from me, I placed my cast, hoping perhaps the little dry fly would improve its appetite on its return. A light breeze saw my fly end up a good three metres off the shore by the time my quarry reappeared. Hugging the shallows with obvious intent, I doubted it would even see the fly. But then, as if suddenly remembering an off-ramp exit, I was shocked to see it deviate straight out to the fly, change down a few gears, and sip it down with an almost compassionate grace. I made no mistake setting the hook!

I appeared to be on a roll this morning; within the space of fifteen minutes, the serenity had been shattered again. Perhaps due to its better condition, this fish did a better job of it, instantly letting loose with a burst of at least four rapid-fire jumps. They did little to help its situation. When a dry fly is properly taken and the strike timed well, if your knots are good and the hook strong enough, there's usually very little a fish can do to shake it.

I spent a bit more time on a few fish that had a school of bullies balled up in the corner of the bay, but I struggled to divert their attention to my fly. Eventually I turned around and fished back towards my camp, the sky overhead now blue.

The couple of fish that I had spotted next to my camp the previous afternoon were there again, but on this occasion, they didn't show the remotest interest in the Adams and caddis patterns. The same could be said for all the trout up to the inlet where the fish had jumped on the bank – they might have had a better memory than I gave them credit for.

Beyond the inlet, I got onto some new water. There were no willows here and doing my best to blend in, I sat down amongst the dry grass at the top of what was quite a steep and precarious clay bank. I sat there for a moment, enjoying the warmth of the sun, and just watched.

Beyond a submerged clay platform no more than two metres wide, the weed-covered bottom dropped away into quite deep water. If nymphs and young fish were your gastronomic partiality, this platform was a prime hunting ground. All the same, it was beyond the edge of the drop-off where there was a good number of trout focusing their hunt. Yep, you guessed it – unidentifiable and virtually microscopic surface prey.

There must have been close to half a dozen brown trout working this stretch of water. Some of them were impressive fish. Trying to make out the larger specimens, ghostly cruising like nuclear submarines in the depths, I suspected that a ten-pounder wasn't out of the question here. The fish out wide were taking dries in a wind lane slick that lay like a landing strip, in a now wind rippled lake. The unfortunate bullies on the other hand, were being harassed over the shallow platform. I decided my primary focus would be the fish opting for surface cuisine.

In the end, though, it appeared they were either too smart, or too fussy to fall for my flies – most likely both – smart and fussy go hand in hand with the challenging trout of New Zealand.

Having tried a blowfly pattern, an Adams, and a small Royal Wolf, I went back to a tiny caddis. Working my way along the bank, I swung the fly across the rippled surface on the light breeze in semicircles as though breaking a horse. I was a good forty metres beyond the clay platform, the little caddis pattern floating high and nearing the end of its run; camouflaged amongst the ripples. The fly had essentially been out of sight throughout much of its drift, but once within a few metres of the bank . . . there was no mistaking an insignificant swirl in its vicinity. That was either a 'natural' being taken, or it was your fly, my brain told me. Thankfully it was enough to persuade me into striking.

Better to be safe than sorry when uncertain in such a circumstance, I say.

Coming up tight to a fish, and seeing another acrobatic brown take to the air, I wasn't sorry in the slightest. Running out across the lake, it danced for all it was worth. Defiant to the very end, if you pick up my New Zealand DVD, you'll see the remarkable resolve of this fish, eluding my hand multiple times as I tried to secure it at the end of the fight.

I suspect this fish wasn't as big as some I saw along this bank, but at about four-pounds and in superb condition, with large dark coloured spots sparsely covering its cream flanks, it was a beautiful fish, and more than welcome. Three fish for the morning, I thought as I watched it swim away. Sadly, up until then that was a record for me on this trip to New Zealand – yep, pretty lame I know!

Back on the water that evening, the little caddis pattern even managed to fool the big fish in front of my camp. Well, actually, I'm not too sure just who got fooled, this fish was some kind of magician!

The fly disappeared into its mouth, just like it had with the other three fish that morning, and I struck, certain that I had finally gotten the better of it. However, this was one incredibly cunning fish and somehow, it managed to avoid the business end of the hook for a third time! I couldn't believe it, and as the, 'was I too slow or too quick?' debate began filling my head again; I had to refrain from hurling a rock at it.

As I skulked along the shoreline in search of more contenders, the fish proved to be challenging. The trout were out in good numbers on the clay bank where the bullies were living a life of chance on their narrow platform. One of the browns lurking above the drop-off had to have been an easy eight-pounds. Much like my morning session though, none of these shrewd trout were willing to let their guard down.

It had been a fun few days here, but the following morning would see me travelling towards some other lakes in the Central South Island.

ᚠ ᚩ ᚳ

I had fished the first lake I arrived at a few times over the years but after a ten-year absence, I was shocked by the extent to which four-wheel-drives had chewed up the shoreline and surrounding countryside. So much like a lot of what I encountered in New Zealand's South Island that summer, it was sad to see. With this cut up countryside before me, and the likelihood that the four-wheel-drive access would see more people on the lake over the upcoming weekend, I jumped a nearby fence and marched off on foot to take a look at another nearby lake. Ten years earlier I had hiked out and fished it for the first time.

Climbing some high ground, I thought I could see it in the distance, and at some stage while in the area, I decided I would hike out to have another look at it. Although I hadn't actually caught anything there ten years earlier, I had seen a few solid looking browns. With a bit of luck, they would be ten-pound plus fish by now . . .

Once back at my camp, an afternoon southeasterly breeze was blowing along the shore on my side of the lake. I rigged up my four-weight; ready to swing some dry flies along the bank.

Keeping a low profile, casting from seated positions as the sun dropped in the western sky, I was starting to lose track of the fly towards the end of its drifts, the glare on the water unforgiving. Leap-frogging my way along the shore, I had moved no more than two times, when I gave the fly a couple of twitches before lifting it clear of the blinding glare. The fly didn't budge! It was stuck down a fish's throat! Pinned to half a metre of wild, angry brown trout, the only way the Royal Wolf was going to move; was with the fish.

Without fail, the trout instantly obliged, taking the fly on multiple jumps through the air, in water that was no more than knee-deep. Unfortunately for the fish, it was late in the day and with my own dinner to be considered, it quickly ended up in my fry pan.

Despite the savaged landscape thanks to morons that couldn't stick to the one track when driving, this fish had quickly shown me the water might have been in decent condition, and still a worthy home for a few trout. I fell asleep that night hoping I might find a few more fish over the following days – not only trout as it would turn out . . .

ʕ ▲ ∝

The following day, the weather was perfect. Over the week I planned to spend in this area, it was predicted to be the pick of the days. The fact that other folk had been watching the weather forecast quickly became apparent. As I had suspected, I wasn't going to be alone. Around half a dozen four-wheel-drives ended up driving out around the lake in my direction that morning, even before I'd finished breakfast. Spin fishermen were amongst them, and it wasn't long before the lake foreshore was dotted with people casting spinners and spoons. It was as good a time as any to hike out and fish the lake I had surveyed in the distance the day before.

Close to an hour later, I reached my lake. Shimmering like a mirage, what I had thought to be the lake turned out to be exactly that, a mirage. My lake was now little more than well-irrigated pasture; a paddock that looked surprisingly similar in shape to what I remembered the lake to be. If I were a trout, a duck, a tadpole, I wouldn't have wanted to call it home – that was a certainty!

Just because people live on properties like this, and perhaps even own them, should it give them the right to destroy a lake that's likely to have been there for longer than European settlers, or possibly even longer than Maori settlers? The add on effect of over irrigation down on the Canterbury Plains might have aided in this lake drying up, but I suspect local irrigation was primarily to blame. I can clearly envisage the line of thought – 'We've got plenty of water up here, why not suck the lake dry and then we can farm on that too.'

I know that years of drought in New Zealand are also to blame, but shouldn't a time of drought mean we live closer to our means: lower stocking density and fertiliser use, work to conserve and retain water, work to reduce runoff and limit erosion, and work to irrigate sustainably? Grazing animals or planting crops most suited to weather and land conditions, also needs consideration prior to anything. If a particular crop or livestock type is no longer viable due to a lack of water and your farming practices have become detrimental to the environment, I don't care if your family has been farming that way for generations, change what you're doing or move – adapt or move out – it's as simple as that! Hopefully government budgets are such that they can assist our farmers to do that.

In my opinion, farmers and rural property owners are an indirect representative of the land, and of the nations in which we live. It's something rural people should be proud of, and we the nation's people should be proud of them. As such, they should always be aiming to farm sustainably. A nation's government should also always be ensuring our farmers are doing so, heavens forbid, perhaps the people will be proud of them too.

It appeared to me that the complete opposite had been happening during the 'dairy boom' in New Zealand; from the top down, dollar signs had been jackpotting through the nation's eyes, regardless of its negative impact on land and water. In New Zealand's defence, I doubt any nation on the planet is entirely innocent of this phenomenon. In my home country of Australia, the rape and pillage of water in the once majestic Murray Darling River system (Australia's longest) has seen it for all too long.

Since colonial settlement over two-hundred years ago, much of the river is literally dying. What the river supports is dying with it, including the communities that rely on it. Sadly, this includes native aboriginal communities who have sustainably relied on the river for well over forty-*thousand* years. We've destroyed it in two hundred! That's *less* than half a percent of the time aboriginal people have lived there! Growing cotton and rice just might not be viable people. So why not take the government payouts and make a life change. Make a planetary change — it's your responsibility to do so — it's everyone's responsibility!

And turning to the consumer side of the coin; instead of the current death throes of Australia's most iconic river system, I'm sure the average Australian would happily pay more for produce rather than have the agriculture industry continue placing an unsustainable demand on the river's water. They would also rather pay a little more than have farmers reduced to such desperation that they take their own lives. Indirectly, it affects everyone, the water the cotton grower takes at the top is water that the citrus growers don't get further downstream, or the vineyards beyond them, and so on. Water management is about working together; it's about making sacrifices for the greater good. After all, what do our farmers and governments, and general public want to leave behind for future generations, really stuffed rivers, or really, really stuffed rivers? Healthier rivers would be a nice alternative!

Looking over the mysterious new paddock in the Central South Island of New Zealand, I didn't need much fishing experience to know that my chances of catching a trout here were slim – it was back to the crowded lake that I was forced to go.

I adopted a similar tactic as the evening before, swinging dry flies on the easterly wind. This wind slowly became more southerly that afternoon and it eventually sent me packing. I drove back up to the other end of the lake, and hiked around to the leeward bank. Boggy ground made for slow progress and also resulted in a sandier shoreline. Compared to the rocks along the opposite bank, it looked like the trout were less partial to the sand and mud; I didn't encounter a fish all afternoon. I hadn't ten years earlier either.

With a few hours of light left in the day, I returned to my van and drove to another nearby lake. Designated for 'fly fishing only', this lake was significantly smaller. It's a good management intention, but it's a shame how it's usually only applied to small lakes.

The wind had backed off by this stage and there was a hive of insect activity along the banks, and on the water. Strangely, though, there wasn't a single rise to be seen. I hadn't fished this lake before, but it looked to me like the water was extremely low. It was far from being a cow paddock, but it did have me wondering if there were actually trout there to be caught. Like many of the lakes in this area, it was popular with water birds and with them seeming to be able to stand anywhere, it literally was little more than a duck pond.

f, ▲ ∝

A howling southwesterly wind accosted me like a mutiny the following morning, it saw me hiding in my van virtually the entire day.

That evening, after a day of tying flies, the wind suddenly swung, I failed to see a fish, and with perfect conditions the following morning producing the same lacklustre result, I decided that New Zealand Fish & Game might want to re-consider their two trout per-person per-day restriction on this lake. I didn't even see two bullies! Other nearby lakes were now little more than dust bowls, but still they were listed in the Fish & Game guidelines. Sorry guys but it's an interesting kind of fishing when you're allowed to take two fish per-person per-day from windblown dust receptacles. Assuming the lake I fished doesn't also dry up in the future, I suspect it was definitely in need of restocking – there were no bullies in the shallows

– and definitely no trout.

f, ▲ ∝

Seeing that everyone fishing the main lake were driving all the way to the other end, I suspected this was a common occurrence. I decided to do the exact opposite. I would try my luck halfway along the track, I'd fish right under their noses as they drove past.

Working my way along the rocks with the little Matuka pattern that had been serving me so well, it didn't take long for one of my angular casts to snap tight in my fingers. It was as simple as that! The plan had worked!

There was no mistaking the hook-up; its confident take had made sure of that. The fish ran to the left and spectacularly leapt a good metre out of the water, but the hook . . . well, it was there to stay.

After a spirited fight, with a few more jumps kindly thrown in for its solitary audience, a beautiful brown trout eventually neared my feet. Despite its dogged resolve, it was only my doing so that saw the hook eased from its lower jaw. At close to fifty centimetres in length, it was another solid fish. No doubt a little dazed and confused, it swam out towards deep water for some contemplation time.

Virtually right in front of where I had parked, I hooked another fish, which, in stark contrast, didn't hit the fly hard at all. It didn't jump either. I was instantly left guessing. A big conservative brown, I optimistically told myself . . .

It was another gritty fight, and I was left speculating about its identity to the very end; when much to my surprise, a big redfin perch stubbornly rolled over in the shallows, like a wallowing pig. Ordinarily I'd have been disappointed, but this was such a good specimen and in such fine condition, that I was actually appreciative of the variety. It might not have jumped, but it had definitely held its own in the pulling stakes. I pried the fly loose from its bucket mouth, and happily sent my best-ever fly caught redfin on its way. In quick succession, the gamble of fishing more obvious water had paid off.

Leaving these lakes, I drove on towards yet another. This next lake was another that I had frequented over the years and although I had never managed to pry any fish from it, I had seen some really big browns here. Driving in its direction, I found myself holding reservations as to whether or not the lake would actually still be there.

When I arrived the wind was blowing and rain threatening like a loaded gun; I decided to take cover. Battening down the hatches in my van, I tied a few more flies, hopeful of being rewarded with an evening glass-off.

It was overcast and the wind not as light as I'd hoped, but blowing in a direction that would be manageable on the water, I finally got out for a fish. In keeping with what appeared to be a sad trend, this lake had also basically turned into a duck pond. Perhaps two hundred metres long and forty metres wide at its widest point, the immediate foreshore was barely ankle-deep. I decided to fish it anyway. Fishing an un-weighted Matuka I had tied moments earlier; I began working my way towards the western end of the lake where I thought I could see an outlet stream. Even with no weight on the fly other than the hook, I was still forced to strip it quite quickly in order to keep it off the bottom.

What I had thought to be an outlet stream actually turned out to be an inflowing stream, in the fading light and gloomy conditions I could just make out the ripples signifying the flow of water. Unfortunately, not enough it seemed. Grass tussocks that I'd hidden behind while sight casting to trout ten years earlier, now stood close to a metre from the water's edge – it really was sad to see.

Many Kiwis had already expressed concerns to me about over-irrigation, but in order for the average Kiwi to recognise the excesses impacting on their country under their noses: dairy farming/irrigation, tourism, housing developments, and immigration to name a few, it might be that a leave of absence is needed for people to truly notice what is happening. It's a global phenomenon sadly, and unfortunately it seems the desire for a select few to make a buck is enough for the wool to be pulled over peoples' eyes. These days it takes me just six months away from Torquay, Australia to be shocked by the amount of new construction on my return; it's like a slap in the face. A year or two away is like a knockout blow. Go away for four years like I did at the turn of the millennium, and entire hillsides disappear.

The wind helped me get a good cast halfway across this puddle of a lake towards the inflowing trickle. In water that couldn't have been knee-deep, I came up tight to a fish. The take was so subtle that I momentarily thought I'd fouled some weed. The style of attack wasn't too dissimilar to the redfin perch earlier that morning. I wasn't rewarded with a jump from this fish either, but that said, I suspect it might have struggled to get enough speed for a jump in such shallow water. There definitely would have been points on offer for the level of difficulty on its re-entry, a broken neck a very real possibility. There

was significantly more weight behind this fish than the redfin earlier that day, and with its opening run quickly getting it on the reel, throughout all its head-shaking shenanigans, I fought it from there. Perhaps the most difficult part of the fight was the now steep bank standing half a metre above the water, not an easy situation when you've ducked out without any waders for a quick fish before dark. Kneeling and reaching down, I managed to get a hand over the substantial girth of its shoulders, flipped it upside down and lifted it onto the grassy bank for hook removal and release. This fish was also around the fifty-centimetre mark, but it was a fat, thick-bodied fish, and until then, easily my best brown trout of the trip. It was a good way to end the day.

In many respects, it was nice to finally have a bit of luck go my way without too much effort – I'd picked up all three fish that day while popping out for a quick fish – perhaps I was trying too hard . . .

ᚠ ᚫ ∝

Sunshine was a welcome change when fishing the same lake the following morning, but understandably, in such shallow water, the trout had a dose of stage fright. With the fish unwilling to step into the spotlight, it was time to move again.

The next lake I drove to was the largest in the area (for now) and, upon my arrival, the warm weather was sucking a westerly wind across it with gusts up to forty knots. In a corner with the wind behind me, I got out there anyway. It was far from enjoyable fishing and, despite my resolve, it also ended up being unproductive.

The frequent and often strong winds in New Zealand help the trout's odds against the angler, of this I am certain! It results in dry fly presentations often being botched and must surely be a contributing factor that makes New Zealand's trout some of the smartest and hardest to fool in the world. There's similar wind to be dealt with in Patagonia, but as you may have seen in my Patagonia book and film, this wind usually means the trout's prey is often large bugs, and even mice, which get blown out of trees and off grassy banks. As I said earlier, flies such as the Chernobyl Ant (which is usually the go-to dry fly in Patagonia) need motion to be effective, a bit of drift due to wind isn't a problem. The virtually microscopic surface prey fed on by so many of New Zealand's trout, even in strong winds, is another story entirely. Rarely does moving your size nineteen dry fly imitation aid the angler in New Zealand. In the days ahead, I would also learn that there was a whole lot more required to secure these fish than just natural drift.

I went to sleep that night hoping I might wake to a suitable wind, or a complete lack of wind, that would enable me to explore the tail-water river flowing from this lake.

ſ₁ ▲ ∝

Optimism, or sheer luck, saw conditions flawless when I stepped onto the river the following morning, and began Polaroiding my way downstream. Yes, with the fish looking straight at me; I know it's not the best direction to be fishing along a river, but as I picked my way through fallen timber and grass tussocks, I kept my distance, hopefully denying the fish any opportunity to see me.

The bank was quite high along the first few hundred metres of river and, with deep weed-filled water below, I'd be as exposed as a dubious clergy if I fished from the very edge. Trout are good at taking notice when danger is out in the open – they don't turn a blind eye either!

Crawling through cow shit to my first casting position, the fish I had seen turned out to be considerably larger than I had first thought. So too was its companion!

As I sat there watching these two fish patrolling deep water on either side of a shallow bottleneck, I contemplated what fly to try my luck with. They weren't rising to anything and appeared to be on the lookout for nymphs. There were a few light brown coloured caddis moths dead on the surface and, although I hadn't seen either of these fish rising to them, there was the occasional rise elsewhere. Despite it seeming like I was late to the party, I figured it still wouldn't hurt imitating the caddis and to try tempting them to the surface – I tied on an elk hair caddis.

With one of the fish momentarily inactive behind a midstream clump of weed, I cast upstream through the bottleneck. The fish flinched as my line landed on the water and as the inconspicuous little fly drifted past it, this was all it took. There was no further reason for this wise old trout to hold its ground and like a camera-shy celebrity, it arrogantly turned up its nose and indignantly meandered upstream through the bottleneck – you think that's going to fool me?

With matching indignation (or so I liked to believe) I turned my back on these two fish and continued downstream onto a lower bank and shallower pools. It was here that I had spotted the occasional fish rising while distracted by the celebs.

Due to my lower vantage point, the fish weren't as easy to spot here, but I was far less exposed and their regular rises were more than enough to keep tabs on them. It was about mid-morning by this stage and despite the fact that I was still unable to identify a hatch of any kind, I still believed I was in with a chance.

Persevering with the caddis pattern in this long and wide pool, I cast upstream, covering what I thought to be two different fish. The water was flowing quite slowly here and perhaps due to the extended time the fish were able to scrutinise my fly, both of them ignored it.

Ever onwards and downstream I went, giving promising looking water a wide berth with eagle-eyed scrutiny, and then fishing back upstream through it.

Passing around a boggy section of bank, I ended up on what turned out to be a boomerang shaped island. Quite fast flowing water was whipping around its outer bend in a narrow stream. There still appeared to be nothing actually hatching, but in the space of ten metres, there were two fish rising on a regular basis; picking up the spent moths I suspected. One fish was holding in slower water towards the end of the bend, and another in fast water at the top. Indiscriminately, I chose to pursue the upstream fish first. Apart from a bit of driftwood here and there, it was quite a barren island to be casting from, my only option for cover was to keep low. I crawled into a casting position like a cat.

With a bubbling rapid at the head of the run, below it, the stream was barely two metres wide. The fish was feeding where the bubbles cleared. In order to keep out of its peripheral vision, but also avoid casting upstream over the top of it, I crawled in towards it at its four o'clock. Ensuring that no more than a foot of my fly line actually hit the water, I cast upstream above it and let the leader and tippet do the rest. This brown trout wasn't a huge fish at about three to four-pounds, but it was far from small, and besides, it was right in front of me. The blood and adrenaline was pumping!

The fish instantly spotted my caddis fly; it moved to investigate, but rejected it as little more than flotsam. "Smart arse!" I muttered to myself, and flicked the fly out of the water. Taking a few deep breaths to let my pulse rate settle, I rolled on my side as if lounging on a beach, and replaced the caddis with a little Parachute Adams. Perhaps the tantalising prospect of an emerging nymph would entice a take.

The fly landed amidst the end of the bubbles with the delicacy of a feather settling on snow; it drifted clear and floated towards the fish, as natural as could be. I had seen it rise twice since my first cast – I couldn't miss – surely not!

Who was I kidding; there are no guarantees in fishing, particularly fly fishing, and particularly fly fishing in New Zealand's South Island! The previous handful of fish I had encountered that morning had proven to be crafty customers (frequently fished I suspect). I was almost surprised when this fish rose to my fly . . . and without hesitation . . . closed its mouth over it.

At a range of just two or three metres, there was no second-guessing on my part, the fly disappeared, and I struck, planting it to the inside of its mouth. Up or downstream were the only options of retreat available to this fish in such a narrow stream and downstream was its preference. Fallen timber in an upstream direction might have furthered its cause more, but as I scrambled to my feet, I saw that I had loops of line caught around the reel; regardless of the direction it ran, I was in a world of woe. With my rod stretched out in front of me as though being dragged by a runaway dog, my line steadfastly tangled, it was I who ended up running. Halfway around the boomerang bend was as far as I scampered, the fish not gaining an inch of line, and the tippet refusing to put up with my blundering. Damn it! I was fuming!

To me, the South Island of New Zealand isn't so much about catching lots of fish, it's about the quality of the fish, and to a certain extent, the quality of the hunt, the thrill of spotting the fish, stalking them and outwitting them. Failing to actually catch and release this fish, I'd only managed to get half the job done. With more and more people living, visiting, and fishing in New Zealand, the fishing was undoubtedly only getting harder, I knew I needed to capitalise on such opportunities.

On a brighter note, I had discovered that the Parachute Adams had worked (on this occasion anyway) so I replaced my tippet, attached another of these little flies around the size sixteen or eighteen mark, and continued downstream, doing my best to brush off the disappointment. I covered a considerable distance before I finally saw another fish.

This dark coloured trout was hugging a steep bank against the very edge of a fast-flowing chute of water. Watching it for a moment, its inactive behaviour might have led me to believe it was asleep. I wasn't going to accept that of course and for no particular reason, I decided I liked my chances of enticing it with a nymph swung off the top of the bank.

In order to pinpoint where it was sitting once I was on the bank, I identified some grass above the fish, then crossed over and doubled back downstream into position – or so I thought – suddenly all the grass seemed to look the same.

With no more than just my leader dangling off the end of the rod like Huckleberry Finn with a beanpole, I crawled and fished my way downstream, totally blind to how my fly looked, or even if the fish was still there. I quickly realised that this approach wasn't my best option, and I hiked back around to the opposite bank.

There was no sign of the fish by this stage. Safe to say that I'd scared it off, I wound in and continued downstream.

The river meandered through deeper pools from here and apart from one fish I spotted from a high northern bank, I was generally forced to fish blind. Downstream from these deeper pools, the river became sparser as its flow rate increased; black, Angus beef cattle spectated from various locations; it was clear to see where cattle crossed the shallower river braids. The more the river lost its uniformity, the less fish there appeared to be. That's not to say they weren't there, perhaps I just couldn't see them. At least that's what I was telling myself to keep the doubt at bay. Willing myself on, it turned out to be a good thing I did . . .

Scanning my way along the larger of two streams from its northern bank, I gave the second, smaller stream, a last glance over my shoulder. Trickling around a bend before entering the main stream, something caught my eye . . .

There wasn't much water in the stream, but on the narrow bend before it re-entered the larger river, there was a nice pool. Whatever it was that I'd seen had stopped me dead in my tracks. With my eyes glued to the deeper water on this dogleg, I waited to spot it again. It had been as if I'd glimpsed a salmon rolling on the surface; or had it been a branch floating downstream and getting caught in the shallows? Surely not, I told myself; there aren't any trees left on these paddocks. Backpedalling downstream, my eyes fixated on the stream, I was starting to doubt myself. When, suddenly, there it was again. There was no doubting it this time. Gentle and insignificant that it was, this rise was as certain as the tide.

Slinking in with a low profile, I crossed the main river, and crept downstream towards the fish. Again, this wasn't ideal, but with the river confluence on one side of the stream and thick grass on the other, I decided to stay on the river gravel. I would try to feed the fly down into the corner where I suspected the fish to be.

Getting down on all fours, I crawled in until I was no more than four-metres away. Carefully raising my head, I could just make out the dark shadow of the fish. It was less than the length of my leader and tippet away from where I lay. And it was big! Really big! Looking virtually straight at each other, like boxers set to clash, I dared not move. How on earth was I going to get a fly to it? Remembering how I'd blown it with a far smaller fish that morning, I reached for the reel and backed the drag off. The friction through the rod guides and the light drag setting would be more than enough to set the hook, after which, I was certain it would take off downstream into the main channel. I definitely didn't want to be tangled up chasing a fish of this calibre, my tippet wouldn't last two steps . . .

As though lounging beside a backyard pool, I manoeuvred and watched this fish for at least half an hour. During that time, it fed off the surface just three times. I hadn't even been able to spot what it was feeding on, let alone identify it, and looking down at the little Parachute Adams, I decided to replace it with the smallest Adams dry fly I had. There was nothing hatching and it appeared to be feeding on virtually invisible midges and sandflies, or possibly even the remnants of an earlier hatch that was equally hard to see. With what

I thought to be the right fly for the job attached and ready to go, the question of getting it to the fish without being seen became my next problem. It was crunch time!

The bend in the stream was a convergence of three currents: the one feeding the pool, the one flowing out of it into the larger stream, and the back eddy that doubled back on itself and fed back into the inflowing current. Lying on my side, I finally worked up the courage to make a cast. Now or never, I figured.

I flicked the leader out, trying to land it above the fish in the first current. Instead, the whole lot unceremoniously landed in the middle of the back eddy. Not quite what I had planned, but I didn't budge. I had no fly line out, and hoping the leader and tippet would sort itself out, I lay there, heart in mouth, and watched hopefully.

Like a slithering snake making its move from a coiled resting spot, the fly led the way, drawing the tippet and leader out behind it into the current. I couldn't believe it; it was going to hit the fish square on the head. As my leader gradually diminished and the speck of a fly drew closer and closer, I crawled forwards, rod poised, pointing straight at the fish. It was clearly a sizable trout and as it casually lifted its head and shoulders up towards the fly, it appeared to grow larger by the second; milliseconds that will be etched in my memory to the day I die. A great thing, had it not been for the subsequent proceedings that occurred with similar lucidity and finality!

It opened its mouth, and in the fly went. Down the top jaw came, and with my arm outstretched, I lifted it upwards and smoothly struck. It was as if I had reached out to give it a scratch behind the ears – it was so close – there was no mistake to be made!

Ah . . . but unfortunately there was! I felt the weight of the fish load the rod and was preparing for all hell to break loose . . . when I heard the drag give, oh so slightly. In the blink of an eye, the fish opened its mouth again, and out popped my fly. The pool was a picture of tranquillity, but the fish thought otherwise. Instantly aware of its mistake, and the danger it was in, it took off. Downstream! As predicted! At least I'd got that right.

I couldn't believe it! As you might understand, there's no way I can publish the words that flowed from my mouth at this stage. Words of utter disbelief! Words of anguish! It was the kind of encounter that simply doesn't happen every day, a big fish easily around the ten-pound mark, enticed to the surface to take a tiny size eighteen fly at a range of less than four metres. To a degree, in this day and age in New Zealand, it was an encounter of my lifetime. I'd got it all right, except for backing my drag off, had I not done this I was certain the hook would have found its mark. Fly fishing, it's a challenge!

I continued downstream until the current flow became so fast that I was certain no trout in its right mind would be living there. It was late afternoon by this stage and with just the two lost opportunities for the day; I started the long hike back to my van. Unable to shake the vivid memory of such a big trout inhaling my fly only to spit it back out, it was a long and solemn walk.

ᶠᵧ ᴀ ∝

I was up with the fog the following morning, eager to catch the hatch I'd missed the day before, and eager to make up for my lost opportunities. A faint glow lit the eastern sky like a warm smile. I made my lunch and had breakfast in readiness for the moment the sun peeked over the mountains.

With the clear light of morning washing over the stream and the fog slowly burning off as I made my way downstream, caddis moths were hatching in the millions. Fluttering from the grass along the river only to crash-land on the water, they were living on borrowed time. In a few places, the trout were making short work of them. There was no deliberation about my choice of fly that morning.

I tied on an elk hair caddis and crawled in towards two fish that were gorging themselves on the abundance of food. It appeared like they had thrown caution to the wind, feeding almost carelessly it seemed – yet still they refused my flies!

Further downstream, perhaps a little too eager for my own good, I spooked a really big fish sitting against the bank on a high undercut corner. I was eager to get to the spot where I'd lost the fish the morning before, and also to the pool I'd missed the massive fish in. Was it the one I'd just spooked? I had to tell myself to slow down! Even so, a big fish like that wouldn't be throwing caution to the wind the day after an encounter like ours, there was a good chance it wouldn't feed off the surface for days.

With the boomerang shaped bend on the river in the distance, I stalked in towards a smallish fish feeding in calm water on the inside of a more abrupt bend. The caddis hatch had tapered off, but with a number of them still on the water drifting downstream, I persevered with the elk hair pattern. To my surprise, this fish wanted nothing to do with it. I'd clearly 'matched-the-hatch', so why wouldn't it take it. Recalling the successful fly-change I made the previous morning, I switched to a small Parachute Adams.

Keeping the surprises coming, I was almost shocked, when this fish darted up to it, and wasted no time eating it. It was like a repeat performance of the previous morning. Only this time, I struck, and failed to hook it. After the devastation of missing the big fish the day before, I barely batted an eyelid on this occasion. I still couldn't get the vision out of my head. It was like a bad dream.

I fished on downstream, past the boomerang pool, and past the big fish's side stream that was still haunting me; there were no fish in either locations that morning, but further on, there was. Two big fish in deep water. They weren't actively feeding, however, and were by no means interested in changing their habits to chew on my fly.

The next big fish I encountered was feeding. It was a dark coloured rainbow. One of the other big fish I'd spotted that morning had also clearly been a dark rainbow trout; it had me wondering if they made up the majority of the fish population on this stream and not brown trout like I'd previously thought. The smaller fish I lost the morning before had clearly been a brown trout. Forced to keep my head low with the big fish I later missed, I hadn't got a good look at it, but I had suspected it to be a big brown. I now realised that perhaps this wasn't the case.

Back to the big dark coloured fish that was feeding, old and wise, it was staked-out at an awkward confluence, various currents entwining like a congested highway intersection. It was taking the occasional dry, but I took more interest in the fact that it was feeding on nymphs; so eagerly that it was actually turning downstream in order to get the ones it missed. At that moment, I should have realised that my best option was to carefully swing a weighted nymph into the current-tangled pool, and hope it picked it up. Instead, I insisted on using the dry fly, and with the haphazard arrangement of currents sinking it, I eventually spooked the fish.

As midday ticked over, the wind was as on time as a Swiss watch. Hoping to escape the stiff westerly, I set my sights on the lower stretches of the river. Who was I kidding . . . ?

The wind-rippled surface quickly had me doubting my use of a dry fly, but it was blowing at a reasonable angle, and the water did look good for a nymph dropper.

As with many things in life though, it's not always about how something looks. If there's no substance beyond the surface there's often no point wasting your time. In this case, it appeared there were no fish willing to back up how good the water looked. The wind was howling by this stage and I'd had enough. I turned back; ready to pack it in for the day and move to the next river before dark.

Taking a direct route well away from the winding river, I was a considerable distance back upstream when I found myself looking across at the water I had been encountering fish in that morning. With rabbits and hares bounding about at the end of the day, and clouds sweeping in from the southwest, it was cold. Although the wind was blowing upstream at thirty knots or more, I wistfully eyed some of the bends in the river that would allow me the use of my indicator and nymph. It was the prime time of day for it. What the heck – I thought – one last crack at it!

I fished the sharp bend in the river with no success and no sign of fish. But further upstream, at another pool where I had encountered fish over my two days here, it took just five casts before the black nymph was taken and my indicator fly submerged. Once more, it was the casual approach that had delivered the goods.

A beautiful rainbow trout was the result. It wasn't as big as the larger trout I'd spotted (and missed) on this river, but after two hard days of fruitless toil and failure, I was willing to take any appeasement that came my way. It was more than that, though . . .

Easily fifty centimetres long, it was one of the better trout I had caught that summer. The deliberate manner with which I'd caught it was also rewarding. Perhaps not as spectacular as the surface take I missed the day before, but as far as I was concerned, I had matched what it was likely to have been feeding on, and fooled it fair and square. With its pink flanks glowing, I felt a sense of self-satisfaction as it swam strongly from my hands.

Not too far from the dirt track and my van, I met a fellow Aussie that was also fly fishing. Going by the name of Bruce, I guessed him to be in his late forties. He had only been on the river for a few hours and although he'd seen a few fish, he'd failed to win them over. On our walk back, I learned that he was a grain and seed crop advisor. He had been in New Zealand for a few weeks visiting properties for work and had some time off to fish at the end. It wasn't surprising that we quickly got onto the topic of the dairy farming industry. He readily agreed that water, and its management, was, and probably always will be, a big issue in New Zealand.

"Incredible considering how much it rains here isn't it?" I said

"They continue irrigating when it's pouring with rain. A monetary value on water is definitely needed," Bruce said. "At the moment, some kind of annual fee is paid here in New Zealand, but nobody ever seems too eager to tell me how much it is. I suspect it's pittance."

I too had seen the irrigators working amidst downpours of rain. Goodness knows there'd been enough of it that summer.

We both also agreed that 'success' shouldn't be gauged by the development of properties and accumulation of assets and wealth. With eight billion of us expected on the planet by the end of 2020, and a rapidly growing middle class in nations who let their rubbish drift across entire oceans, that's a hell of a lot of holiday homes. Bruce's final thoughts he shared were this – "If any species overpopulates somewhere, they destroy the environment and end up disease-ridden. They usually end up eating each other."

Seeing that so many of the world's viruses in recent decades have come from the world's most populated nation, and one of the most densely populated, perhaps there's some amount of fact in his theory.

We appeared to have a lot in common with our views on conservation and I could see that his line of work might have resulted in him having a difficult balance of beliefs. Despite the possible clashes, getting sustainability-minded folk like him in the research, consultative, and management fields is what's required – it could only be a good thing.

Back at the track, I wished Bruce all the best for the following day, which would be his last day fishing, and hoped we might cross paths again one day. I was moving on towards what I planned to be my last river in the Central South Island.

After sleeping in my van near the Orari River, I quickly discovered that the mid stretches of this river were basically finished. Barely flowing in the midst of the Canterbury Plain's new 'dairy-farming mecca', it appeared to be another victim of obvious mismanagement. There was a trickle of water, but in the heat of summer, the trout wouldn't have been too happy living here – their growth most definitely inhibited.

Pulling into Ashburton for a few days, I caught up with my aunt and grandparents, picked up my kayak and headed south towards Otago and Southland. Hopefully I would find more water, more isolation, and more than a few spawn-run brown trout in the southern extremities of New Zealand.

The larger rainbow that climbed onto the dinner table.

The largest rainbow I managed in North Canterbury.

Calm conditions on the two-fish/day fishless duck pond.

Trying to avoid the wind on a lake with more water.

Headed downstream in an attempt to escape the wind.

Consolation after a loosened drag blew my chances.

Walking on water in order to find solitude.

Fences falling into rivers, sadly not an uncommon sight.

A nymph caught brown at the mouth of the flooded slough.

One of the 'penthouse pool' rainbows.

4. OTAGO & SOUTHLAND

4

It was late in the afternoon before I reached the first river I planned to fish in Otago, but with the sun shining and the summer days long, there was plenty of time to get out for a fish before dark.

Flowing through rolling hills and primarily sheep grazing countryside, willow trees lined the river. I couldn't wait to get down on the shingle banks and explore my way downstream. Not the ideal direction again, but the river hugged the dirt road further upstream and I was hoping to get as far from vehicle access as possible. I forced myself not to bother with the pools close to the bridge, but some hundred metres further downstream; I couldn't walk past the head of the first large pool.

Despite the rural countryside, this river appeared to be one where the landowners and users had managed to get things in balance. The amount of water and its quality looked relatively good. I would discover over the days ahead that the farming practices weren't perfect, but I had definitely seen worse.

With a blowfly imitation and nymph-dropper on my four-weight, it took just two drifts beside some fallen willows at the head of the pool for a nice brown trout to take an interest in the dry fly. I clearly watched this fish as it made its fatal mistake. It hesitated as the fly drifted over it, clearly thinking twice about eating the fly, and then made the mistake of veering downstream to take it. Instantly airborne and cavorting across the pool, it was a good introduction to Otago, particularly considering how close I was to the road. I couldn't wait to explore further downstream, surely it could only get better.

Unbelievably, I didn't even get beyond this pool before I was rewarded with another enthusiastic and wild brown trout.

On a long cast to the trees lining the opposite bank, it wasn't as big as the first fish, but again rising to the dry fly over the nymph; it quickly put a good bend in the rod. Releasing this fish after a lively battle, I realised that these two fish represented the most rapid success I'd had since being on the road – two fish, basically back to back. I only covered a few more pools before the shadows had closed in on the valley floor, the show had come to a close for the day and it was time to make my way back. A brief but rewarding show it had been.

A handful of fish had been rising that evening, but imitating the flies hadn't been the best means to catch their attention. With a bit of luck, the sun would be shining the following morning and the fish would be equally hungry.

ᶠᵧ ▲ ∝

The sun was shining and despite the fact that I was on the more isolated rural stretches of this river, it didn't take long for me to discover how much fishing pressure the river received – particularly on such a beautiful day.

I was up early, but a guide and his client were up earlier than me. As I pulled my waders on, they were on the river and heading downstream on foot, well ahead of me. To make matters worse, I'd only just finished licking my wounds when a four-wheel-drive pulled up and headed down a farm track following the river, access prearranged it seemed.

This wasn't exactly the kind of proceedings I'd been looking forward to. It had me wondering if I had fished water the previous evening that had already been fished that morning. What to do for the day . . . ?

Not to be outdone, I decided I would hike further than them all. Presumably I could get further downstream from where the guide and his client decided to start fishing back upstream, therefore I reasoned that any further river miles I covered should be mine for the day. From what I had seen the night before, I also suspected the vehicle track would only get the people in the vehicle so far.

Rather than fight my way along the bank of the river, I also decided I would hike along the vehicle track. Presuming they would all be fishing upstream from where they hit the river, I set off on a forced march, paying little attention to the river as I went. My sole intention was distancing myself.

Sure enough, I came across the four-wheel-drive at the end of the track, little more than a kilometre downstream. Just in case they had fished downstream from their vehicle, I covered another two or three long pools with barely a glance at the river.

I must have been over two kilometres from where I had parked, when a small side-stream branching off the main river caught my attention, I couldn't bring myself to walk past it.

Slowly snaking its way beneath some overhanging willows, it looked like the kind of water that might go unnoticed by the average angler, especially if fishing in an upstream direction. And still with no sign of the guide and his client, I figured why not have a go before they appeared from behind the willows. Talk about a game of cat and bloody mouse!

The water I was looking at was the perfect scenario for me to 'walk the dog' into. In other words, feed a dry fly out and drift it in under the willows. It was there that I suspected a lazy brown trout might be picking off its breakfast. Seeing that I would remain stationary in my casting position, it would be more a case of feeding the fly out and 'letting the dog run.'

I drifted the fly down the side stream and under the edge of the willows three times, but was forced to lift it out and recast on each occasion. It looked too good not to give it a fourth go.

Landing the fly halfway to the willows in the open, I began feeding the excess line out, allowing a natural drift, yet still keeping the fly on a tight enough lead not to miss a take. Just as I was losing sight of it as it edged into the shadows beneath the willows, I halted the drift and was on the verge of pulling the fly out, when I suddenly came up tight to a fish. As discussed earlier in this book, I suspect the slightest pause in the drift had imparted 'life' in the fly, and triggered the take. A few twitches to the fly just before re-casting can't ever hurt; you never know what might be ogling your offering and itching to pounce, if it hasn't done so by that stage, you've got nothing to lose.

The only downside with drifting a fly into cover like this is that the fish is essentially feeding on home delivered takeaways, there's usually very little stopping them from scoffing their meal on the doorstep and then slamming the door in your face. On this occasion, with the trout eager to get back inside to its favourite television show, it was a real tug of war; I wasn't accepting such rudeness, however, and neither of us conceded an inch. As it splashed and scrapped for ground, my four-pound tippet was put to the limit, the fish easily weighing that much or more, but in the end, it was just enough to drag this home-delivery-guts off its couch, and out into the outside world.

This brown was possibly a touch bigger than the biggest fish I'd caught the evening before. I successfully tussled it clear of the willows, but it wasn't finished with me yet. Cartwheeling across the surface towards faster water like a kite lost on the breeze, I tightened my grasp on the line, applying steady pressure, willing the fish to abort that route too. Complying admirably, it stampeded straight at me in the shallows. Thankful to be fighting it by hand, I quickly adapted, whipping the line through the guides until my quarry nearly hit me in the feet. From that dead-end it fled for the weed against the bank, but once encouraged out into the open again, it finally conceded defeat.

Flipping this thick-bodied and superbly conditioned fish upside down, I whipped the fly out of its top jaw and watched it swim directly back into the shade of the willows; to sit on the couch and reconsider its eating habits perhaps.

Climbing out of the river onto a paddock, I skirted around a fence falling off the bank, and then hiked downstream, past fifty metres or more of willows lining (and stabilising) the bank. It was at the head of this long pool that I spotted the guide and his client. I knew they were likely to be as happy to see me as I them, so I set a direct course across the paddocks towards willows I could see in the distance. For all they knew, I hadn't yet made a cast – the perfect crime!

I knew I'd get back onto the river at the willows in the distance, but what I couldn't see was the twist and turns of the river in between and it wasn't long before I was fishing a few of the open pools along the way. They looked too good in the early morning light not to drift a fly through them.

There were fish here, that quickly became obvious, but they weren't overly big from what I could see, and they didn't appear very convinced in my blowfly imitation. I briefly hooked one little scrapper, but it threw the fly and I wound in, happy to head through to the willows and perhaps fish these pools again later in the day.

Quite probably due to the presence of the well-established trees, there were some long deep pools at these willows too. Thanks to trees stabilising the riverbanks, these kinds of deep pools can hold a substantial amount of a river's water. In times of excessive rain they help manage an entire river system; taking the stress off lesser riverbanks, they act as natural dams. And in a time of drought, deep holes on a river can help limit evaporation and promote water retention, particularly if there's sturdy foliage shading the deep pools. Yes, a grazier might end up with shade on their pasture at that edge of the paddock, but at least the river is less likely to eat away at their land, and if cattle access drinking water elsewhere, they also won't degrade the bank and pasture in that area. Vegetation also provides shelter for livestock and whether from excessive snowfall, cold wind, or too much sun, it can help increase an animal's fattening rate, and ultimately, its profitability. Another positive aspect of having trees on the edges of rivers and paddocks is that over time, the carbon and other good stuff in the leaves, bark, and timber, can gradually find its way back into the soil, again promoting profitability. Not to mention the positive offset trees have on carbon dioxide and methane produced by livestock. I'd already seen fences falling off the top of riverbanks where there had been no trees that day – it's not rocket science – and the mind-boggling thing is that it's not overly expensive to promote a bit of vegetation growth, particularly in New Zealand where the survival rate and growth rate is likely to be quite high.

The next fish I came across was courtesy of another 'letting the dog run' episode. Crossing the river from where the large trees stood on the inside bend (large trees and boulders required on outer bank to stop erosion), I fed the exact same blowfly imitation down some faster water into a really deep pool. Tucked behind some younger willows, this pool was close to a fly line in distance from where I stood and must have been over my head in depth. It was the kind of deep, weed-filled pool that you'd think twice about swimming into its darkest corners as a kid – that was where the eels would be . . .

The water was incredibly clear beneath such a sunny sky and despite the distance, I watched with ease as a big trout boldly drifted out from the depths of this pool, came into broad daylight, and confidently sipped the fly off the surface. As they say, presentation is everything . . .

Why this fish didn't turn and dive back towards the roots of the willows, I have no idea. Instead, it did exactly what I needed it to do; it ran straight out into the open. Warranted it did so in a downstream direction, but there was no structure down there and I was confident some steady drag pressure would eventually have it back upstream in the shallows. Much like sailing, or even motoring a boat against a current, this was best done on angles, work it one way against the current until it refused to budge, and then do the same on the opposite angle. Two big runs back downstream saw me having to repeat this process, but is this not what fishing is all about, a strong fish making you work hard for your goal? This brown was definitely such a fish. Holding at the head of the deepest pool I'd yet seen suggested it was one of the larger fish in the area, if not the river. It was definitely the biggest fish I had hooked there.

In the end it was in a small side-stream above the willows where I managed to get it under control. Well, partially under control . . . it avoided my outstretched hand as I applied the finishing touches, but eventually it capitulated and let me get ahold of it. Easily five-pounds and with sparse dark dots, it swam straight back downstream on release, and disappeared around the bend back into its deep pool.

I was now miles from the dirt track where we had all parked earlier that morning and despite the fact that I continued even further downstream, the fishing only proved to become more difficult. I progressively saw fewer large fish, but did manage two around the three-pound mark. One of these fish must have jumped no less than half a dozen times, bouncing around like a puppet on a string, no sooner was it in the water and it was back in the air again. It quickly winded itself with these antics and once unhooked, was swimming free again in no time.

It wasn't long before it came time for the long hike back. Keeping a keen eye on the water, I fished a few pools here and there, but little more eventuated for the day. It was dark by the time I stepped through the fence back onto the track by my van. With the hour arm at ten o'clock, it had been a long day.

$$f_{\jmath} \ \Delta \ \propto$$

A rainy day followed, but after that, the forecast looked good for a five day stretch, in fact it looked to be the best long-term forecast since I'd been in New Zealand. I decided it was time to paddle out onto one of the larger lakes.

Having slept in my van parked on the lake's foreshore, the weather report for the first of the five days proved spot-on.

The water was like sheet glass as I paddled out from the eastern end of the lake, slicing through it like butter, even if my inflatable kayak did handle somewhat poorly compared to more regular craft. I was loaded up with a six and four-weight rod, and enough food and camping gear for two nights. My primary focus was an inflowing river at the far end of the lake. I was hoping to find a few brown trout starting to edge into the river, and I was hoping to outwit them before their hankering to spawn would see them stop feeding entirely.

I'd seen a number of helicopters flying overhead with deer hanging beneath them that morning. Fly in fly out hunters I presumed, but apart from these choppers, I now felt like I was finally getting away to some less frequented water. I realised the car park I'd just left must be full of boat trailers at times, but I hadn't seen any that Monday morning, and I did my best to remain optimistic.

With mountain peaks in all directions, their summits now bare of snow and bare of trees in the alpine reaches, the blue water of the lake sparkled below, green jungle-like vegetation overhung rocky shorelines, and with the air as fresh as could be – it was worth the paddle for the scenery alone.

After two or three hours paddling, I finally reached the primary river I had come to fish. Everything was glorious out on the water and my expectations were high, I couldn't wait to step ashore, stretch my cramped legs and hopefully spot some fish.

Ever careful of submerged timber, the river was a lot smaller than I expected as I tentatively paddled into it in the kayak, miles from nowhere, a punctured craft out there would have presented some serious complications for my return. I did have a repair kit, but only so much patch material.

As I stepped ashore and slid my kayak onto a beach of river stones as smooth as bowling balls, it took just seconds for my good mood to vanish entirely.

They were onto me in seconds and they were bigger than anything I had ever seen! So thick it was difficult to breath! SANDFLIES!!! I kid you not; a respirator wouldn't have gone astray. Struggling to get my tent up, it was only when I put my waders on that they finally stopped savaging my lower body. The second I stopped moving to do something, they were onto me. I dug out my rain jacket, adding it to my body armour before finishing with the tent. It didn't look like rain was going to be an issue, but without that tent, I suspect the sandflies would have carried me away.

Glad to keep moving, and otherwise excited about what such a beautiful little river might hold, I rock-hopped my way upstream to see if all the effort was worth it.

Sadly, it seemed it wasn't. The stream thinned out so quickly that any kind of fish population was out of the question. Fish from the lake may have spawned in the lower gravel beds of this stream, but with a huge lake full of food just a stone's throw away, no trout in its

right mind would have chosen to live in any of the pools I came
across.

Back down on the lake, the afternoon breeze was blowing and was
coming straight into my end of the lake. Dressed for fishing, I figured
I might as well.

Grabbing my four-weight, I attached a Matuka and waded out
behind the small breakers. Paralleling the shoreline scanning the
water ahead of me, it wasn't long before I spotted a big brown eel,
and then another one. Finally I found a trout, and quite a solid one;
eight-pounds I estimated. I couldn't determine if it was a rainbow or
brown, but it was little more than two rod-lengths away and looking
straight at me. Facing into the current and waves, no doubt waiting
for its food to be delivered to it, I drifted a blowfly pattern down to
it a few times. But when it came time for me to make a move, it
turned out the trout had as well, it was nowhere to be seen. If you're
fully exposed on a lake with an eight-pound trout staring at you, it's
usually safe to say your chances are blown.

With the sun creeping behind the western mountains, I decided
not to continue fishing along the lake that day. With lots of fallen
timber, weed beds, and structure in the shallows, it looked good.
However, with the afternoon breeze and chop washing ashore, I felt
like I wasn't doing the water any justice. Instead of simply spooking
fish in poor conditions, I would wait for the calmness of dawn.

ʃ₁ ▲ ∝

If I had any illusions that I might wake up and discover the sandflies
gone, it was quickly shattered. They were still lining my tent fly in the
thousands, struggling desperately to get inside and harness a feed of my
blood. Their feverish determination sounded like light rain on the tent
and when I say thousands – it's not just a figure of speech – there were
literally thousands of them!

It was no surprise that getting out of the tent to go fishing wasn't very appealing. I didn't have any repellent with me, but I honestly don't think it would have made much difference.

I dashed out, grabbed my billycan, and jumped back into the tent for a breakfast of rolled oats, raw peanuts, sun-dried dates, and sultanas. And on this occasion, all that was served with plain old river water as I'd forgotten the milk powder. Yes, I'd be writing a good list before casting off next time.

As I had expected, conditions were calm that morning, but once on the water I was surprised to see very little surface activity. Even during the three-hour paddle the day before, I still hadn't seen a single rise. The trout were there, the large fish I had spooked the evening before had proven that, but their numbers weren't consistent with the smaller lakes and rivers elsewhere. On this larger water body, perhaps there was just too much water between them.

As I set out to fish the stretch of water I'd forfeited the evening before, I knew it was perfect trout habitat – particularly for brown trout. Knee to waist deep flats with plenty of submerged timber and weed beds; it was a big brown trout's paradise. Surely I could find one out there . . .

I started fishing within range of where I had seen the fish the evening before. Casting the small Matuka to imitate trout fingerlings I'd seen in the shallows, I covered no more than five metres, when I missed what I was certain to have been a fish. It was one of those takes that left me guessing: was it a big fish taking a cautious 'sniff', or was it a small fish boldly picking off more than it could chew? The bottom line was that I'd missed it, but seeing that I had only just started fishing, I was naively still full of optimism. Little did I know, I would cover another hundred metres and not see another fish. Over the days ahead, I would discover there was a good chance it had been quite a nice sized fish.

Wearing chest waders, a long sleeve shirt and rain jacket with the hood pulled low over my cap, I had managed to avoid the worst of the sandflies that morning, but it was a warm day and it was far from the kind of attire I wanted to be fishing in. My hands were exposed and swollen from all the bites and to be honest, it was simply hard work – far from enjoyable.

I got back to camp for a lunch of two muesli bars and a can of sardines. I'd also forgotten my bread, peanut butter, and jam. Yep, I was definitely in need of that list.

Paddling out on the lake towards a smaller tributary and a stretch of sandy beach, I had a welcome respite from the sandflies. Once ashore, I briefly thought I might have avoided them entirely, had I camped in the wrong spot, but no, they found me soon enough; it wasn't long before the rain jacket was back on and the hood pulled low.

Stowing my kayak in the shade under some trees, I went for a look around. Nearby were remnants of a fairly well used camp. Sadly I'd even seen footsteps on the beach that didn't look very old, and the telltale markings of a V-bottomed boat being put ashore. The most disappointing thing to find here was the discarded plastic chairs and empty beer bottles left in the fireplace. Not to mention the many beer bottle caps uncaringly thrown around the place. It wasn't the kind of thing you like to find after a three-hour paddle . . .

Although this stretch of water probably got regularly flogged judging by the nearby campsite, I made my way along the shoreline and quickly spotted a pair of fish in the shallows. The sun was shining straight on the beach and it was hot! The sandflies were nailing me! An alternating and constant slapping of both hands was required to maintain some form of sanity. If tying on a new tippet and fly were required, I'd be destined for an asylum. Due to the handful of failed knots I'd recently been experiencing, I was putting five twists into my blood knots when attaching flies to the lighter tippets, but on this afternoon, the sandflies and my sanity allowed just the usual four. I still ended up with no fewer than a dozen sandflies gnawing on my hands; even blowing on my hands while tying wouldn't deter them.

The only fish I saw along that beach were the brace of fish sitting off the inflowing stream right near the filthy campsite, one of which must have been close to six-pounds. I did my best to cover them with the Matuka, but after seeing the fresh footprints and rubbish nearby, my heart just wasn't in it. They weren't rising and I knew they had probably been fished quite recently. They emphatically showed no interest in the Matuka.

With the wind blowing along the beach, it was a good scenario to drift a dry fly and nymph-dropper. I reasoned that this technique would also give me a free hand to swat the sandflies off my rod hand. I realised I was in the market for a pair of gloves!

Things just weren't going my way, though. I'd only just rigged up a large blowfly dry with a black nymph, and had barely fished twenty metres, when I was stricken with an evening glass-off. For the first time that summer, I wanted the wind to keep blowing. It simply wasn't the kind of water to be casting a dry fly and leaving it to sit. There were no fish rising and I wondered if I should have been fishing a nymph or streamer. However, as I said, my heart just wasn't in it.

As far as I was concerned, there was very little on this part of the lake that was worth staying for. The following morning I would be paddling back with a fly rod rigged and ready to make a few casts along the way. It would have to look extremely promising for me to put ashore and camp another night.

ᚠ ᚪ ᚳ

Paddling out from my campsite, the lake was bathed in glorious sunlight and still conditions. A part of me felt disappointed to be wasting such perfect weather in an area that hadn't fished as well as I thought it should. I set my course directly down the lake, shaving the corner of some mountains where they plunged into the water, the thick rainforest at their base in stark contrast to their barren alpine heights.

Just as I neared the first craggy slope, I heard the trickle of a mountain stream tumbling out of the rocks and old-growth jungle. I instantly thought of the trout hanging around the small stream near the rubbish-filled campsite the previous afternoon.

I tied a large, bead-headed Matuka to my six-weight, and sank the fly down around the inflowing creek and fallen timber. It looked like perfect brown trout water; I could clearly imagine a big old brown trout sitting amongst the timber, patiently waiting for a hapless trout fingerling or galaxiid to make the mistake of venturing under the wrong log. It never did happen, and my demeanor dropped to even greater lows. Where on earth were the fish . . . ?

I paddled on, continuing along the shoreline when my direction of travel allowed it, and crossing open water when it didn't. With the shoreline becoming less mountainous, I must have covered another kilometre or more, when a small cove caught my eye. "That looks pretty good," I thought to myself, and for a moment I debated whether or not I could be bothered stopping. It was only the added thought of, I bet none of the powerboats bother stopping to fish there, that had me stealthily pulling into casting range.

Sinking the fly down against submerged timber, it was on my second cast, after perhaps half a dozen strips, that it was immobilised in its tracks. It went no further!

This was a decisive take and I knew the potential danger the timber posed – I did little more than hang on – my eight-pound tippet and knots at their limit!

Gratefully, this was enough to deter the fish from diving into the maze of wood, and taking me to the cleaners. It so easily could have! Instead, much to my delight, it launched into the air with three jumps, the water glittering like gemstones in the early morning sunshine. Realising the airborne strategy wasn't helping its situation, this fish then made the mistake of running for open water, putting a good ten metres or more between it and the safety of its timber-footed shoreline. Perhaps realising its folly, it desperately tried one more jump; again, well over a metre clear of the water and as clean as they come. They weren't necessarily ten-point no-splash reentries, but safe to say that I was putting it off balance, I was suitably impressed. A good tug-of-war ensued from here, but I let it run when need be, usually as it neared the kayak. Right when I thought I had it in the bag, it would near my outstretched hand and then take off in a splash of anger; wine flung in my face on a date gone wrong. Not that I'm speaking from experience there, but I continued hanging on, keeping it within range of leader and tippet, until it tired and allowed me to get ahold of it with my left hand. And what a beautiful thick-bodied fat fish it was (not good dating talk either!). I did suspect it to be a hen, though, and covered in a myriad of spots with a blunt bullet-like nose and vivid sash of pink along its flanks, it was one of the healthiest looking fish I had seen that summer. A part of me couldn't believe it. It had been as simple as that, make a cast in the right place, and bang!

Letting it go, I paddled on, eagerly looking for new locations to repeat my good fortune.

Murphy's Law usually has it that I have a headwind on my return paddles after camping on lakes like this, but in this case, luck was on my side and a light westerly was tentatively ushering me along the lake. However, the wind was so gentle it appeared not to know if it wished to reach the other end of the lake. After catching such a beautiful fish, I could relate.

The next stretch of shoreline that caught my eye was some reed-lined shallows that were bookended with thick vegetation at one end, and submerged trees at the other.

I had no success in the corner with thick vegetation tumbling down to the water's edge, nor along the weed-lined drop-off in between, but in the furthest corner, just a few casts towards the submerged timber did the trick again – I was instantly onto another fish!

The similarities to the previous hookup stopped there. This fish dove to the bottom and charged towards the timber like any dirty fighting trout would. Or, I guess, like any sensible trout would. Is it a brown, I wondered? No offense to the rainbows, but the cunning European brown trout is reputed to be a bit more of a thinker than the flamboyant North American rainbows. Not once did this fish jump and it kept me guessing through numerous last-minute splashing dives to the bottom. Until, finally, I managed to secure an almost identical rainbow. Unpinning the Matuka from its upper jaw, I happily watched it swim strongly to the safety of the depths below.

After two long and trying days, these fish had suddenly appeared from nowhere, I couldn't help but expect the ball to keep rolling throughout the day. Much like life, though, the game of fishing can often fail to deliver on what one might expect. I guess its uncanny ability to do this is part of what keeps us hooked. I did, however, finally see a fish rise.

After paddling across an expanse of open water, I found myself pausing to have something to eat. By the time I had finished, I realised I had drifted into a wind lane. Ten metres wide and running along a stretch of steep, timber-clad shoreline, there was a smorgasbord of dead insects mixed amongst the bubbles and scum on the surface. As I cast towards the submerged trees and fallen timber lining the bank, I saw a rainbow trout boldly venture out into the open water, and brazenly take something off the surface. It then practically swam straight towards me, and casually inspected my kayak. With the water so clear and this rainbow's colours so bright and vibrant, I felt like I was drifting across a tropical reef.

This fish's boldness to leave the cover for a meal got me thinking. Perhaps fishing a fly that offered a bit of movement on the surface would prove productive. Something like a damsel fly imitation, or even a Chernobyl Ant. I wasn't totally sold on the idea, and I decided if I saw another fish rise, only then would I make the change. A big part of me didn't want to waste time re-rigging while on such a user-friendly drift. Over the next hundred metres or more, I never did see another fish rise – or anywhere else on the lake for that matter.

The fish were discreetly absent throughout the remainder of the day. Sadly, the boat traffic wasn't.

It was only two or three boats, but as I drew closer to the eastern end of the lake and the car park, it was enough to dampen my enthusiasm. Still, after what could only be described as three days of hard slog, I was glad to have been rewarded with the two rainbows.

I was in the market for a new six-weight rod by this stage and I decided it was time to venture further south in Southland to Invercargill, the southernmost city of any substantial size in New Zealand.

Although it amazed me at how many roads and villages crisscrossed this southernmost extremity of the country, there were still plenty of rivers to be fished. The majority of rivers flowed through privately owned agriculture and milk tankers on the roads were more prevalent than ever. Pushing it from my mind, I tried to remain positive.

It seemed New Zealand's wilderness wasn't very isolated with all the boats, four-wheel-drives, and helicopters these days anyway, so who knew, perhaps fishing under everybody's noses could outperform the apparent 'isolation'.

꜀ ⋀ ∝

With the dawn of a new day, I headed out on foot to fish the river I had camped beside.

Unbeknown to me, my morning of fishing and run of good weather would suddenly come crashing shut like an All Black's front row. The clouds were as black as a coalface, the wind savage and the raindrops like stones plunging from the sky. I never even fished my way out of the first pool!

By late afternoon the wind was still tearing in from the west, but incredibly, the sun was shining. By this stage, I was still amidst grazing countryside and I made my way out on another river.

There had been a lot of didymo in the river I briefly fished that morning, but thankfully, this river wasn't as badly affected. Had it been flowing out in true wilderness; it really would have been a thing of beauty. Nevertheless, flowing crystal clear and at a medium pace, I was confident of finding a fish or two, even if dairy herds and suburbia were just around the corner.

I failed to achieve much with my blowfly pattern in the first pool, but as I cautiously made my way onto the tail of the next long pool, stretching ten metres or more, I detected a couple of tiny rises in the riffle. The fish were there; their conservative rises suggesting they were quite reasonable sized fish. They showed no interest in my blowfly imitation, and I changed to a tiny Adams.

This little fly rewarded me with an aborted take, which, from a distance of just four metres, I witnessed as clear as day. They were brown trout, and as the evening progressed, they proved to be typically fussy. I worked through my fly box at a desperate pace that evening, so much so, that after an hour I needed to replace my tippet due to so many knots wearing it short. I tried a Craig's Nighttime, various sized caddis patterns, a Parachute Adams, and a number of other emergers, including two emerging midge patterns. Based on what I could see on the water, and in the air, I even tried two different dun patterns. There was a lot of insect activity, some of it large and some small. The swallows and trout were having a field day. Unfortunately . . . I wasn't!

The only thing showing any real interest in my flies were the swallows. Incredibly, after more than two months, this was the best rise I had seen in New Zealand all summer. I retired for the night, frustrated and beaten. I was, however, adamant that I would have another look at this stretch of river in daylight hours.

I was quite sure this river got the kind of attention a family fish bowl does, but there was definitely more than just the one goldfish here. There had also been no one else on the water that Friday evening. With a bit of luck, Saturday morning might be the same.

f⅂ ▲ ∝

It was an overcast morning as I pulled on my waders, and to the south, the All Blacks front row was threatening once more. With a bit of luck they'll go for a run up the west coast, I told myself.

Flowing in a north-to-south direction, the westerly wind was quite manageable on this stretch of river. Added to which, large willows sheltered the water from both banks in many places, on occasions even allowing me to cast directly into the westerly wind. These willows and the surrounding fodder crops and pasture all appeared to be an ideal breeding ground for insects, and as I parked near the long pool that had been alive with fish the evening before, I could clearly see the occasional fish rising.

My plan for the day was to have a brief fish that morning, visit a nearby town for a coffee around midday, tie a few flies, and then maybe hit the river again for an evening session. Seeing that the fish had shown little interest in my assortment of dry flies the evening before, I had lay awake in my sleeping bag pondering things the evening before. By hanging the 'carrot' of a nymph-dropper behind the dry fly, I had decided I would try to lure them away from their surface prey.

The first nymph I opted for was a stick caddis nymph. Drifting like snowflakes the evening before, there had been a lot of white caddis moths amongst the variety of insects and a quick dig around the bottom revealed stick caddis nymphs in good numbers. My plan quickly proved effective.

Even if it was just a little two-pound scrapper that had picked up my nymph at the end of its drift, the fact that it had chosen the nymph over the dry fly was proof enough to me that a larger fish might do the same. I had started the day using an elk hair sedge caddis imitation as my dry fly indicator, but as the day started to warm, I eventually changed it to a large blowfly pattern.

Before I knew it, my quick fish before a midday coffee had stretched well into the afternoon and I hadn't even progressed beyond the first pool.

Crouching on the opposite bank at the head of this pool, I could see a number of trout. Two or three of them were quite big and I was hooked on trying to betray their feeding habits. They were dominating the headwater to ensure priority over the food entering the pool and I suspected they also knew they were safe there due to the wind making it virtually impossible for me to present a fly. The water was also quite shallow, and flawlessly clear. These were adult fish, they had been around the block more than once, and long before I could get a fly anywhere near them, they were spooking.

It was a unique kind of river compared to many I had been fishing that summer; there was an incredibly large fish population, but the majority of them were only around two to three-pounds. In a strange turn of events, I now found myself on a river where I wasn't too bothered if I spooked a fish – I knew there would be a few more just a bit further along the bank.

The interesting thing, however, was that despite their lack of age and maturity, they were remarkably prudent. They definitely weren't about to feed on the first thing I threw at them.

The fact that this river was quite slow flowing also may have been making life difficult for me. The fish had all the time in the world to scrutinize what I was presenting to them. In a fast run linking this slow flowing pool to the next, this pattern of behaviour suddenly changed.

A fish of about three-pounds pulled my blowfly indicator under, and ended up with the tiny bead-headed nymph hooked to its lower jaw. It exploded from the water with a couple of jumps and after a few strong runs in the faster flow; the dependability of my hook placement was quickly exposed.

Someone watching from afar could have easily been mistaken for thinking I'd lost a double-figure fish. I wasn't happy! The fish were numerous, but just like the evening before, they were proving to be quite a challenge, especially the larger ones. I was getting pretty hungry by this stage, but this lost fish was the thorn in my side – now I really wanted to catch one!

I went on to feel the weight of what felt like two more decent fish in shallow water beneath the willows, but I only felt their weight long enough for them to break the surface and brusquely throw the hook.

My best fish for the day was in another shallow and slow flowing pool.

Using an even smaller black nymph by this stage, and on my second cast, I clearly watched this fish casually swim across open water towards the flies. There was a flash of white as the nymph disappeared in its mouth, and I struck, the deed done. Well . . . so I thought! Suddenly its demeanor wasn't quite so casual! Four-pounds of brown trout flew into the air, cartwheeling back towards the cover of the willows from whence it had bravely ventured. Apart from this explosive opening to the flight, it was generally quite a subdued affair from that point on. Until it came time to get ahold of it for release that is . . .

This fish turned out to be quite the poker player. Just before the bell, with all the aces up its sleeve, it was ready for one last knockout punch. There I was, the fish in the shallows, me thinking it was 'in the bag'. I got ahold of the leader, and got a hand on the fish, but I might as well have been opening a bull rider's gate. Blasting from the shallows, showering me with water, it left me standing there in disbelief, the inert leader hanging from my hand.

I should have been content with this catch and 'release', but again, it made me even more determined. I prefer removing the hook myself thank you very much.

However, determination isn't always the required condiment when it comes to fishing and, eventually, I got back to the car with the clock reading 9:00 PM; my empty stomach growling. So much for a midday coffee break – I hadn't even had lunch!

It was time to move on, out of the dairy fields and hopefully back to some version of wilderness.

ᚠ ᚪ ᚳ

I didn't get too far the following morning, the sun was shining when the weather report said it shouldn't be, and as I took my time over breakfast, I contemplated having a 'quick' fish back at the same river; perhaps I'd try my luck in the opposite direction.

In the end I decided against it and by mid-afternoon I was into my second coffee at the bar of a nearby hotel. The weather report wasn't looking too good for the next two days, but Wednesday through to Friday after that was looking like it might improve. This got me excited about venturing out onto another of the large Southland lakes. Knowing the sandflies would be just as bad, I still wasn't sure if I would leave the sanctuary of my van for more than a day. No doubt I would make my decision upon seeing the lake, but the last day kayaking back at the previous lake had made me realise how much water I could cover and fish in one day. Day trips might be the order of the day.

After finishing my second coffee, I decided I'd better get out and make the most of the afternoon before the two days of foretold rain arrived.

The river I reached that afternoon wasn't too far away from the lake I was hoping to fish later in the week. It wasn't exactly out of the rural countryside, but it definitely felt more isolated than the infuriating river I had been fishing over the previous few days. It was a grey blustery afternoon by that stage, but the wind was blowing upstream on a slight angle and was manageable.

It was a significantly smaller stream than the one I had just left, but I'd only fished upstream through one pool and one riffle, when I spotted quite a nice fish. I could see it sitting at the head of a narrow and deep pool, and I knew there was a good chance it could see me. I froze to the spot, and still fishing with the 'there's plenty more where you came from' frame of mind, I dropped a medium-sized Royal Wolf just above it. Of course it ignored it entirely and upon seeing it the third time, it shot-through. I hadn't expected anything more. I wound in and continued upstream, fishing along quite a lengthy chute of water that I suspected most people wouldn't bother with. By the time I reached the top of it, I hadn't found any reason why they should.

The pool at the top of the chute was beautiful, though, it was well worth my time. With a crumbling cliff lining the back of the pool and a deep slot flowing along its base, a shallow pebble bottom stretched between this 'money zone' and me. Judging by the sizable fish I had just seen in a smaller pool, there had to be a fish or two sitting along the base of this cliff. Late in the day as it was; I imagined fish backed up at a drive-through – nymphs would be on the menu – I was certain!

Back from the water's edge, I took the time to attach a black nymph-dropper to the dry fly. Either option could have been on the menu, but on this occasion, I had a feeling the nymph would be the draw-card. At about size fourteen or sixteen, I had chosen a slightly larger nymph to what I had been fishing in the shallow water the day before.

Not wishing to spook a lone fish in the shallows and blow the entire pool, I covered the lower third of it from a distance, flicking my line over a few exposed rocks in the shallows while mending the drift. As the white of the Royal Wolf drifted through, floating high and clearly visible, I couldn't believe it when it failed to dip beneath the surface. I caught myself talking out loud – "Come on, you've got to be there! Surely?"

But it seemed there wasn't a fish ready for a nymph here. I edged upstream to cover the upper two thirds. The uppermost stretch of the run had too much current disturbance for a clean drift, and I put all my belief into the central stretch.

Dropping the flies in at the end of the disturbed water, literally casting straight into the dirt cliff so the flies fell to the water as naturally as could be, I waited with abated breath. Despite how good it looked, the flies drifted through this stretch untouched too. I must admit; I was gradually starting to lose my enthusiasm. When the dry fly casually dipped on my second cast, my brain and my heart told me it was nothing but the bottom. You can imagine my surprise, when I struck, and instead of the flies flying back over my shoulder like they so often do, they held firm in that glorious 'giving but not giving' sensation of hooking a fish. Some people call indicator nymph fishing 'bobber fishing', and to a certain extent I agree with them, it is, but geez it's a great feeling when you hook a fish, especially a good one like this.

It didn't jump. In fact it didn't even really run; this old dog of a brown was the top dog in this pool and he wasn't going anywhere, unless he really had to. He definitely didn't want to leave the deeper water to cross the shallows; his obstinate head-shaking and rolling on the surface made that perfectly clear. All in all it was little more than a tug-of-war this fight, albeit with a bit of dogmatic surface commotion, especially when the shallows drew near. Applying as little pressure on the hook and tippet as possible, I ended up using the current to lead him downstream, and across the shallows in the one motion. I didn't want a repetition from the day before; if I had any say in the matter, this was going to be a clean release.

Eventually I got my hands on the fish in the shallows and he was by far the best brown trout I had caught that summer, easily the largest from a river. Glowing with a rich golden brown colour, and sporting large dark spots earnt from a life hiding in the rock and timber-filled corners of the river, he was a weathered old fellow, but in beautiful condition A large white scar at the corner of his mouth near where my fly had found its mark suggested that he'd been caught and released before. At the very least, it had been hooked. Having acquired a few battle scars myself over the years, my heart kind of went out to the guy, and with affection; I happily watched him swim back into his favoured deep water.

Heading back towards my camp in the gathering darkness, my mind wandered.

The day before I had fished all day on an empty stomach for just two scrappers, two lost fish, and two or three missed fish. Life and fishing can be strange at times . . . sometimes the less you try the more you get, and then, other times, much like this unfortunate fish who was just trying to get a meal and stay alive, sometimes all you get for your effort is hardship and pain.

What will tomorrow deliver, I wondered?

ᶠ₁ ▲ ∝

Although rain was forecasted, I was pleasantly surprised to wake to sunshine and relatively still conditions. I had imagined spending the day fishing in waders and a rain jacket, but instead, it was in a long-sleeved shirt and rolled down chest waders that I set off. It wasn't a very big river and I was unlikely to be wading very deep.

I had only passed one pool and a lengthy rapid when I came to the pool where I had seen a fish the previous afternoon. It was there again, but it wasn't sitting in the same awkward position at the head of the pool. Instead, it sat halfway along the pool behind a slight dogleg in the bank, a stand of willows drooping from it like un-kept hair. Perhaps it was feeding on prey falling from this tress of leaves.

I could easily present a fly to it here and I wasted no time crawling into a casting position off its flank. Mid crawl, I watched its calculated behaviour as it took a dry. Despite the rise, I went ahead with the Royal Wolf and nymph-dropper from the evening before; if presented well, there was no reason why it shouldn't have taken either of them. There was no interest shown in either fly on my first cast, but with my heart in mouth on the second, it turned and followed the dry fly downstream for two metres or more, its snout so close to the fly, it had to be sniffing it.

The natural dry that had been taken earlier had appeared to be a blue dun. I didn't have any specific blue dun patterns, but I was confident the little Adams that had been proving effective would be more than adequate. And so onto the business end of my tippet one of them went. It took just the one cast.

Just like it had with the real thing minutes earlier, the fish's pointed nose came right out of the water like a periscope, and it climbed on top of what it thought to be its morning breakfast. Clearly watching its mouth close over the little fly – I struck!

The tranquil pool suddenly erupted into chaos, water flew as it leapt into the air, and then charged downstream in an attempt to exit its pool. I wasn't going to allow that, and with some persuasive pressure, I managed to keep it on home turf. We stood there stuck in deadlock for some time, the fish stubbornly holding its ground, and me insisting it give it up. In the end, it was my stubbornness, and my lack of patience, that saw the fish come out on top. Or perhaps it was just my bad luck. Either way, the hook pulled and my sudden run of good luck came to an abrupt end.

Putting this early downfall behind me, I pushed on further upstream, past the old brown trout's pool, and a considerable distance beyond. I had the occasional cast here and there, but the runs and pools I was encountering appeared too shallow to support fish of any substance.

I'd covered perhaps a kilometre of fruitless water, when I thought I spotted a fish sitting in the middle of a steadily flowing riffle. Having lost my patience after two hours of fishing with the assumption the river was thinning-out; I sulkily walked straight out into the current to confirm it was a fish. At that point, I was almost certain it was a rock or a log. But no! It was a fish! And quite a good one!

"Well . . . they're still here!" I said to myself, somewhat stupidly. Then, realising what I'd done, I told myself out loud just to make sure I didn't do it again, "Good one! You just spooked a damn good fish!"

Across the stones and through the sparse grass and flax, it took another few hundred metres before I came across another decent pool.

About as long as a tennis court, with a grandstand of willows down one side, I spotted a sizeable fish sitting off a shallow bank near the head of the pool. Judging by its movements, it appeared to be pursuing nymphs. However, while crawling into a casting position, the same thing happened as had happened all those hours ago that morning; I watched a sizable blue dun drift towards it, and then disappear down its pointed snout.

"Ah, you're mine," I said to the fish.

I had reverted to the dry fly nymph-dropper approach while fishing the previous lackluster runs, but I now wasted no time changing back to the little Adams. I knew it wouldn't last a second . . .

By the time I finished tying it on, I looked up and realised the fish had moved. It was now just below some willows, tight in the corner, immediately below the inflow of the pool. It was virtually right in front of me! I didn't need any line out, and from my seated position, I flicked out the leader. The little fly landed delicately and drifted straight towards the fish, my rod poised and ready to strike.

With equal care, the fish's snout rose up and over the fly and at a range of less than three metres, there was no mistake to be made. The sting of the hook hit the fish's nerve endings and it responded with an immediate head-shaking jump. This failed to remove the bothersome fly and it quickly absconded in a downstream direction. Up to the challenge, I was on my feet and stumbling after it instantly, my stealthy approach a thing of the past. Bringing the fish up short of exiting the pool, it ran back upstream straight at me, and like a bus out of service, it kept on going.

Clambering out of the pool onto the bank I ran after it, only just managing to get a workable angle on it as it dove for the roots of the willows. With generous palm pressure on the spool, my four-weight rod bent tip to tip, I somehow managed to draw it short of threading me into oblivion. Again it tried the downstream approach.

Only making half the distance this time, I knew we were into the final stages of the fight. I was back in the water ready to perform my duties as a welcoming committee, but from day one that summer, I had learnt that these wild Kiwi trout weren't truly beaten until you had them safe in hand. I took care applying the finishing touches, eager to get what I now realised to be a rainbow trout, firmly in my grasp. And what a beautiful fish it had turned out to be. At around the four-

pound mark, the tiny fly pinned to the corner of its mouth had me marveling at such large fish feeding on such tiny prey. Trout, you've gotta love them! In my eyes they really are one of a kind in the piscatorial world. I happily watched this one swim strongly from my hands, straight back into the depths beneath the willows.

A little further upstream from this pool, I came to another. Long and narrow, I saw very little along its length, but I did manage to spook a big fish sitting in slack water adjacent to the rapid feeding it. I couldn't be certain, but I suspected it might have been a brown trout.

If I found pools with a reasonable amount of debris lining their banks, or with some form of vegetation offering food and shelter, it seemed I was in business. The trout weren't there in big numbers, but at around the five to six-pound mark, they were beautiful fish. I made a mental note of this one, and moved on.

The stream left the willows and other shrubbery from here and tracked into the open across the wide riverbed. It wasn't until I reached some shrubbery standing alone like an oasis, that I found another pool large enough to hold a fish. A pool established by a lone tree and some scrubby vegetation, their roots tapping into the ready supply of water they were helping to retain. It's not a complicated science – nature and a handful of plants had created this pool – and virtually every decent pool on the river! With a helping hand, so much could be done by New Zealand's landowners lucky enough to have such rivers flowing through, or adjacent to their properties. It would be a win-win!

This pool I had come across was relatively small, but it was quite deep and with timber in the water for shelter, and shrubbery on the bank, I was confident it would hold a fish.

Creeping into position to present a cast, a small fish, or at least what I thought to be a small fish, broke the surface and confirmed my suspicion. I was back to the dry fly and nymph-dropper by this stage and I made just the one cast into this beautiful little pool.

The dry fly was barely past the submerged branches, when it dipped beneath the surface. I struck! Expecting the little fish to be the culprit, I was surprised to feel my rod load dramatically, and seesaw downwards to something far more substantial. Easily five-pounds of rainbow trout threw itself upstream with a big jump. In a reenactment of the previous fish's capers, albeit in less water to make a stand, it then fled downstream, doing its utmost to exit-stage-left. Realising it couldn't make it; it shot back upstream and at the base of what was principally a solitary tree, it dove for the safety of the sticks and sunken branches. Battling out there in the stone-covered dusty expanses, it was like a shoot-out at the Grand Corral. This fish gave me everything it had but I put the brakes on, and with my knots and tippet holding strong, I dragged it kicking and screaming out of its hole. Surprised to see that it was the nymph that had earned its keep in the now sunny conditions, I quickly released another beautiful rainbow.

Fishing on for another kilometre or more into the evening, I failed to see another fish before turning back.

It was late by the time I got back to the lower reaches near my camp, and I was basically stumbling around in the dark. Eventually I crossed the last pool, clambered up the bank and into the bush – I'd made it!

I had plenty to think about over the long walk back, but the main thing I couldn't fathom was the bag limit for this river being four fish per person per day. I'd only seen five fish all day.

Whether it was due to water being pumped out for irrigation, or the supposed drought, or there not being enough snow-melt to sustain the summer flow, or global warming, or, most likely all of the above, the river appeared to be running quite low. There was barely enough water to support four mature fish, let alone every angler being eligible to kill them. I thought back over the day. I caught two, lost one, and spooked two. I'd fished all day, and covered well over five kilometres of river, I'd only come across five fish. Do people really need to kill four fish per person, or, as some waterways allow, six? From a broader perspective, I don't think these kinds of numbers in the regulations do New Zealand's trout fisheries any favours. Even if there were fish numbers that could sustain these excessive kill quotas, it suggests to anglers that those kinds of numbers are acceptable. Some anglers are then less likely to abide by the rules. "It's okay at River X . . . you can keep four fish per day there . . . and at Lake Y you're allowed six, so let's take these three fish here even if the limit is one, it won't matter . . ." And so the story goes.

The question is this; do people really need four or more fish? I personally think that trout bag limits on wild fish stocks should be one or two fish per person. There's no way this river I had fished that day had a trout population threatening the native galaxiids and bullies, or any other native flora and fauna, so why not take your one fish for the day, if you really have to, and give the fish populations every chance we can?

Recognising this river couldn't offer me much from a consecutive day of fishing, I drove into the night and camped at the lake I was eager to explore.

ʕ ∆ ∝

It had been a cold night camped in my van and come morning; the lack of clouds explained why. It was beautifully calm on the lakeshore as I inflated my kayak and got ready to head out for the day. Seeing that I wanted to fish in two opposite directions from where I had reached the lake, I was kind of happy there was no need to paddle all my camping gear out onto the lake. And perhaps more importantly, I was glad to avoid camping with the sandflies.

My only disappointment for the morning was seeing a jet boat loading up with passengers in readiness to voyage across the lake, and down the river I intended on fishing. As I paddled out onto the lake, the sun having crept above the mountains and burnt off the morning fog, the jet boat roared past me. Moments later, a helicopter buzzed overhead, also heading towards the river!

"Geez, what exactly are they preserving in this national park," I wondered out loud? And on that note, I decided to head in the other direction, perhaps the following day there wouldn't be people making money out of the river I was hoping to fish.

This lake had much steeper sides than the previous one I had fished and if it was wade-fishing for trout in shallow water that I was after, the area I had cast off from probably offered some of the best water. Deep water can mean big trout, but it's in the shallows where their food is usually most abundant. Not letting this bother me, I concentrated instead on the 'deep water big trout' theory.

Paddling around the first rocky point with a light wind blowing in my favour, I started a drift along the lush tree line. Casting a heavily weighted Matuka towards shore much like I had at the other lake, I hadn't covered more than ten metres, when I came across a narrow entrance to a little side lake. Perhaps just larger than a tennis court, it was little more than a blister off the main lake, but it oozed with potential; I felt like I'd been let in on a local secret whispered on the wind.

Peaking in from a distance, I could see there was a footing of timber and reeds around this little backwater, but unfortunately, I could also see that there was a bright green alga coating everything. Through my Polaroids, it almost looked fluorescent. Still, this was the perfect honey-hole, no boats were able to get in and it was perfect brown trout habitat. I was led to believe there were no rainbows in this lake.

From a distance I made a cast straight through the entrance, landing the fly alongside a submerged log. I gave it plenty of time to sink, the water so clear that if a fish did come out and take the fly, I'd see it with ease. It didn't happen unfortunately, and as I carefully stroked around this perfect little harbour trying to spot a fish, I didn't see a thing. Even for immature brown trout that weren't yet thinking about migrating to spawning beds on rivers, this was perfect habitat for them. The reeds and assortment of submerged logs must have offered habitat to an abundance of prey suitable for hungry young trout, not to mention the overhanging vegetation that would rain down a swag of insects given a decent blow. So where were the fish? I was at a loss as to why they weren't there. Even if I had spooked them, I was sure I'd have spotted one or two in the process. The algae, however, was disappointing and as I went further around the honey-hole's shoreline, it lit up the shallows like a 1980's roller disco. Blanketing the rock and river stones and filling the cracks like radioactive poly-filler, it must surely have impacted on nymphs and other trout prey being able to live there. It also made me wonder about the oxygen levels in the water. Was this bay too sheltered perhaps?

Eventually I made it all the way to the river that interested me in this direction. No number of casts towards rock drop-offs and fallen timber had revealed a thing along the way, all my hopes for the day appeared to depend on the water around the river.

A steady southwesterly breeze was blowing by this stage and was funneling a substantial swell down the deep lake, there were small waves breaking in the bay where I put ashore.

Walking around to the river cascading down a near vertical mountain slope, the lake foreshore looked good. The river on the other hand, was too short, too steep, too shallow, and flowing too fast to realistically be adequate fish habitat. The gravel in its immediate lower reaches and outflow area was where I hoped to encounter brown trout starting to congregate for spawning. As it turned out, it was the occasional weed bed along the top of the equally steep drop-off on the lake foreshore that caught my attention.

Regardless of it looking good, my casts proved futile and it wasn't long before I was back in the kayak, dealing with the headwind and chop on my return trip. It was a long, arduous, and ultimately wet paddle back, but I eventually made it back and pulled ashore with half an hour to dark.

Now that I had the kayak rigged up and ready to go, I could be on the water much faster the following morning, and with a little bit of luck, perhaps I would find the brown trout amassing near the other couple of rivers I wanted to investigate.

ᚠ ᚨ ᚩ

Another beautiful day dawned, but with two boats already launched ahead of me, and two more jockeying at the back of the ramp like racehorses, I couldn't help but wonder if I was wasting valuable days of good weather.

Paddling out across the lake with the sun shining and mountains towering in all directions, my kayak slicing through glassy water like butter – there were worse ways to be wasting my days!

Thankfully, the tour boat operator was heading to the other end of the lake, so with a little bit of luck, there wouldn't be anybody going down the outlet river that day. Just how much of it I would actually be able to fish, whether from my kayak or on foot, remained to be seen, but with at least two of the boats heading in the opposite direction, I garnered some hope.

It was a slightly shorter paddle than the day before. Well, at least it felt that way without the twenty-five knot headwind and waves.

Reaching the end, sparkling white sand beaches created a funnel into which the sea of lake water flowed. With beautiful native bush land backing the beaches, it really was an idyllic scene. The crystal-clear water, the white sand beaches, and beautiful sunshine, it almost seemed like there should have been a few coconut trees to complete the tropical illusion.

The river turned out not to be remotely tropical in appearance. Armored with ferns and a jumble of temperate rainforest hardwood logs, thick vegetation lined the riverbanks – the water ran deep, narrow, and fast.

Pulling into some slack water and coming ashore on the white gravelly sand, I clawed my way downstream through the bush to see what I could see. And what did I find?

Well, let's just say there was no way I would be fishing this river on foot. Had I attempted to explore downstream in the kayak, I could have paddled back upstream against the current for the first thirty to forty metres of river, but beyond that it was a raging torrent, it would have been one-way traffic – downstream!

Besides, in the back eddies and other slack water, I couldn't spot a fish here either.

This lack of fish had me absolutely baffled. I've visited a lot of rivers and lakes in New Zealand during my life, and I can recall seeing trout with ease. As a kid, it was often a case of simply stopping at road bridges and looking down into the rivers. Much like the Avon River in the middle of Christchurch, you could spot fish in the middle of cities. You still can in the South Island's largest city of Christchurch, but I hazard a guess that it's not as easy as it once was. This lake I was on had an incredible amount of insect activity on the surface, but not once did I see a fish of any substance rise, surely trout would find enough food here, what was wrong?

Lining everything like a lead blanket, the only thing I could foresee impeding the availability of fodder for trout, was the didymo. Even so, it was prevalent in many other South Island lakes and the trout still managed to survive in decent numbers. So, where were they?

Sneaking downstream in the kayak, I paddled back upstream against the flow, which began its surge from well above the beginning of the river. Balanced on the precipice as I was, it was then that I finally saw my first fish. It leapt clear of the water, feeding I presumed, but I couldn't really tell. At around three-pounds, it wasn't a big fish, but it was enough to at least confirm there were trout in the lake.

With so much water drawing from this lower arm of the lake, I was able to drift along the lakeshore, casting towards fallen timber scattered in the shallows. Considering the fairly constant flow of water able to deliver prey, it was the most likely location for trout to live. More likely than all the other locations that had failed me, anyway.

My first drift down towards the vortex of water was unsuccessful, but another from a little further along the lake wasn't.

On the verge of pulling my fly out of some timber before it got hung up, a brave little brown beat me to it. Snatching the fly and turning back to its hideout, this fish was a gallant little fighter and saw me struggling to keep pressure on it from the very beginning. I managed to get my hand to it beside the kayak, but it's last-minute capers included flipping free and shaking the hook. I guess it saved me the trouble of removing it myself, but it still would have been nice to get a better look at it. The brief glimpse that I did get confirmed it was a brown, and despite its tenacious showing, I could see it was a bit on the skinny side. Perhaps there wasn't as much food to go around as I thought.

Giving up on this outlet area, I was taking a look at where some other small streams flowed into the lake, when I found another fish.

Winding in after fishing a stretch of water along a deep, weed-covered drop off, I detected the slightest of bumps. It felt out of the ordinary, and as my leader and fly neared the rod tip, so too did an almost identical little brown trout. It must have given my fly an investigative tap and kept following it. Luck had been on the fish's side here because I had been debating whether I should strip one more retrieve or wind in. Had I not chosen to wind in, I suspect I would have detected the take far better and prompted a strike. I'd seen three fish over two full days of fishing and at about two to three-pounds each; they had all been virtually identical.

Something obviously wasn't quite right on this lake! The fish numbers were surprisingly low and their growth rate appeared to be stunted. I know two days isn't a good research period, but something was definitely restricting the trout growth rate here, and what it was, I had no idea!

I fished a number of other picturesque looking spots that afternoon, but I was doing little more than wasting my time it seemed. I decided I would leave the following day, dry out my kayak in the sun (hopefully), and then head back down to the paddocks in search of a small creek that I hoped would be big enough to hold a few fish.

$$f_1 \; \blacktriangle \; \propto$$

With my gear dried out and stowed away, I got back down on the plains and was surprised to suddenly be bestowed with an ashen day. Given the gloomy skies, I called in for a coffee at a café I knew of. It was mid-afternoon by the time I got back on the road.

I took a drive along the coast and immediately got distracted by a good-sized swell steamrolling New Zealand's southwestern shores. I had no surfboard with me, but still I couldn't help puttering along the coast checking out the different breaks. Eventually I tore myself away from the possibilities and was headed back north. With the sun occasionally sneaking from behind the clouds like a breeze-hungry ember, I found my way back to the river that had proven so frustrating a number of days earlier. It was early evening and I knew there was a good chance the mayfly or caddis hatch might be in full swing.

I accessed the river at the same bridge, and having always fished upstream from here, I chose to try my luck downstream. There appeared to be such a large number of fish in this river, I didn't really think it would matter.

Covering my options with a dry fly and nymph-dropper, I quickly had a little two-pound brown at my feet courtesy of the nymph. Continuing downstream, I persisted with the nymph-dropper combination well into the evening, but my success didn't endure.

Just on dark, with barely enough light left in the day to tie on a caddis pattern, I had one last crack at them with the solitary dry fly.

With the rises so abundant in the poor light, it was hard to distinguish what was being taken, the naturals, or my fly. In the end, with darkness approaching, I ended up striking whenever there was a rise in the general vicinity of my fly. They were delicate rises and I was certain some of them were on my fly, but for the life of me, I couldn't hook any of them. The following day it would become clear why . . .

ʔ △ ∝

Clouds prevailed when I woke the following morning and I decided to head back to the river I had fished before venturing out onto the lake, the river where I'd actually had some success. Having caught the brown trout and two rainbows in an upstream direction, I decided to explore downstream here too. I accessed the river perhaps half a kilometre below where I did previously, and would fish upstream to that point. With limestone cliffs sculpted over millennia lining the river course here, it was vastly different to the river's upstream reaches. I found a pool that was deeper than the rest; it had plenty of bank-side vegetation at the base of the cliffs and looked perfect. I couldn't see any fish, but I was confident there would be one hiding somewhere.

Faster water in the top half of the pool saw me crawling in at the halfway point, ready to drift a large Royal Wolf and black nymph-dropper through the lower half of the pool. I managed a reasonable drift, and just as the flies neared the limestone cliff, something took the nymph and the dry fly went for a swim. I had quite a large belly in the line due to slack water on my side, but still I struck, and well within time I thought. A fish broke the surface almost simultaneously, and my flies went flying back over my head, the fish gone.

I obviously hadn't been in time, the fish savoring the nymph a touch too long. I had been a split second too slow and was thoroughly disappointed! The sun had confidently found a gap in the clouds, and it would have been nice to chalk up a fish so quickly. I knew there weren't a lot of fish in this river and chances like this were few and far between.

Proving this point to myself, I continued upstream all the way to where I had started fishing days earlier, and I didn't see another fish. I decided to continue upstream.

I had a few casts in the pool where I had lost the rainbow first thing in the morning, and also in the pool against the cliff where I had caught the brown trout. With no rain for the four or five days since then, and the snow in the river's headwaters long gone, it was about half a metre lower. There was still enough water in these two pools, but I couldn't find a trout for the taking that day.

I continued upstream, eager to get to the pools where I had spooked the two fish, the first being where I'd foolishly stepped out midstream to confirm it was actually a fish.

With the pool in sight, I was eager to get there and spot a big brown. Walking along the top of a head-high bank on a run that had no vegetation lining it, I again became my own worst enemy. I should have been looking at the foreground in the river and not getting ahead of myself, but the water looked so barren. On the two days I had fished here, it had been as unproductive as it looked.

Of course, on this day, there was a nice rainbow trout sitting right in the middle of the now shallower run. With a clear view of me standing above it like some kind of grandiose Soviet monument; it couldn't not see me! I saw it the second it moved, and swore at myself in disgust. It wasn't sitting in an easy spot to target, but it helps if you don't walk on top of them.

Hoping there was more than one fish in the neighborhood that day, I continued up to the pool. With one dead looking tree backing this pool, and flowing at no more than a hand-span in depth, it was incredibly low. Other than the deeper hole in front of the tree, a large fish's options would have been limited. Sitting right in the middle of the shallow stretch of water, however, was a big dark-coloured fish. I wondered if perhaps it was the big brown trout I had spooked in the upstream pool last time. Maybe both fish had moved downstream a pool each.

I crept around this big dark shape sitting next to a limestone coloured rock, still not one hundred percent certain it was a fish, but also not willing to take any chances. I knew the fish would be extremely flighty in such thin water.

Once in a suitable position, I made the cast and drifted my flies straight down to the fish. Unfortunately, they continued straight past. They did so on three occasions, before I decided to drift them over the deeper hole in front of the tree. They made it untouched past here a number of times too, before I finally got up to confirm that I'd been casting at a fish moments earlier, and not a branch. Edging my way back downstream scanning the water, sure enough, the lump of yellow limestone rock was sitting there all alone; the fish having vanished like a ghost.

The next pool was where the big brown trout had been sitting days earlier. There wasn't a fish to be seen this day, it really did seem like both fish had decided to make a move to the house next door. The next pool was the one backed with willows where I'd managed to catch a rainbow on the little Adams.

I spotted it here again, just below the willows, exactly like last time. I was certain it was the same fish, and I crept in to see if he'd learnt anything from our previous encounter. In retrospect, I wish I'd used the exact same fly, but instead, I decided to show it something different – perhaps it would be interested in sampling one of my nymphs.

The flies drifted by naturally enough, but I never did see the fish again after that first cast, it appeared to have wizened up to my game. It was definitely time for me to find a new river.

ʕ ▲ ∝

The usual weather patterns in southern Australia and New Zealand see a period of generally good weather as high-pressure systems swing out of the Southern Ocean from west to east, there's usually a good sized low-pressure system that get pushed down and out of the way in the process. The lower leading edge of these highs pair up with the trailing edge of the lows to form what are often quite savage 'fronts'. The leading edge of the next low often does the same thing with the back end of the high as it passes. Marching in from the southwest out of the Southern Ocean like some kind of production line: low, high, low, high, low . . . , this is exactly what I woke to that next morning. It wasn't necessarily a 'savage' front, but I wouldn't like to have seen what the west coast looked like. I was inundated with drizzling rain and skies as black as coal. The weather forecast suggested it would only last a couple of days in the south of the South Island, so I decided to make a move towards Lake Teanau to see it out.

Lake Teanau and the town of Teanau is another key tourist hub in the South Island. As I pulled up in a car park overlooking the lake to have some lunch, people were boarding a helicopter for a sightseeing flight. Despite the grey skies and rain, a large catamaran full of tourists also pulled up at a nearby dock. Keen!

By the time I had finished my sandwich, two or three coaches had driven past behind me and a similar number of private powerboats had passed by on the lake. A jet-boat fishing charter operator had also driven past towing his boat. The town had grown significantly in ten years and with the cafés and shops sharing the high street with the usual real-estate parasites, it was clear to see the beginning of the end had been some years earlier. This doesn't bother the real-estate vendors, though, the development that marks the end in my eyes is little more than dollar signs in theirs – hoping for business from out-of-towners walking the main drag, or even out-of-NZers – they don't care! Flogged you might say? Most definitely!

I joined the hordes of Chinese, North Americans and Europeans in the supermarket, where I stocked up for the next few weeks on the road, as far away from that supermarket as possible. I then popped into a café for a coffee and to confirm the weather report. Interestingly enough, listening to the accents floating around the cafe, the clientele was strictly from the States and Europe.

Drizzle was on the cards again for the following day, but it looked like there might be a decent three-day window after that.

I filled up on fuel, left the 'NO FREE CAMPING' signs behind, and headed out to investigate one of the many nearby rivers.

I donned my rain jacket and waders, and trekked up a stream that was little more than a trickle through cow paddocks. Once upon a time (just twenty years ago), such a river would have been crawling with trout. There was a well-trodden path through the grass along the banks here, and although at times it ran far too close to the water to be discreetly spotting trout from, it was hard not to follow. It was that or negotiate my way through head-high weeds.

I covered perhaps half a dozen pools before the lack of light got the better of me. I hadn't seen a fish in any of them. Come morning I planned to check another river, and by day's end I would drive out to the next area I wished to fish. Hopefully the weather report would hold true.

$$f_{)} \; \triangle \; \propto$$

Like a black-and-blued boxer going the full twelve rounds, the dreary weather had held through the night. But not deterred by the dark skies and a few wind-blown haymakers, I still made my way out onto the second river. In fact by day's end I was fishing a third – I didn't see a fish in any of them. There was no shortage of didymo in the third river; that was unquestionable!

Some people might wonder if I was patient enough with these rivers, but any river that had proven its worth that summer had done so by revealing a fish or two early in the piece. Not my catching them necessarily, but at least being able to spot one. Like I said, it used to be a lot easier. I was more than happy to strike these three rivers off my list.

$$f_{)} \; \triangle \; \propto$$

Having camped the night amongst trees near a lake I intended to explore, I woke to the passing of traffic: vehicles coming and going, the rattle of boat trailers – it did little for my enthusiasm!

If I'm totally honest, I was feeling pretty disheartened by this stage, there were people everywhere and the fishing just wasn't what it once was. Yep, I know, the jaded old man at just forty years of age, but perhaps that's a reflection on how quickly things had changed. Ten years earlier I had spent a few days around the lake I was parked near, and the only person I saw was a solitary ranger.

Eventually I got the motivation to get up and I wandered along the shoreline of a smaller lake where no boats were permitted. The water was beautifully clear, the trees bearded with lichen in the pristine alpine air, and the birds gleefully singing at the first hint of sunshine after days of rain – happy days . . .

Personally, I think it would be great if there were no boats allowed on many of the lakes in New Zealand, particularly down south in Fjord Land, surely there is enough water out there to leave some of lakes free from being trolled to death?

I didn't see any fish on this first reconnaissance, and driving on towards the lake I wished to fish, passing campsite after campsite busy with peoples' morning routines, I took a walk along the shoreline. With four-wheel-drive tracks cutting through native grassland, and burnt out rubbish-filled campfires scarring the landscape even further – I'd seen enough!

My plan had been to paddle out and fish here, but with so many people around, and their impact so noticeable – I just felt like running – I'd had a gut full!

I had looked at a nearby stretch of river on maps and had liked the fact that the clear-felled farmland finished in wooded reserves, which appeared to line both sides of the river. Both from a fisheries officer and people working in fishing shops, I'd had confirmation that the fishing was particularly good there, one store worker referring to it as the 'Trophy Zone'.

"Sounds like it's common knowledge," I said.

"Yes, it is, and the guides hit the area quite heavily."

With that kind of knowledge, ten pound plus fish or not, it was the last place I wanted to fish. Intrigued by the theme-park-like attraction, I drove out for a look to see what all the fuss was about.

As expected, a nice shiny four-wheel-drive covered in stickers suggesting it belonged to a guide, was parked at the upstream access point. I noticed that somebody had discreetly written 'Wanker Zone' on one of the fisheries signs. I couldn't help but chuckle to myself and think; yeah, you got that right.

I turned my back, eager to get away, and into a new area. On the way, I took a look down the track leading to the southern access point. I got halfway down it and saw another shiny four-wheel-drive with personalized number plates relating to trout, and stickers. Guides at both ends, and for all I knew perhaps more parked further along the downstream access point. I drove away pondering the situation.

Tourism clearly doesn't benefit everybody and this was a perfect example. And that's coming from someone who's half Kiwi and half Australian, imagine how the local Kiwi anglers must feel. There I am with my NZ$140 fishing license and I basically can't fish a stretch of water because there's a guy at either end making close to NZ$1000 for the day. Yes, I hear you saying I still could have fished it, but these are smart fish, I knew I would have been wasting my time following in other anglers' footsteps, particularly on the same day. Besides, for me, the fact that I'd need to walk past other vehicles just to get to the river makes for an un-enjoyable experience even before I've set eyes on the first pool. I'd know I was behind the eight ball from the outset, that's not the nicest feeling in anyone's terms.

Sadly, with the current rate of the world's population growth, I can't see it getting any better in my lifetime. I think I might have to buy a boat and sail away (keep an eye out for book-8 in the series).

I ended up stopping to fish a stretch of water in the same river towards the end of the day, a lesser stretch of water, out in the cow paddocks of course.

But wait, is there anything to be learnt from this situation, or perhaps even proven by it? Yes! There is! As I've been harping on about throughout this book – bankside vegetation does help to support a better aquatic environment.

It's a bit of a no-brainer for most of us anglers, but from the amount of fencing I'd seen getting washed away by rivers that summer, on properties one hundred or more years old, you'd think that somewhere along the 'fence-line', these NZ farmers might have cottoned onto the fact that trees help riverbank stability. More paddock stability + less financial loss on wasted fencing + livestock shelter in harsh winters/summers + less livestock in rivers + less agricultural runoff + enhanced soil quality + trees assisting in neutralizing methane/CO_2 = healthier rivers + happier fish + more 'swimmable' rivers + LARGER PROFIT MARGINS.

Better river flow could even help flush out the didymo more effectively. That's probably wishful thinking on my part, but you never do know. None of this will happen overnight, but just think, all it might take is some effective tree planting.

So, did I see any fish during my afternoon session? Well, I did actually, the first in a long time. It saw me at the same time, and in a cloud of didymo, it was off like a rocket. I was back at my van well before dark.

I got a meal of pasta going, had a splash in the river as it boiled, and then drove directly out of there, the meal cooling in my billycan as I drove. Travelling towards my next river of interest, I was almost certain I would find a few fish the following day . . .

ſ₁ ▲ ∝

I think it's good to be optimistic in life, but at times it also pays to be realistic.

The upstream reaches of the river that I had driven to and camped at the evening before turned out to be both lacking water and lacking fish. There was plenty of farming going on, though, and some classic examples of vertical cliffs getting chewed out by the river – pasture right up to the very edge of course. My hopes were dashed once again . . .

Getting on the water for a look anyway, I covered little more than a kilometre before turning back. I would drive further downstream; hopefully more water would mean more fish.

On the positive side, it was a beautiful sunny day, but judging by the shiny four-wheel drives parked on the edge of the road in places, it looked like there were others out fishing as well.

Along a dirt road on foot, I eventually got down onto the river. I had intentions of fishing upstream, but on reaching the water, there appeared to be more vegetation lining the river in a downstream direction, so I headed that way instead.

At that very first pool where I reached the river, there were fish in its lower reaches. It was a wide and quite long pool and I could clearly see at least two fish. Within seconds, I had achieved more than I had in the previous few days.

Fishing my way back up the pool with a blowfly dry and tiny black nymph-dropper, it took at least a fifteen-metre cast to get the flies across the pool and up against the willows. I could just make out one or two fish repositioning or unsettling with my first few casts, and they didn't touch the flies.

Edging into the upper reaches of this pool, I instantly spotted a large, dark coloured fish sitting in slow flowing water. Two-thirds of the way across the pool, it was as obvious as a shipwreck. Standing back from the edge, I placed a cast well upstream from it. The faster water was against the willows, but there was still enough movement in the main body of the pool to slowly drift my flies towards the fish. The fact that I could see it so clearly from such a distance indicated just how big it really was. With both brown and rainbow trout, it's an evolutionary trait that I've never really understood. The backs of some bigger trout (particularly males I think), get so dark that their camouflage is often blown entirely.

As my flies drifted closer, the fish casually recognise the fact that there was food on the way; I could tell by its body language that it had spotted them. Just as they came into range, with a languid flick of its tail, the fish moved forwards – my eyes glued to it.

I was certain it was going to take the dry. At least that's the mode my brain was in. Close to a fly line length away, moving in slow motion, it was as though the fish was swimming through jelly. Completely mesmerized, my concentration was in a different world, when, from nowhere, the dry fly slowly dipped beneath the surface.

The trout was as alert as a lioness. I was not! No sooner had the dry fly disappeared, and the trout was gone, rocketing towards the cover of the willows – quite literally – it had been let off the hook!

I felt like hitting myself over the head with a big piece of wood! I knew I wasn't going to get many chances like that, especially in the middle of the day with the sun shining brightly overhead. And at the first pool I had fished no less. "Wake up Julian!" I said to myself, along with a few other unprintable words.

Covering a couple more pools in a downstream direction, I came to yet another shiny four-wheel-drive, sitting pretty much in the middle of the braided riverbed. There was no one to be seen. I hadn't seen anybody further upstream, and I figured it was unlikely the fish would have been sitting out in the open like they had been if somebody had fished there earlier that day. So I turned around, and headed back upstream, bypassing the pools I had already fished.

I started spotting a few fish here and there, big ones. They were sitting in the heads of the pools in very shallow water. I spooked two, but managed to get what I thought to be clean casts to three others: two sitting in awkward back eddies, and one really big fish in the very head of a rapid. It was barely deep enough for the fish itself at the top of this rapid; I should have done away with the nymph-dropper and tried feeding a small dry fly down to it, but that's fishing, you never do know for certain what's going to work.

I finally had some luck in an even-flowing run that flowed into a dogleg against a stretch of willows.

Just in case there were fish convening in the shallows, which a lot of them appeared to be doing, I crawled in keeping a low profile, and cast from a seated position. To first 'clear' the foreground, my first cast innocently drifted past at little more than a rod length in front of me. My second cast went two thirds of the way across the run, straight into the stretch of water that would allow the longest and cleanest drift of the flies. It's not always these optimal stretches that produce the fish, but on this occasion it was.

I managed to spot the white 'wings' of the blowfly pattern amongst the bubbles quickly, and with a quick mend of the line, the flies were drifting perfectly. As they neared the leading edge of the willows; my eyes glued to the dry fly, pleading for it to dip beneath the surface, I was stunned to see the mottled brown head of a big trout's mouth open wide, and greedily engulf the dry. My jaw must have dropped open just as wide, but I wasn't resting on my haunches this time, even if I was actually sitting. I struck, scrambling to my feet in the process. I was perhaps as shocked as the fish. I'd seen its head clear as day, this was perhaps the biggest brown trout I'd hooked that summer. I couldn't mess things up, not now . . .

It fought downstream towards the willows a number of times during the fight; a tangle of branches and roots that really would have caused me problems had it reached them. Time after time it went for them and I only just managed to cut it short each time, slowly sapping its will – losing this fish wasn't an option!

Behaving like big brown trout often do, it never once looked like jumping, it adopted a traditionalist approach over flamboyancy and we paced each other up and down that short stretch of river as though stubbornly negotiating an armistice, neither of us willing to concede an inch. Eventually, however, it did.

Edging this beautiful fish into the shallows, it remained subdued, willingly letting me get a grasp of it, and remove the troublesome fly. And what a spectacular fish it was!

The late afternoon sky was as blue as could be, the air flawless after days of rain, and the light razor sharp. The water clinging to the fish glinted as though it was swathed in jewels, its unblemished powerful body easily eight-pounds or more. It was a thing of beauty, reward for months of hard work that had been a long time coming!

On this extraordinarily positive note, I called it a day. I would be back on this river the following morning, somewhere along its length, at the crack of dawn.

ſ₁ ▲ ∝

Another flawless, sun-drenched day dawned. Even if it was mid-March, it almost appeared like summer had finally arrived.

I had camped downstream from where I fished the afternoon before and with the sun shining and birds singing, I set out in an upstream direction. It seemed the spawn-run adult browns were on the move in this river – my expectations were high!

It didn't take long to start spooking the occasional fish sitting in the larger pools. Lurking in the shallows, or in the middle of these pools, their camouflage was infuriatingly effective. The fish in the slower pools were incredibly flighty; they seemed to have an uncanny ability to sense my movement, even when crab-crawling into casting positions with my rod clenched between my teeth. I finally spotted a fish in a pool that offered a user-friendly rate of flow.

You simply can't cast over these fish; it's a case of sneaking past them, and then crawling in towards their flank as close as you dare, then casting upstream on an angle of around forty-five degrees.

Sometimes, particularly with fish sitting on the very edge of shallow rapids at the head of pools, it was often a case of sneaking in upstream from them and feeding the fly downstream.

Despite my cautious approach, I was still struggling to find fish willing to cooperate and by early in the afternoon, I decided it was time for a break. I retreated to a nearby town for some coffee, but unable to keep away, it wasn't long before I was back on the river – even further downstream on this occasion.

The fish were there and they were equally capricious. By the time I had vigilantly skirted around to the head of the pools, keeping what I thought to be a safe distance from the water, there would often be up to four or five fish that had sensed my presence and taken flight. Always in an upstream direction!

I spent well over half an hour on a fish that evening. Gracefully sipping down tiny mayflies, it shunned my fabricated assortment entirely. I even tried a blowfly and nymph-dropper, but after a brief pause as though ignoring a knock at the door, it went straight back to taking the naturals. A nearby flock of ducks appeared to be watching my futile attempts and having a good laugh at my expense – from a safe distance mind you.

By the time the sun had gone down and I was walking back, one of the pools I passed was alive with fish slurping down mayflies. At first, they were taking the emergers, but as the hatch tapered off, the trout made short work of any moth that spent too long near the surface. I tried a parachute Adams, and then a blue dun, but again, the trout weren't easily misled. Considering how much food was available, this didn't come as much of a surprise. I eventually walked on and left them still feeding.

Later that evening, I found a spot to camp upstream from where I had finished fishing that morning. With the trout essentially getting the better of me, the following day would be a full day on the water – I wouldn't be outdone!

ᚨ A ∝

It was a crisp morning that I woke to and by no later than nine o'clock, I was heading upstream with lunch packed.

The previous two days had shown me there was a significant number of fish in the river, and they could be anywhere. Even so, much like salmon when they are running, any location that enabled the fish to rest was always going to be in high demand. Unlike salmon, the trout continue feeding throughout much of their spawn-run; it's only towards the latter stages, when they're in their spawning beds, that they become extremely aloof and generally uninterested in feeding. The fishing season is usually closed by that stage.

Apart from behind obstructions, there are two key locations on New Zealand's braided alluvial streams where fish rest and continue feeding: in the slow flowing shallows at the lower end of pools, and in the very shallow back eddies that usually form on either side of the main inflow, at the head of pools. This latter location is often the last spot a fish will rest before tackling a rapid. Once fish are really moving, they can often hold in water that you most likely wouldn't look twice at under normal circumstances. It can make for exasperating moments if in a rush!

On this day, on this particular river, I was determined to cover the water thoroughly; I firmly told myself that I wasn't going to spook any more of these fish in the shallows. At the very first pool I came to, my ploy proved its worth.

It was quite a long pool, perhaps thirty metres in length and ten metres wide. I didn't fish the lower end of the pool as I chose to start fishing two thirds of the way down. I approached it from the side. As I said earlier, you cannot cast over these NZ spawn-run fish, or any trout worth its merit for that matter. I was fishing a four-weight outfit, but I'm positive that even a two or three weight line cast over these fish would have spooked them.

I put my rod in my mouth and crab-crawled the last five metres, getting into a seated casting position a rod length from the water. Fishing that section of the pool, I then proceed as follows: Cast upstream at a forty-five degree angle, let the fly and line drift past like the arm of a clock, mending the line when necessary until it finishes its natural drift roughly forty-five degrees downstream; 10:00 to 2:00 or 2:00 to 10:00, much like your recommended rod arc when casting.

Your line drifting over the top of holding fish will usually spook fish too, particularly on a sunny day like that I had been blessed with. It is for this reason that I keep talking about 'clearing the foreground'. There's nothing worse than casting straight out over the best-looking run you've seen all day, only to have a massive trout take flight from just beyond your rod tip. If you walked in and cast, it was gone before you unhooked your fly. It's a slow approach, but if you can't spot the fish due to ripples and depth, it's a patient and slow approach that often reaps rewards. After my two short casts, I'll then drift two casts at a similar distance beyond that, and then the same again beyond that. These last casts usually cover the far side of the river.

Still rigged up with a blowfly and nymph-dropper, it was on the first of these midrange casts that a nice fish of about five or six-pounds, took a liking to the dry fly. Generally I hadn't been fishing blowfly imitations until the day heated up, but this fish proved they must occasionally find flies on the surface at all hours. A little over halfway through the drift, the white calf tail 'wings' sitting upright and enabling me to spot the fly, I clearly watched it disappear – sucked through a trapdoor – straight down the throat of a trout.

Early in the morning, and on the very first pool, it could have easily taken me by surprise, but I had my wits about me on this occasion.

I struck and stood up in the one motion, as the trout responded in unison, leaping well over a metre high, and untidily splashing back down in the still conditions. This fish wasn't quite as big as a few evenings earlier, but I later suspected her to be female, and as they often do — fight she did! Only the one jump was pulled from her repertoire that morning, but she definitely appeared to be partial to the other side of the river. Keeping my movements as smooth as I could, the steady pressure took its toll, and eventually saw her guided into the shallows ready for release. With strange, almost blotchy colourations, it wasn't the most beautiful brown I'd ever seen, but she was in good condition, and to get a fish on the board so early in the day, I couldn't have been happier. With a worn lower tail a badge of honour from many successful years of spawning, I was glad to let her go so she might continue doing so for many years to come. Fanning the eggs to keep silt off them is primarily the role of the female trout.

I continued upstream, giving shallow water a wide berth in order to spot fish from a distance, and meticulously covering water that was too deep to spot fish. The long open pools backed by willow trees revealed the occasional fish, but not as many as I had expected, or hoped. I drifted nymph-dropper rigs along the edges of these willows, but was surprised by my lack of success.

That said; the second fish I managed to hook did come from one such pool.

Like many of these pools, the majority of the shallow water was virtually motionless, but on this occasion, there was a steady flowing stretch between the motionless eddy and the bank. As I crept along it, carefully scanning the water, I saw and heard some minuscule rises. The tiny dimpled rises were so inconspicuous! Their greatest giveaway was the kissing noise of the fish sucking in their prey. Again the rises were in the slower water, perhaps two thirds of the way down the pool. Here their prey was delivered to them at a reasonable speed, and they weren't wasting energy while waiting to intercept it. I suspected it to be tiny mayflies on this occasion.

There were two or three fish feeding in this area, and as I crab-crawled my way into range of the upstream fish, either it stopped feeding, or moved downstream. I was definitely getting a good workout crawling around like this, and I scurried downstream to target the next fish.

Attempting to match the hatch, I tied on one of the little Adams dry flies. I drifted it through the area twice, but despite another rise during that time, my fly was ignored.

"I bet you don't knock back a blowfly," I said to the fish, and set about changing flies.

Sitting upstream from the fish at a suitable distance to keep me out of sight, it also allowed me to cast and let the fly drift down to the fish naturally. I did just that, mending the line with little rod flicks and stripping in the slack so as to keep well within striking range. I'm sure a subtle sip would have been enough for this fish to get the fly down, but perhaps it viewed the blowflies as a bigger challenge. Instead of the dainty rises it had earlier been feeding with, it attended to my blowfly imitation with the grace of eating the entire cake. I watched the fly plunge down the fish's throat virtually right in front of me – there was no debating when to strike!

This was a smaller fish, perhaps just three-pounds, but as it bounced around the pool like there was no tomorrow, I kept my eyes glued to the prize; I wanted to do the honours and remove the hook myself. There had been plenty of no-fish-days that summer, but there had also been plenty of one-fish-days. To finish a full day of fishing with just two trout to my name wasn't exactly remarkable either, but it was better than none and one. With a bit of luck I could make it three or four.

The fish swam off strongly from my hands, good karma on my side I hoped. Well, despite the trauma I'd just put the fish through, I guess. Even so, I am a firm believer that catch and release fishing, when done carefully and quickly, is as good a form of education for a fish as any. A fish that's been caught once or twice is far harder to catch than one that hasn't, therefore it's more likely to grow older and procreate more; in the long run, the fish and angler are winners. The primary concern with catch and release fishing, however, is that it's done CAREFULLY and QUICKLY'.

The wind started blowing not long after I released this fish, and I mean really blowing! As the afternoon progressed, the sky to the southeast grew darker and darker. I hate to say it, but it was like a scene out of Lord of the Rings. I think this looming weather even put off two separate carloads of duck shooters. It was enough to put me off, and after a knotted tangle in the back of my fly line had me sitting on the rocks for no less than half an hour, I turned back.

The low-profile approach to stalking trout works well, but a lot of patience is required in order to keep picking your line out of all the loose river stones that prevail in New Zealand. My line had just about had enough.

Passing another stretch of willows with reasonable flow under them, I added a grey nymph-dropper. Earlier that day I had observed a number of grey nymphs in the shallows, and with mayfly hatches seemingly common at times, I speculated that it was a good colour to match the dun nymphs.

On my very first cast, I must admit that I didn't actually see the dry fly go under, it was more a case of letting the flies linger at the end of their drift, and a trout taking a liking to the nymph, which must have suddenly 'sprung to life'. The calm band of water under the willows sprung to life too, but far more abruptly I suspect. The explosion of white water saw a dark fish rocket skyward, how it managed to land back in such shallow water and not break its neck, I don't know. A game of tug-of-war then ensued, the fish trying to head downstream into timber amongst the willows, and me holding on, doing my best to persuade it otherwise. Perhaps the tangle in my line and my turning back, had put me in the right spot at the right time? Then again, who knows, perhaps there had been a ten pounder with my name on it sitting in the next upstream pool. Either way, three fish for the day wasn't a bad result, maybe the karma was with me. After a night of wind and rain, would it still be there come morning . . . ?

ᚠ ᚨ ∝

Come morning I was amazed to see that the storm had dispersed and the air was clearer than ever. My weather karma was with me finally – better late than never I guess . . .

I wasted no time getting on the water, but it quickly became obvious that my fish karma had forsaken me. By midafternoon I was still without a fish. I must have spotted and stalked close to half a dozen fish that day, some of them in the exact same places fish had been on my first afternoon. Perhaps just two of these fish were sitting in locations where a simple cast-and-drift presentation was required. In other words, they weren't making life easy for me.

Because I had to crawl to casting positions out of sight of the fish, I was unable to identify exactly when they were spooking. Was it when I approached, when making the cast, or even when the fly drifted past them? You can only see so much from ground level, but the simple fact of the matter is that if you can see the fish, it can definitely see you.

The majority of the fish were in awkward locations: close to back eddies, and-or in ultra-thin water on the edge of rapids at the head of pools. There's rarely a certain approach on how to present a fly to fish holding in these kinds of scenarios, and invariably, you usually only get one cast at these fish. For the average angler on a new river working out how best to deal with individually unique and awkward current flow situations, success is seldom likely. Perhaps in another forty years' time, when I'm in my eighties, I'll have a far deeper bag of tricks. In the meantime, I'll take comfort in the age-old adage of, 'that's why they call it fishing and not catching'.

When I did finally manage to outwit a fish, it was in a scenario not too dissimilar to my last fish the evening before.

I had just finished fishing upstream through quite a fast-flowing stretch of water beneath some willows, and was in the process of securing my leader and nymph-dropper, when I glanced back downstream and spotted a dark shape in the shadows. From a distance, it looked a lot like a fish.

I unhooked the flies and cast them back out, walking them downstream towards the supposed fish; my eyes glued to the white of the dry fly. I'd gone past where I thought the fish to be, and was just on the verge of pulling the flies out, when, as meek as a mouse, they crept past some branches hanging in the water. My mind was expecting the nymph to get hung up here and it didn't come as a surprise when the dry fly dipped beneath the surface. I struck with the hope of clearing the flies more than thinking a fish had taken the nymph. However, similar to the evening before, the narrow and shallow strip of water suddenly sparked to life with frantic surface commotion, as a beautiful four-pound brown abandoned its cover. Having fled the opposite bank so eagerly, it quickly showed a dislike to the shallow bank I stood on, and found itself wishing it was back where it had come from.

Time and time again this fish fled the shallows where I patiently stood waiting for it to tire, and come to hand for a quick release. Like an ankle roped beast, it eventually realised it was in a no-win situation, and almost submissively, allowed me to get a grasp across its broad shoulders. Keeping it in the water as much as possible, I carefully removed the hook, snapped a few photos, and promptly sent it on its way.

In some regards this had been a lucky capture, but at that stage of the day, I was ready to take any ounce of luck I could muster. The little grey nymph had struck again and I fished on upstream into the evening expectantly.

I fished through the pool where I picked up the big fish three evenings earlier, and with conditions almost identical, I had hopes of bigger and better things. Unfortunately, they went unanswered.

As darkness began to gather, the mayfly hatch went into overtime. They were thick as thieves and with so much food on the water for the fish; my various attempts to match the hatch were akin to a younger sibling searching for attention. Stepping forward into my teenage years, I eventually thought, stuff you lot, and I tied on a mouse pattern. This I stripped and drifted through the melee as contemptuously as a staff sergeant. And the trout . . . ? Well, they took no notice of it whatsoever.

As I trudged back on the main road, I decided it was time to move on, there must surely be other rivers with large spawn-run fish moving in them, and with the kind of hatch I'd seen that evening, I was confident of finding dry fly fishing conditions in full swing elsewhere.

It was ten o'clock by the time I got back to my van and I just caught the ten o'clock news on the radio. The weather report was predicting gale force winds in the days ahead and it looked like my run of perfect weather was going to come to an end.

I decided it was a good time to find a few smaller streams, deep in some valleys somewhere.

ᚠ ᚨ ᚳ

It was mid-afternoon by the time I reached the first stream I had singled out on my maps. It was in rural countryside, but it was off the beaten track, amongst hills and relatively sheltered from wind if it were to eventuate – or so I thought . . .

Despite the forecast, it was a nice sunny afternoon where I was and I wandered over to the river through some trees. Leaning up against one of them so as to keep out of sight, I peered into the rocky little stream. Quite to my surprise, I spotted a fish almost immediately.

"Why, hello there," I said to myself.

It was a brown trout of about three-pounds. Sitting in a narrow chute of relatively fast flowing water that was weaving through larger rocks like a scrumhalf, I stood there watching the fish for quite some time. Despite the steady water flow, it didn't budge, and didn't appear to be getting much in the way of food either. The water itself was slightly tannin stained (or something having the same effect), but it was still fairly clear. As though exiting a washing machine rinse cycle, it was also foaming with white bubbles. I knew this was due to high nitrogen levels in the water; it's common in the rivers of southwest Victoria, Australia, and even in the grazing countryside of Montana and Patagonia. Due to high levels of fertiliser and stock effluent runoff and seepage into ground water, I was glad I'd filled up my water bottles elsewhere.

I tried not to let the water quality deter my mood, I'd spotted a fish! Besides, with flax and tussock grass and trees lining much of the watercourse, I'd seen a lot worse. With no other anglers for miles around, I couldn't wait to get on the water.

The fish I had previously seen was gone by the time I returned with a rod, and with the river appearing to thin out in an upstream direction, I chose to fish downstream.

The watercourse was no wider than an average car and the pools no more than ten-metres long. Both banks were quite high; the opposite covered in scrub, and mine with plenty of flax and tussock grass to provide me with cover. It was possible to scan much of the water from the positions I crawled into.

Movement against the opposite bank of the first or second pool I came to suggested I had spooked a fish; I wondered if it was the one I'd seen earlier. It wasn't until a few pools further downstream that I finally spotted a fish I was able to cast to.

At little more than a pound and a half, it wasn't a big fish, but if I had any say in the matter, it still wasn't going to get off lightly.

I crawled in through the grass, and knelt beside a tuft of tussock grass for concealment. The head of the pool was quite turbulent. This fish was sitting halfway down in a position where the water had sorted itself out. By the time I'd unhooked the blowfly pattern from the rod guides and sorted myself out to cast, the fish was nowhere to be seen. There was a lot of weed in the water here (another sign of unnaturally high nutrient levels) and therefore plenty of cover for the fish to hide amongst. Assuming it was still in there somewhere, I presented the fly anyway. I covered the water along the opposite bank with three casts, before looking upstream towards the faster water at the head of the pool. Looking straight into the sun, I made a few casts here too, but with the sun, the white bubbles and turbulent water, I had no idea where my fly was, for all I knew it might have been completely submerged.

After my second cast, I went to pull the fly out of the water for one last cast, but instead, the rod started kicking in my hand – I was onto a fish – a particularly unlucky one!

Sometimes the angler has to have a little luck too. It wasn't in the bag just yet, though…

The fish soared into the air with an instantaneous jump that almost brought it to my eye level on the bank. The water sparkled in the sunshine, and it splashed back down like a kid belly-flopping off the local pier on a summer's day. Cunningly, it then dove straight into a weed bed in the middle of the pool. This saw me straight off the bank, almost belly-flopping into the water myself. I dug amongst the weed as though I'd lost my marbles. With my line buried into the weed and out the other side, somehow, the fish still managed to get its head up for a jump, just metres from my left shoulder. I managed to catch this jump on film too, so if you watch the film, you'll see it. As I'd earlier predicted, hooking a fish in this tiny stream was quite a show.

"Bloody hell," I mumbled to myself with admiration. Eventually I freed the line, but the fish wasted no time heading upstream and across to the opposite bank, where it dove straight into another weed bed.

I stomped and kicked my way along this weed bed, hoping to scare it out the other end. This tactic, along with a bit of digging around with my free hand, eventually had it free, even if it was now dragging quite a bit of greenery around. I guess a three-pound trout can be a handful in an open river at times, but put it in a living room sized pool full of weed and you've got fireworks. I was really excited to have caught this fish and I let it go with high expectations for the remainder of the stream.

Incredibly, apart from one or two small fish spooked out of rapids, and a few tiny fish nervously investigating my fly, I didn't see another fish that evening.

ꜰꞱ ᴀ ∝

As anticipated, it was blowing a gale the following morning and even though I was deep in a valley, there was still no way I could find the motivation to go fishing.

By the evening it had backed off slightly and I investigated my way upstream, perhaps the fish were up there. I spooked two small fish out of a rapid in the tail end of the very first pool, but didn't see anything else all evening. Despite what appeared to have been an opportune one-off capture, luck had definitely been on my side the day before. Even so, I was intrigued by the possibility of catching fairly big fish in these small streams – it had me looking at my maps in a whole new light!

ꜰꞱ ᴀ ∝

A cold grey morning dawned and it saw me heading back into civilisation for much of the day.

By late in the evening, I was back on the road, heading out to another stream, when, on impulse, I turned down a dirt track and met some friendly people who were kind enough to point me in the direction of some relatively un-trodden water.

I was deep in a valley, perhaps even deeper than the last, and with deciduous trees starting to change colour along the beautiful bubbling brook, it felt like I'd found myself an English chalk stream. I threw some boots on and went for a wander along the bank before dark.

With a lot of weed in this river too, I didn't even end up making a cast that evening, I knew that hooking a fish here would mean getting in the river. Even so, the fish were there! I didn't openly spot them, but I did see movement on the surface, and two or three rises over limestone rock bars. Forming natural barrages along the river like rungs of a ladder, there were a number of these solid stone rock bars. One of the fish I saw rising absolutely belted something off the surface as it drifted amidst a trickle of bubbles above its hiding spot. So violent was this rise that for a second I thought New Zealand had acquired a beaver population. Beavers belt their tails on the water in an attempt to scare off intruders and more than once they have had me thinking I'd come across the grandfather of all trout in North America and Patagonia. I couldn't wait for the following morning, and to make matters even more appealing, I was almost certain I wouldn't have to beat anyone onto the water.

ᚠ ᚪ ᚲ

Unfortunately, I found myself on some great-looking water, but the weather wasn't looking so promising. Strong winds were blowing downstream beneath overcast skies, and the autumn leaves were flying. In places, the river looked like I'd need a garden rake in order to fish it.

Curious about how the river looked further downstream, I explored that way for a few hundred metres, passing perhaps half a dozen rock bars on the way. The third or fourth of these rock bars was bowed in a downstream direction, either end of it eaten away by millions of years of water flow. In the recessed slack water close to the bank, I spooked and saw my first fish for the day. Easily four-pounds, but most likely more, it had me angry with myself for spooking it, and excited about what the day might bring.

As a means to get the wind across my left shoulder, I decided to cross the river on one of these rock bars, and fish from the opposite bank.

There was a lot more vegetation on this bank and it made for interesting casting conditions, but I persisted and steadily worked my way back upstream, focusing the majority of my efforts below the rock bars. Although there wasn't the usual well-trodden track signifying heavy fishing pressure along this river, it was still clear that the fish weren't about to roll over and surrender.

Fishing a dry fly on this river quickly proved to be a challenge. I knew the fish would prefer to be holding, just below, or even amongst the jumbled rock of these natural weirs, but they were far from uniform in shape. The river flowed through the various gaps in the rock, but behind the larger rocks, the water lay in relative peace. It was very difficult to get a natural drift, but I tried my best, working the closest water first, and then attempting to progress further across.

Halfway across the second rock bar I fished there was a deep hole that allowed a reasonable window for my line and fly to drift. It was here that I finally found a fish willing to show some form of interest in my fly. It was a fast drift and a brief window of opportunity – but sometimes that's all it takes!

On my very first cast, the fish took a swipe at it, like a poorly timed punch. In actual fact it was possibly testing out its opponent with a left jab, possibly trying to sink the fly, much like I'd encountered the rainbows doing in the Central South Island. Or perhaps it was just checking to see if it was alive, trying to prompt it to move. Of course my first instinct was to strike. I got nothing but air; it was my counterblow that was mistimed.

I cast again. I should have realised what had happened and told myself to grit my teeth and to NOT strike if it took another swing, but happen again it did, and there were no gritted teeth on my part. I struck, and in a repeat performance, achieved nothing.

Eventually I crossed back over to the other side of the river and before I knew it, I was back at my camp.

Instead of a deep pool behind the rock bar in front of my camp, the rock bar itself was particularly broken up and wide. I fished a couple of the closer channels, and then made long casts towards the other side. I was losing sight of the fly amongst the bubbles and to a certain extent; I couldn't really tell if the flow was pulling it under or not. On my second or third cast, a huge head emerged from the water, its nose regally pointed and lower jaw hooked. Dark, almost red in colour, its shoulders climbed from the water – even from such a distance – it was all so clear!

Much like watching waves break on an offshore reef, if it looks big from a distance, then once you get out there, it's REALLY big. This fish that I saw casually rise up to my fly was easily ten-pounds or more, quite possibly one of the biggest fish I had ever had rise to a dry fly. Did I hook it? No! Unfortunately not . . .

It was hard to tell from twenty odd metres away, but at a guess, I think I struck too quickly, and pulled the fly out of the side of its mouth. Unlike the previous fish where perhaps I needed to refrain from striking and let the fly sit, a strike *was* needed with this fish, but I think I was a split-second too quick. It's a funny old game fishing

dry flies for big trout, particularly brown trout, and particularly in
New Zealand. Although I might not have given it the split second of
extra time needed to close its mouth over the fly, they can also spit
them out just as quickly. This fish definitely left me with some visual
images that would plague my mind for some time, if not throughout
my life.

Just a few pools further upstream, I spotted a fish of about three-
pounds sitting over a bed of green weed. I quickly lost sight of it, but
placed a cast a few metres to the side of where it had been. Midway
through the drift, with a tantalisingly slow rise, the fish took the fly, I
waited . . . and struck. For a brief second I felt the weight of the fish,
but failed to hook it. Why? Because; on this occasion I was probably
a split second too slow. I couldn't win!

Moments later it started raining. It was then that I met the retired
fellow who owned the adjacent property I had now fished my way on
to. He was about to move a mob of lambs, but came down to see how I
was going. And more than anything, for a chat I think.

Throughout their working life, he and his wife had run sheep on a
larger property further south.

"Twelve years ago we bought a place in Wanaka with plans of
retiring there," he said from behind his dripping specs and beneath a
hat, which, like mine, was probably serving to keep the drizzle off his
head more than the sun. Listening to him talk in his friendly jovial
manner made me want to both laugh and cry.

"Wanaka has changed a bit in twelve years hasn't it?" I said
searchingly.

"Oh, hell yeah! That's why we're here; we sold that place and
bought this property here. It's basically just a hobby farm, but
Wanaka's not much of a retirement place anymore! Everything is so
damn expensive there now! And there's too many people! If you want
a coffee you need to line up . . . if you want groceries you need to line
up . . . if you want . . ." His voice trailed off in disappointment.

Although there were a number of decades between us in age, it was both satisfying and interesting to hear him voice similar concerns and dislikes. Ultimately, though, it was saddening!

"We bought here, four . . . nearly five years ago. You see all this shit," he said pointing at the river. "All that weed, none of that crap was here five years ago when we arrived. Now look at it... That's from dairy farmers upstream in the watershed. Everybody blames the farmers, the dirty farmers, but when it was sheep, back when you guys in Australia were cracking all the jokes about how many sheep we had, it wasn't a problem then. It's because of all the nitrogen-based urea fertiliser. Those dairy 'cockies' (a term used for farmer in Australia and NZ), they spray that crap all over their paddocks, literally until the cows come home. You see, your average dairy farmer thinks they're in trouble if they don't have six-inches of pasture yesterday."

"Would you drink that water," I asked with a laugh. "Oh, shit no!" He said.

"Yeah, I don't really want to, but I'm going to have to," I said with a hesitant chuckle. "Boiling water is usually to kill bacteria, I don't know if it'll be much help with toxicity levels, perhaps the nitrogen will come out as a gas like chlorine does. I don't know, but I'm definitely going to boil it!"

The rain started falling heavier and we bade each other farewell. I pretty much called it quits with the fishing at this stage, and headed back to my camp. I was eager to catch a fish, though, so once back at my van, I pulled out my six-weight outfit and fished downstream casting a small Matuka.

It was all to no avail, the fish came out on top that day, and like some kind of Loch Ness Monster, I knew there was at least one really big trout out there. Who knows, perhaps one day I'll be back, maybe the weed will even be gone . . .

ᶠ₁ ▲ ∝

The following morning was overcast again and after breakfast I scouted downstream for another sortie on the pockets where I knew fish were holding. Experiencing little success, I pushed on further downstream.

Although there was the occasional small fish, I found very little of substance, nothing like the jaws I had seen rise over my fly right in front of my camp the day before. Of course I repeated those casts as well, but there was nothing at home in the camp pool that day.

Further upstream I found some fish, but they were all relatively insubstantial. They were the kind of two to three-pound trout that might spawn for the first time the following season. The only thing they would be heading upstream for was to harass adult trout for a meal of their eggs.

Having found little to keep me interested, I was ready to move on in search of . . . dare I say it . . . greener pastures. No shortage of those!

Wishing to beat the crowds, I reconnoitered back down onto the flats to take a look at a stream that I hoped might go under the local angler radar. Lined with willow trees and flowing through the cow paddocks, I wasn't expecting pristine conditions, but despite the fact you wouldn't wish to swim in the water yourself, these rivers sometimes still produce fish.

I made it to the bridge where I'd chosen to access the river, and with plenty of white foam scum on the surface, I was glad I'd filled my water bottles at a petrol station. The Labor Environment Minister David Parker wanted all of New Zealand's rivers to be swimmable by 2030. It's an interesting goal, and a worthy one I feel, because just twenty years earlier, I suspect people wouldn't have batted an eyelid at people swimming in the Avon river in downtown Christchurch. The times had most definitely changed in New Zealand, and much like global warming, it's not a case of 'is it changing?', the issue is HOW QUICKLY it's changing.

If anyone had been out testing the South Island's rivers that summer, it was me, and believe me, within ten years, it had changed dramatically!

No sooner had I stepped amongst the bubbles of this stream I was prepared to grovel in, and I realised there was a man heading upstream with a fly rod in hand, just ahead of me. Despite the rural landscape, and its close proximity to a large town, the river looked reasonably good, and besides, I was ready to go and have a fish for the afternoon, the sun was even shining. But, realising someone had just fished the stretch I was about to fish, I went back and sat in the driver's seat of my van. Disheartened, yet again, I just sat there shaking my head. There were people everywhere!

For quite a while, I just sat there feeling disillusioned. What's New Zealand coming to I wondered, you can't go and find solitude in isolated areas because people access it with boats, four-wheel-drives and helicopters, so you resort to fishing in nitrogen loaded streams with cows gawking at you over the fences, and there's people fishing there too.

About half an hour later, I looked up from my map and saw the man cutting across the paddocks as though he was done for the day.

"Well, we're in luck," I said to myself. "We'll have a fish after all."

It was a tight little stream, and with willows lining both banks, casting access was at a premium. Due to the narrow nature of the river, it also meant that casts were more likely to be landing over, or near fish. Although there were some deeper pools with nice undercut banks full of tree roots, at times the watercourse was barely wider than the length of my rod – nine feet.

In the second pool I came to, I kicked up a decomposing fish lying on the bottom. Once upon a time it would have been a nice four-pound-plus fish. Chances were somebody had caught it and got a

little trigger-happy with the camera, forgetting the simple fact that
fish acquire their oxygen from water. Clean water anyway.

The first live fish of any size that I saw, was sitting just to the side of
some faster water at the head of a pool. I was in the water by this stage
and was standing directly behind it; had it not moved on the surface, I
never would have known it was there. I made a cast over it, letting no
more than the leader and tippet land on the water ahead of it. It showed
no interest in the blowfly pattern I was fishing, but moments later, it
moved to the other side of the pool and a few metres downstream.
Apart from the fact that I was frozen to the spot, eyeballing this fish
from against some willows, it had moved into the ideal location for me
to cast to it.

So as to draw as little attention to myself as possible, with a flick
of the wrist, I made the cast. No doubt a little apprehensive about the
strange figure inspecting its left flank, the fish ignored it again.

"You won't ignore a nymph," I confidently told the fish, as I
retrieved the dry, and set about attaching a nymph-dropper.

By the time I tied on the nymph, I looked up, and the fish was gone.
No doubt sitting under the willows with his mate, having a laugh from
the   back   row   like   a   pair   of   smug   school   kids.

The only time I managed to get a fish to show interest in the dry
fly that evening, was at a ninety-degree bend in the river, quite a way
further upstream. It was here that I literally had a mob of young steers
lining the fence, watching the show in the riverbed down below – the
attentive front row kids – future scholars.

In what was an awkward pool to fish, I had an audience and was
under pressure to perform. There were fallen branches to be
considered, but perhaps more importantly, the awkward current and
eddies. This was one of those pools where you think you're reading
the water correctly, but in the end; your fly gets drawn under the
water anyway.

After what seemed like a handful of casts into different corners, I placed one last cast, directly into the primary flow coming out of the corner, straight at me. Fish sitting in such a location are ordinarily picking up food brought to them on the current, not falling out of the sky, but the second my fly hit the surface – something hammered it!

It was more like a bass taking a surface plug than a trout, and even now, when I think about it, I don't know if I should have waited, or struck instantly. Of course I did strike, but it didn't result in the hookup I was hoping for.

Was this fish just trying to injure its prey? Did it swing downstream to look for it? I'll never know, but it definitely got off lightly, and I finished another day with no reward for my toil.

f₃ ▲ ∝

The following morning there was still a little bit of sunshine on my side of the river and I went back upstream to see what I could see.

Knowing there were a few respectable fish to be found here, I showed caution with my movements, casting to similar locations where I had encountered fish the evening before. But despite my attentive approach; there were even less fish to be found in the morning. Were they still tucked in under the willows? I didn't see a single rise that morning and apart from the fish trying to demolish my fly, I hadn't the evening before either. It was time to look elsewhere!

The next river I fished was relatively famous in Southland and renowned for producing good numbers of brown trout. The fact that I was somewhat in its lower reaches had me concerned that many of the larger fish might have already moved upstream on their spawn-run, but even so, I was still hopeful of finding a few fish. I tried to push from my mind the fact that local anglers, travelling anglers, and even guided anglers, had no doubt been flogging the river all summer, and I picked out an access point that offered a lengthy upstream stretch of inaccessible water. I arrived in time for a few hours on the river before dark, with conditions perfect.

Even as I rigged up, the vast stretch of river in front of me slowly became more and more dimpled with rises, as the evening insect activity clicked into gear.

Knowing I would fish upstream come morning, I contemplated fishing downstream, but realising I wouldn't get very far before dark, it was upstream that I decided to go.

I was on a high bank, no more than twenty metres from my camp when I spotted a trout hugging the bottom, just to the front of a clump of weed, quite a distance from the bank. Creeping closer to the top of the bank through tussock grass, I made my first cast with a blowfly pattern. Fifteen metres or so off the bank, I watched the fish hesitate slightly as my fly drifted over it, but it turned up its nose and paid no further attention. I decided to change flies to a tiny size eighteen Dad's Favorite, and while doing so, glances at the water revealed a few other fish milling around the same area, all of them about three-pounds respectively. In the general vicinity, there had also been a few rises, not as many as elsewhere on the river, but it did seem their evening meal was being found on the surface this day.

Again these fish spotted the fly, indecisively wavering in the current like wind vanes, I could clearly see the interest a number of them had in it, even drifting downstream, well beneath the fly, peering up at it, deliberating about its authenticity.

The next fly I trialled was a small Parachute Adams. Perhaps emerging nymphs were being taken.

This fly elicited the most interest yet from the largest fish, which was still sitting in front of the weed; but still it was unconvinced. Almost certain they wouldn't ignore a nymph; I set about rigging up a Royal Wolf with a lengthy nymph-dropper to account for the chest-deep water. My knees were getting sore and my left foot was falling asleep by this stage, but I was up for the challenge, I was interested to see if I could fool one of them.

It was also about then that I spotted a man back downstream near where I had parked. I estimated him to be around sixty years of age and with a fly rod in hand; he was wandering along the very edge of the bank, straight towards me. Not ideal practice if you don't want to spook fish. I continued rigging up, assuming that common sense would eventually prevail and see him head inland and continue upstream around me; rude that this is in itself when it comes to river etiquette. Concentrating on my knots, he got to a distance of about twenty-five metres when I stopped and looked across to explain the situation. "Please don't come any closer, I've got a few fish here and if you come too close you'll spook them. I'm also fishing upstream. I don't think anyone's gone downstream, there are no cars parked there."

He hesitated for a moment, but to his credit, he must have turned around and headed downstream, as I never did see him again. I know – my actions sound harsh even to me as I sit here writing them, but at the same time, I'd been trying to outwit these fish for half an hour, had he come any closer – they would have fled for sure!

His actions had me dumbfounded, as they might some other readers. As such, I'll take the opportunity to share my thoughts on river etiquette for such an instance. It doesn't have to be just for fly anglers on rivers either, I've experienced the same thing miles from land in the open ocean with boat anglers, so whatever your passion, here's some food for thought.

First, just let me say that I'm all about friendliness and openness, it disappoints me that my 'hellos' to people are becoming more frequently ignored with our ever-expanding populations. However, for the majority of anglers, particularly fly anglers on rivers, unless already with people they know, I don't think it's a social event for them. Perhaps back at the car park, bridge, or boat ramp it can be, but while people are out there fishing, chances are they're enjoying the peace and solitude and the opportunity to get away from people. Add to this the fact that I was crouched down in grass stalking flighty fish that already see too many people. If there's someone already on a river or lake fishing in one direction, give him or her space and fish in the opposite direction. If you do have to fish in the same direction, get well past them at a distance like I did on my first river in Otago, and distance yourself. DO NOT pass someone and start fishing twenty metres ahead of him or her in the same direction, this is the pinnacle of angling rudeness. Friendliness is great, I'm all for that, but so is respecting other people's space. Goodness knows there's already too many of us on this planet, and with population growth predictions the way they are; it doesn't look too good for the future.

In the end, these fish I was pursuing may as well have been spooked, as they showed very little interest in anything I had on offer, including the nymphs – too many anglers hurling flies and lures at them from the very edge of the bank perhaps.

Fish continued rising as I progressed further upstream, but they continued ignoring what I had on offer. Like a number of evenings in the previous few weeks, there seemed to be too much natural prey available for them to warrant taking something that didn't look quite right.

Is it instinct for a trout I wonder, or is it a conscious decision? Do they let the fly drift by and think to themselves, "Gee that twig looked a lot like these mayflies we've got on offer tonight, lucky I didn't eat it by accident!"

I did end up managing to fool a little two-pound brown into taking a nymph, and after my track record over recent days, it had me feeling better than walking back to camp having caught nothing. I went to sleep that night, intrigued by the number of fish so close to my camp and curious about what I might find further upstream the following day.

ʕ ▲ ∝

The weather had deteriorated by morning, the wind had strengthened and although there were patches of blue sky, it was generally a grey day. I wasn't feeling overly optimistic, but doing my best to ignore the elements, I accepted my fate and pulled a rain jacket on beneath my fly vest.

Starting my fishing where I'd finished the evening before, my first cast swiftly saw the blowfly taking another dive. The grey nymph had done the job again! It was another small two-pound brown, but beneath a slate grey sky, it was a positive start to the day.

Further upstream, I came to perhaps an even longer and wider pool. Suggesting shallower depths, and plenty of standing room, vast flocks of ducks and other water birds, despondently took to the air as I approached – raucously voicing their distaste like a Parisian protest.

By the time I reached the pool, the feathered rabble was long gone and the water had settled. Recalling how a number of fish had chosen to sit close to small clumps of weed in the pool near my camp, I zeroed in on an assemblage of submerged timber, some of it protruding from the thigh-deep water.

Dropping my first cast above the largest log, I fed the flies out as they drifted downstream and past it. They were perhaps ten metres past the logs when the dry fly disappeared in a remarkably untidy take; not dissimilar to the fish I'd missed a few days earlier. I struck, and on this occasion, the fly was in the fish's mouth. It stayed there!

The fish jumped frantically and then freight-trained downstream on a long run; extraordinarily long considering it was probably only a three-pound fish. It had me thinking otherwise at the time, but once I had played it out and safely brought it to hand for release, a healthy three-pound brown it was. I doubted it was a spawn-run fish, but it was still good to pick up something a touch bigger than the previous two.

Further upstream, drifting the flies past a solitary log out in the open, the dry fly took another impromptu swim. I was fairly sure I detected the weight of a fish on the nymph when I struck, but I was a fraction too late on this occasion. You win some, you lose some . . .

There was the occasional small rise a little further across the stream and I waded into a position where I could get a clean drift. Anticipating the dry fly to be taken, I was surprised when it suddenly plunged beneath the surface as though crashing through the gallows. I made no mistake timing my strike this time, and set the hook in another two-pound troublemaker. The juvenile fish definitely had a preference for the nymph it seemed. Or, being an overcast day, perhaps there simply wasn't much food on the surface.

Upstream and into the next big pool, I found an oil-calm stretch of water with a trail of bubbles drifting through it. I almost heard the rises before I saw them. There was definitely food on the surface here!

Surely the dry fly has to get taken over the nymph this time . . .

Neither fly drew any interest on that first cast, but the blowfly was to the liking of at least one fish on my second, thus proving my assumptions correct. The sting in its jaw quickly had it questioning its taste, leaping from the water in panic, and then bolting downstream, where it jumped again. They might have been small fish, but they were full of fight! In the end, it was almost identical to the previous fish that had taken the dry fly, a healthy and well-conditioned three-pound fish that was probably enjoying the chance to rule the roost for a little while.

Quite a bit further upstream, around four o'clock in the afternoon, I finished my day when another two-pound fish showed preference to the . . . yep' . . . you guessed it . . . the grey nymph. I hadn't altered the flies all day!

They hadn't exactly been big brown trout, but with three two-pound fish and a couple of three-pounders for the day, it was my best result yet as far as numbers were concerned. But where were those bigger fish?

ʳ₹ ▲ ∝

The weather turned really bad for a couple of days and with three or four days of sunshine predicted after that, I couldn't will the rain away fast enough.

When the skies did finally clear, I headed up into the mountains. I intended to spend a couple of days kayaking on a lake whose inflowing rivers were of particular interest to me.

The weather appeared to improve the further into the mountains I went, was it a sign telling me to stop scrounging amidst the agriculture on the plains below – was the tip of the iceberg the place to be?

I reached the lake with enough light left in the day to inflate my kayak in readiness for an early morning departure. Sadly, it also gave me time to throw some not so old campfire rock circles into the lake. This was in a reserve area where the NZ Department of Conservation allowed fires in their prebuilt fireplaces. As is always the case, it didn't stop people lighting fires wherever they felt like it. Not to mention the surrounding vegetation being stripped for fuel. In pristine places like this – a total fire ban I say! Cook on a portable stove and enjoy the true wilderness. If a campfire is someone's priority, there are usually plenty of opportunities for that near built up urban areas. Why can't we keep the wilderness truly wild and leave behind just footprints, not burnt out fireplaces full of beer bottle caps? No fires NZ DOC as simple as that; it would make your job a lot easier and, dare I say it, more effective!

ⅎ ∆ ∝

After a cold star-filled night, I woke to fog hugging the tree-clad mountains like a pre-shave lather. I had prepared my lunch the evening before and after a quick breakfast, wasted no time getting on the water.

There wasn't a breath of wind, the lake like a mirror, and the alpine air pristine; it was a picture of perfection.

Of course it didn't take too long for the buzz of a helicopter to snap me out of my reverie. I tried hard not to let it break my spirits.

From my position out on the water paddling, I had noticed a four-wheel-drive track running along the shore through the trees: the sparseness of the undergrowth at the end of the track was unmistakable. As I paddled further, I spotted a hut amongst the trees. Presumably people lit fires outside the hut, or who knew, perhaps there was even a wood stove inside. The impact of the hut's users on the vegetation was clearly visible from a distance. Eating outwards into the bush like a disease. A disease limited only by people's laziness, how far they could be bothered walking to find wood. Or driving too, I guess!

Just what is it exactly that has New Zealand so excited about having cabins everywhere in the wilderness? My mother and her family are from there and I've spent a lot of time there while growing up, but I still don't quite understand the state funded huts in the 'wilderness'. To me it seems like a waste of taxpayer money that has a negative impact on the environment. Particularly considering the fact these huts invariably end up being shot up, vandalized, and filled with empty beer bottles.

Generally speaking I suspect the designated hiking tracks in New Zealand (your Milford Track etcetera) are overrun with people, and most likely have a substantial backlog of bookings too. Sure, these are great government money-spinners, but one way to reduce the numbers and create a less crowded experience (and perhaps even increase profits) would be to get rid of the cabins and have designated camping areas, ideally where trees are sparse, or nonexistent. No firewood would help enforce no fires! In all honesty, though, from my experience, 'real' hikers appreciate the value of these kinds of rules and simple peer pressure would see that no fires are lit. Cook on portable stoves, get water from the rivers, and take out what you bring in. Long-drops and/or eco-toilets could be erected at these overnighting locations if the number of hikers remains high, which I'm certain it would. But, by making people have to carry a tent with them and 'rough it' a little, I think it would definitely see some folk less likely to hike. Or, you never know, perhaps they get a tent, hike the tracks, and feel like they've had an even more rewarding experience.

As I paddled further, it became clear the four-wheel-drive track continued through the grassland; the scar across the countryside couldn't have been due to foot traffic alone. And here is the key to environmental protection and conservation in my eyes: a couple of well-placed boulders across the four-wheel-drive track and some hefty penalties for driving beyond. It would have done the whole region a huge favour!

Thankfully there were no boats on the lake that day and two hours of paddling later, I was nearing the furthest corner of the lake. I'd put all the human impact behind me, but then . . . like a slap in the face . . . two more cabins materialised.

Standing grotesquely like toilet blocks, there was one on either side of the lake. I couldn't believe it; it was an otherwise spectacular landscape! Four-wheel-drive tracks cut up the mountainside behind one of the huts like open wounds, the lazy route to higher ground and a view no doubt. Four-wheel-drives, all-terrain vehicles, jet boats, cabins, helicopters . . . whatever happened to camping; wasn't it all meant to be about getting back to nature?

Coming ashore near the mouth of one of the rivers a bit over an hour later, the water was clear, the wind still light, and the river a perfect shade of blue; the entire setting was perfect. Perfect that is, except for the four-wheel-drive track cutting across the pebble beach to the water's edge – a middle finger right in my face!

I did the only thing I could, I turned my back on it and focused my attention on the river, but in all honesty, by this stage, I wasn't really expecting much. I imagined the river to be so frequented by anglers coming in by boats (and four-wheel drives I now realised), that I presumed my chances of success would increase the further upstream I reached.

There was even didymo! All the way out there! Dispersed by four-wheel-drive wheels perhaps? Not a lot of 'CHECK - CLEAN - DRYING' going on between river crossings there I suspect. Likewise with ATVs and dirt bikes! Pushing the negatives aside, I was there to fish, and the weather conditions were perfect.

The river was quite wide prior to spilling into the lake and getting within casting range of the opposite bank required some wading. The tussock grass lining the cutaway bank hadn't stabilised it enough to prevent some decent sized rocks from falling into the water. Revealed as darker patches through my Polaroids, it was behind these rocks that I envisaged a trout or two holding, casually picking off the occasional early morning dry.

Still with the green blowfly dry and grey nymph rigged up on my four-weight, I saw no need to change it and began working my way upstream, vigilantly wading from one casting position to the next, and swinging the flies on the current. Reflecting on this as I sit here writing, I'm horrified by the fact that after a full day fishing with this rig a few days earlier, I don't even think I checked my knots and tippet!

At the third location I cast from, the water was flowing a touch faster. It had also narrowed enough to mean that I could cast from dry river stones.

Maintaining a low profile with my crab-crawling technique, I fired out my first cast across the uniform flow. The flies drifted perfectly through the top half of their drift, all the way until they were level with me. With my eyes glued to the white of the dry fly all the way, I eagerly waited for it to dip beneath the surface and signify a take on the nymph. I did my best to mend the line without disturbing the flies as they drifted past, but still there was an unavoidable belly in the line, I was sitting down after all. I fed them downstream further, craning my neck to keep them in sight. When suddenly . . . as though in dreamlike slow motion . . . a hook-jawed mouth opened wide . . . and confidently gulped in the dry fly! It was as though it had never seen the business end of a hook in its life!

I struck, springing to my feet in the one swift movement. My rod bent double, the fish urgently boiling the surface at the other end; it was a substantial weight I'd suddenly found myself tied to, the stubborn mass of a fish accustomed to having its own way, the water it displaced must have seen my pulse rate skyrocket. A short run downstream enabled me to get it onto the reel quickly. I was smugly feeling quite happy about this, until, it abruptly aborted its downstream run and ran upstream, twice as fast, and straight at me! I stood my ground and concentrated on winding the one-to-one gear ratio of the fly reel as fast as I could. Somehow I managed to keep up with it and kept the hook firmly set. From then on, it was a battle of attrition, a big fish dictating its own terms, unwilling to concede ground, and not very partial to the idea of being brought into the shallows. It was a high-shouldered thick-bodied fish, easily over eight-pounds, and time and time again it fled from the shallows – my heart in my mouth as I dreaded the hook pulling.

Somehow it didn't and, in the shallows, the fish eventually accepted defeat. I wrapped a hand around its tail wrist, and what a beauty she was! He actually . . . judging by the hooked lower jaw. It was a solid fish: high shoulders like the mountainous backdrop, jaws as expansive as the plains below, and a large adipose fin typical of big adult trout. With his battle scars and spectacular markings presented like the wrinkles of an elderly man that should have known better, it looked like wisdom with age had eluded him that morning. But, as he swam strongly from my hands, straight back to the hole he had risen from, I was sure he would be none the worse for wear; he'd live to tell the tale. With a bit of luck, hopefully this fish would return to the river and spawn for a good number of seasons to come.

Standing there watching this fish swim away, I was a little bit shocked at what had happened. And so quickly! With the simplicity of two plus two, this was one of those rare occasions where everything had fallen into place. I'd paddled to the other end of the lake, fished through no more than thirty metres of river, and been rewarded with the best brown trout of my summer (at that point).

Continuing upstream, I couldn't help but expect the fishing to get even better. After such success in the first thirty metres, how could I be blamed for presuming there would be a number of spawn-run fish strewn throughout the river, much like the previous few rivers I'd been fishing?

Incredibly, it wasn't to be, it seemed my chances of finding another fish became less likely the further I went. Apart from the didymo, the river looked in pristine condition, but as the water continued thinning out, the fish simply weren't there. Before I knew it, it was mid-afternoon and I indignantly turned around, went back downstream, and turned off on a tributary that I'd crossed on the way up.

Lined with clumps of tussock grass and toetoe flowers, this stream was like a small version of the main river. Much to my surprise, I quickly spotted a few fish. Not big fish, but trout nevertheless, and worthy of my time. Unfortunately, it became apparent that my flies weren't worthy of theirs.

In what appeared to be the last pool of any size worth fishing, I spied a large fish sitting against the opposite bank. I drifted a selection of flies past it, but as had sometimes happened with larger fish that summer, it didn't feed once while I stalked it, and it didn't appear likely to change its behaviour for the likes of my feather and fur.

I gave up on these rivers and cut across barren ground to the lake and my kayak. With so few fish in the river, perhaps there was still some shoreline-based foreplay going on. I would paddle back and have a fish from the shore on the way – perhaps I could interrupt some trout sharing a romantic candlelit dinner of nymphs somewhere.

Being quite a steep-sided lake, shallower stretches of shoreline were relatively scarce. The specific kind of shallow water I was looking for was also scarce! Trout will inhabit barren river stone and shingle shorelines on a lake, but I'm adamant that a few trees and-or grass on the water's edge creates a far more productive stretch of water – particularly coming into early evening like it was. Trout prefer to sleep in the shallows of an evening, and if there is shoreline vegetation aiding their concealment, I think they're even more content. Prior to slipping under overhanging branches as though snuggling under a warm blanket, the shallows are their hunting grounds.

Coming ashore at the kind of bay I was looking for, not with trees as such, but with enough grass tussocks to keep me happy, it didn't take long to spot a fish. Sitting no more than two metres from dry ground and around the three-pound mark at the very least, I thought it was a fish! By the time I had crawled within casting range, it suddenly started looking very much like a rock. A part of it was even sticking out of the water. Was it doing that before I crawled in? It had been a long day and I couldn't remember, but with the water shimmering like tinfoil despite my Polaroids, I was starting to doubt myself, was I down on my hands and knees for a tailing fish, or for no reason at all? I wasn't too concerned; after the fish I caught that morning, it was going to take a lot more than a spooked three-pounder to bring me down.

Kneeling up slightly to try and confirm it was in fact a fish, sure enough, a reasonable sized brown trout darted towards deeper water. At least now I knew there were fish in the area to be pursued, but had I blown my only opportunity? You would think I'd have learnt to just make the cast by this stage, wouldn't you? Only human I guess!

As I progressed, I saw a few fish philandering along the abyss-like drop-off, but this first fish was the only one I saw in the shallows that evening. By the time I got back to where I had spotted it, it had returned and was much easier to see. I couldn't be certain, but I was fairly sure it was the same fish.

A steady breeze had been blowing down from the mountains for much of the afternoon, but the conditions had now calmed across the shadowed lake. I knew I should probably try to tempt it with a smaller fly, but in all honesty, it was getting late, I still had a long paddle ahead of me, and after such a long day, I simply couldn't be bothered. In water barely deep enough to keep its dorsal fin submerged, this time the fish was less than a metre from shore. Seeing that it was so close, I made my cast from four metres away. Oh so delicately, and just a few metres to its side, the end of my leader and tippet caressed the water.

The trout instantly swung around! It swaggered towards the fly with the boldness of a gangster. Stopping just millimetres from it, it tested its prey's resolve. Testing mine! Provoking its prey, checking to see if it were alive, I watched with wide-eyed disbelief as it gave the fly a nudge with its snout. Despite it being just a three-pound fish, my heart was in my mouth . . . but only briefly. It quickly sensed something wasn't right, and took the exact same evacuation route to deeper water. Should I have given the fly a twitch perhaps, given it some life I wonder?

The river had produced an exceptional fish for me that day, but it was the lake that I was most interested in fishing the following day. All the same, I doubted I could keep myself away from the lower reaches of the river for the entire day. For all I knew, an even bigger fish could move in from the lake overnight – come morning it might be there waiting for me!

ʕ ▲ ∝

If at all possible, the weather the following morning was even more perfect. With sunshine only just creeping onto the western shores of the lake, fog clung to the lower mountain slopes and the water was as calm as a millpond.

The sun had edged over the eastern mountains by the time I started paddling and it looked certain that I was in for a beautiful day. Paddling across the undisturbed surface of the lake, flies and the occasional mayfly and butterfly sat on the water as though resting on pavement. By the time I was halfway down the lake, I had already stopped twice to cover rising fish with a dry fly. Tiny emerging mayflies may have been what were on the breakfast menu, but as usual, it was hard to be certain.

My intention for the day had been to repeat the previous day's run of events: hit the lower reaches of the river first, but then leave more of the afternoon to explore the lake. These rises on the lake were hard to ignore and with the sun in a good position to sight-fish the eastern shoreline, I found myself drawn towards a grassy shoreline. I was hopeful of finding some fish in the shallows again.

Much of the bank dropped away into deep water, but there were a few five-metre wide strips of rock offering shallow thresholds to the reticent depths beyond. A doormat of didymo covered these rock shelves, but with intermittent rises beyond the drop-off distracting me, it was over this filthy carpeting that I spooked the occasional fish. Despite this, it was the rising fish that held my attention.

Concealing myself amongst the thorny invasive vegetation as best I could, I tried a range of flies while covering the rises: emergers, midges, and tiny dries, I even tried a handful of different black fly imitations. Despite my efforts, I couldn't get anything to take a second look at all I threw at them. In close there was even a small fish of about two-pounds whose parents appeared to be out. He or she was recklessly raiding the fridge, gobbling down anything and everything that moved – everything but my flies.

Perhaps it was just too calm and too late in the summer; they were well fed and had seen enough hardware thrown at them from boats for the one season. I wonder how I may have fared had there not been a four-wheel-drive track just a stone's throw away, and no powerboat access allowed!

I paddled on, reaching the river mouth with the afternoon breeze still a distant fact of life. After the previous morning's events, I couldn't help but expect fireworks!

I fished my way upstream through the water where I caught the fish the morning before. The pool looked as perfect as the day before, but I found no success here that morning. I set my sites on faster water at the head of the pool.

Due to the fish running rampant through the pool the day before, I hadn't bothered fishing here, but it was a new day and I was eager to see if anyone was home. This faster water marked the top of what was effectively the first pool before the river hit the lake – if you had to place a bet – it most likely would have been here.

From my seated position, my now favorite green blowfly pattern landed just below the disturbed water at the very head of the pool. Perfect! It drifted through this optimal stretch of water just as perfectly. With a large belly of line held up in water I'd been forced to cast over, the fly was just on the verge of being pulled under. But then . . . without warning . . . a large fish got to it first!

My fly didn't stay beneath the surface for long, the fish instantly hurtling towards the heavens. All of this I caught out of the corner of my eye as I scrambled to my feet, backpedalling frantically in order to remove the belly in my line. Of course it pays to stay in close contact with your fly when presenting it, but sometimes it just isn't possible. This had been one of those occasions but with a prompt downstream run from the fish further helping my situation, the gamble had paid off. Another spectacular jump was thrown in at the end of this first run. With it flying through the air like a bar of steel in the midday sun, I started realising that I may have tied into a rainbow. Even if this fish possibly fought better than the brown the day before, a part of me was a little disappointed – I've definitely got a soft spot for the ol' *salmo trutta*.

Still, I wasn't complaining! After a few last-minute scrambles from the shallows, I eventually secured a long-jawed and perhaps slightly under-conditioned rainbow. Once more, it all suddenly seemed so very easy. Or had I just timed things well?

I hiked upstream, scanning the water from a distance. I'd only gone perhaps ten metres, when I heard a boat pulling ashore behind me. I tried to ignore it and looked back upstream. But then, straight ahead of me, were two women, backpacks on, hiking downstream on the other side of the river, a white 'handbag dog' tagging along at their heels. Back to reality with a thud!

Again, the river failed to reveal any more fish, and when I reached the tributary I had dabbled with the day before, I was happy to make the turn.

I hit the pools where I'd seen fish, but my reliable fly failed me again.

In the pool where I'd seen the big fish sitting close to the bank, I fished from the opposite bank; hoping it might still be in the same location. Perhaps it would drift out and intercept my fly.

In the end I fished this pool from three locations, covering my options well, but none of them produced a result that day either. Assuming the fish was sitting in the middle of the pool, or in deep water at the top, I gave up on the river and decided to hike back to the lake. Sure enough, there it was, boxed into the lower corner of the opposite bank, right where I'd seen it the day before. Cornered and spooked, it didn't know which way to go for a moment, but finally snuck past my legs and out into the pool.

"Why didn't you take my fly," I asked it affectionately. "Smart-arse!"

And down to the lake I went.

Daylight got away from me again and wishing to pack up so as to reach the next river that evening, I only managed to have one shore-based fish on my return paddle. It consisted of having a few casts with a streamer and dry fly around a much smaller inflowing stream. Although I saw one solid looking fish as I came ashore, my efforts amounted to little.

I did manage to get back to my camp earlier that night and with everything stowed as darkness set in, I drove towards the river I wished to fish. The long-term weather reports were predicting it to be the last day of reasonable weather for a while.

ſʒ ᴀ ∝

As I watched a helicopter to ensure it wasn't dropping anglers in the headwaters of the river I was planning to fish, the skies were relatively clear, but the weather brooding. I lost the chopper in the early morning sun. I couldn't be sure, but as I got my things together for a full day on the water, I was fairly confident I would have it to myself. With rod in hand and sunshine prevailing, I set off.

Similar to a few other rivers I'd been encountering, the lower pools of this river were long and flowing slow. As I crept through the tussock grass lining the banks, thistle seeds were floating upstream on a light breeze like snowflakes and the early autumn air was crisp.

Sneaking along the margins on a high bank, I stepped out from behind one of the tussock grass mounds and spotted my first fish. Quite a good one too! Sitting in fast water at the top end of just the third pool I'd come to, it was a promising start.

I froze, sank to my knees and retreated backwards. There was no way I could approach this fish from the elevated bank without spooking it. I took a look across the river for a landmark to gauge where the fish was, and then backtracked, crossed, and crawled into position. The loose river stone bank was virtually at water level, and despite keeping the lowest profile I could, I felt as exposed as an ant on a New York City footpath. Off what I presumed would still be the fish's right flank, I crab-crawled into a casting position.

I laid out my first cast at roughly forty-five degrees and with slow water creating yet another belly in my line, I did my best to mend it. Why must they always sit in the most awkward positions? It keeps life interesting, I guess . . .

As we've already determined, trout don't always take a fly the same way either. On this occasion, it was done slowly, almost hesitantly. Was it attempting to submerge its prey before swallowing it, or was it appraising its meal of choice, or had it simply realised its mistake at the last minute and wisely chosen not to close its mouth? I tend to think it was the latter, the water was flowing faster than elsewhere, but it was still relatively slow, there was ample time for the trout to inspect the fly, and in this case, identify its oversight. Before the day's end, I would see that when fish on this river genuinely wanted to take the fly – they took it!

Giving this fish the benefit of doubt, I changed flies to a small Adams and made the cast again.

This achieved nothing. Considering the fish's anticipated meal of a blowfly had flown out of its mouth at twice the speed of sound just a few moments earlier, I wasn't surprised. Conceding defeat after two more futile fly changes, I moved on.

Upstream from here, the next pool was narrower and shorter. I ignored the lower portion of this pool, deeming it to be flowing too fast, and offering trout little in the way of cover. I approached the top of the middle stretch where the river had a dogleg in it and there were a few larger rocks on the bottom. It looked like the best lie-up spot in the entire pool; if I were a trout, I would sit here. Generally, though, I thought the pool looked too small to support much in the way of fish life. Good thing I'm not a fish, as my first cast suggested otherwise.

My fly landed right next to the bank in the dogleg corner. The water there was motionless and it took the current flow on the line to draw the leader and fly out. Drifting out of this sheltered backwater, the second it hit the main flow, a pointed brown trout snout rose up over the fly, and with the grace of a ballet dancer.

It was a repeat performance to the previous take (or aborted take). Due to simple reflexes, I had struck again. Had I gritted my teeth and held back from doing so, I would have loved to see what might have happened.

I went through the same fly changing process as before, but practically confirming that both fish had sensed imminent danger, my flies were wisely ignored again. Judging by the size of the fish's mouth that I'd caught a glimpse of, I suspected this fish to have been a touch smaller than the previous. Or was it? All I'd really seen was the tip of its nose, you never truly know for sure . . .

Despite these two quizzical contenders getting the better of me, I stood up and continued upstream with optimism. "Wow! There's fish here!" I told myself.

The next pool I came to was longer and slower than any I had yet seen on this river; I knew there had to be a fish or two in it. Potentially quite a big one judging by the two fish I'd just encountered in lesser pools.

Flowing wide and transparently clear, the lower two thirds of this pool was quite shallow. I decided to cross back over and approach it from the high bank. This would keep the sun behind me: helpful when spotting fish, but risky due to my silhouette and fall of shadow.

Keeping my distance to avoid these risks, I was confident I could spot a fish before it saw me, and then plan my angle of attack. How wrong I was!

I was halfway along the lower two thirds of this long pool, well back from the bank, weaving my way through golden grass tussocks, scanning the riverbed with the ease of reading a newspaper – when there it was – I found what I was after!

Halfway across the river, sitting in the centre of the pool with the boldness of a leopard tank, was a massive trout. Easily a double-digit fish, I froze to the spot. I didn't sink to my knees as I previously had. It was facing upstream and I was well behind it; it couldn't see me . . . surely? I was even behind a large tussock of grass!

They don't get this big by being foolish though, and as I stood there frozen to the spot, partially in awe of the fish, and partially daring not to move, the fish broke the standoff. It drifted further across the river towards the shallower bank, but somehow, miraculously, it still managed to disappear.

Right there and then, I decided there was no point scanning the rest of the pool, let-alone fishing it. I slunk backwards, meekly trying to disappear into the grass – a defeated man! It might have swum off with the coldness of ice, but I knew where it lived and by day's end, there was every chance we would meet again.

The next few pools were significantly smaller and even though I drifted a fly through the more likely looking stretches, there appeared to be nobody home.

From here, an almost swamp-like, flax and tussock grass clad stretch of river followed. It saw the river split into two smaller channels. Following the larger of the two, which was still little more than two metres wide, the water was just as clear, and surprisingly deep in places. I was confident there would still be some larger fish to be found. What a show it would be if I managed to hook one in such a small stream!

Creeping along behind the grass and flax, I came to a gap that allowed me to glimpse down into the narrow channel and for the third time that day, I froze! But, having been schooled by the larger fish just moments earlier, I slowly sank to the ground, melted backwards into the limited cover, and disappeared downstream . . . unnoticed. Perhaps!

There was no way for me to know if I'd successfully evaded detection or not, but I optimistically doubled back downstream and crossed over to the shallow bank again.

I crept back upstream, pausing below the stretch of water where I'd seen the fish, a finger of sand created the channel margin on my side, the tip of it likely to be level with the fish. Weighing up my options, I stood there surveying the scene from a safe distance. Do I cast upstream across to the fish and run the risk of spooking it due to how close my line and fly would need to land, or do I creep down onto the top of the sand spit, and feed the fly down to it? As you so often do when fishing for trout like this in New Zealand, I'd only have one shot at it.

I opted for feeding the fly down to the fish, purely because I felt there was more margin for error. If it wasn't drifting quite right, I could easily abort the drift before it got too close to the fish. Feeding a fly downstream in tight confines is still no easy task and although the first drift was reasonable, I had more line out on the second, and would have preferred it to have been my first presentation. All the while, I had a voice inside my head, it was quietly saying, "Hey! The fish could well have spooked the moment you saw it, you might be drifting that fly down to nothing!"

Despite the fact this 'voice' was speaking the truth, I view these missed opportunities as good practice. Much like the bigger fish that morning, I knew I'd be coming back this way before the day was done. There was every chance I could still be rewarded with a good show in this extraordinarily confined stretch of water.

Another long and quite wide pool followed this marshy stretch. The 'voice' spoke to me in a positive manner this time, "There's gotta' be a fish or two here!"

Locating the fish without spooking them, that was the challenge! With a heavily vegetated opposite bank and the sun now high in the sky, I decided to fish this pool blind, leapfrogging my way along the shallow shingle bank, covering the water as thoroughly as possible.

I had crawled into and drifted flies through perhaps three locations before I reached the deeper water at the head of the pool.

The river was slightly narrower here and there were a few large boulders creating some interesting flow patterns, but generally, it was a case of crawl in and cast upstream at forty-five degrees, then strip accordingly to keep in contact with the fly. On my first cast, the fly had only just landed, when a small fish latched onto it with reckless abandon.

Instantly Recognising this suicidal rise to be from a juvenile fish, I struck – somewhat angrily! The fish felt the hook, tumbled across the surface with youthful disregard, and threw the fly. I myself had been let off the hook! Or had I? I knew this brief disturbance was more than enough to disturb any descent fish in the pool, and I had a few words with the little scrapper as it disappeared downstream. Sorting out my line, I repeated the cast.

Nothing happened on this cast. Or the next! Still seated in the same position, my third and final cast landed the fly a few metres further up the pool. The green-bodied blowfly imitation was perhaps halfway across the deeper water, vulnerable as an unharnessed tightrope walker, defenceless and exposed, when it abruptly vanished into a slurping rise. I struck while scrambling to my feet – confident of a secure hook-up!

This hadn't been a halfhearted nudge at its prey, this was a big fish and I'd clearly seen it swallow the fly; straight down the hatch, there had been no speculation, no tenderising, no taste testing, it was completely fooled, just the way I like it.

The fish headed downstream. Not at a great rate of knots, but like really big brown trout do, steadily and intractably, a bull led by the nose. Its dogged back and forth pacing of the deeper water was only broken by the one jump, an end-over-end launch that seemed to have it hanging in the air at my eye level, before untidily splashing back down. It was a heart-in-mouth moment, but right at what was perhaps the most vital moment of my NZ walkabout, the hook and my knots, all held true. The stubborn nature of this fish had me more worried in the latter stages of the fight; just as that unhelpful 'voice' returned . . . "How many fish have you lost in the shallows right at the end this summer, those so close, yet so far encounters?"

Time and time again it fled the shallow water, obstinately refusing to tire. I didn't dare attempt to get ahold of it – it was so close, yet so far . . .

This fish was undoubtedly in the eight to ten-pound range, and that's being conservative, my actual guess was that it was easily a double-digit fish, the best fish of my summer, the best trout I'd ever hooked on a dry fly. It wasn't one to be lost! This was undisputed by me, and any voices that cared to listen. There wasn't any by that stage. It was just me and the fish.

Its mass was too large to be bullied around on a four-pound tippet and I knew better than to rush things. Nevertheless, every time it ran back to deeper water, it gradually did so with less and less conviction, before, finally, it accepted defeat. It calmly let me kneel beside it, respect and gratitude almost overwhelming me. The girth of this fish was immense, its tail-wrist a stretch for my hand, an adipose fin the size of a large coin, its lower jaw hooked and long – I was in awe! The most joyous moment of all, was watching this beautiful golden-brown fish swim strongly from my hands, straight back into the deep boulder-strewn pool it called home, and no doubt dominated.

It would have been close, but I had a feeling that this fish was a touch heavier and longer than the big brown I'd caught a few days earlier. I couldn't have been happier, a big New Zealand brown that would have easily been close to double figures, and on a dry fly no less.

I continued upstream . . . buzzing! If no more fish came my way I wouldn't have been bothered in the slightest. Even so, I fished on expectantly. The river wasn't crawling with fish, but every pool appeared to hold at least one. How far upstream would that trend continue?

The next two pools were significantly smaller and I couldn't find a fish in either of them. However, the pool beyond that was something quite beyond the ordinary.

Bedrock was at the surface here and had formed an extremely deep, almost circular pool. Although beautiful, the intricacies of fishing this pool extended far beyond the fact there was a wall of trees encircling it. The only conceivable place I could see to cast a fly was where the river flowed into the pool. If anything, this pool was an ideal spot to sit under a tree and soak a worm. I did see a good-sized trout while crawling through the grass doing my best to present a fly at the head of the pool, but it treated my synthetic surface prey with nothing but scorn.

I fished on upstream through two or three more pools, and was surprised not to see a fish in any of them. Were they not there, or were they just hiding well?

With the sun edging behind the nearby mountains, and a couple of fish back downstream that I wanted to 'check in on', I decided it was time to turn around.

Wind and bad weather was approaching from the southwest as I hiked, but just as I reached the narrow sand spit pool, the sun peeked through the clouds. Had destiny finally sided with me?

I came onto the pool downstream from the tip of the sand spit. Earlier in the day the fish had been sitting against the opposite bank, virtually adjacent to the tip of the spit – I quickly found it again!

This time it sat out in the open, two or three metres downstream from the tip. As I crept in from behind it and slightly off its right flank, it innocently rose to the surface, and deftly sipped down a dry. If I needed a confidence boost, this was it! There wasn't going to be any feeding the fly down to it this time! With a good window of water upstream above it, there was more than enough space for me to gently lay down my leader and fly, it would be none the wiser. The light was soft, the wind in my favour for once and surrounded by flax and tussock grass, I wasn't even going to have to crawl. Thankful for the simplicity of being able to cast while standing – I wasted no time!

There was no mistake with my presentation. The tip of my fly line landed just level with the fish, and my twenty feet of leader and tippet stretched out beyond that, landing delicately so as to not startle the fish. The fly settled upright as it should, and its drift trajectory saw it likely to pass the fish just a metre to its side. It didn't get that far, though!

The fish saw it coming. It casually drifted across and upstream for the intercept. I clearly watched all this from my vantage point and when it's mouth closed over the fly; I made no mistakes.

Feeling the hook, the fish broke the surface and darted downstream, straight past where I was busily negotiating my way into the water. It was a tight little stream and I knew I didn't stand a chance trying to dictate its movements from the bank. I managed to turn its head, and it shot back up upstream, straight past me again. The deep water against the bank where I spotted it earlier that day was its goal this time, and it made it with ease. I didn't realise it at the time, but I was in serious trouble!

It dogmatically held its ground here for some time and I relaxed into enjoying the fight, ignorantly admiring its tenacity. Eventually I realised it might have got me in some weed, or worse still, a cave under the bank. Keeping pressure on the fish and still not realising the severity of the situation, I waded upstream to investigate.

It turned out to be the latter. The entire bank was undercut, undercut deeply and when I kicked around the fish hoping to scare it into the open, it ran a good four metres upstream – under the bank the entire way!

Moments later, like some kind of illusionist, it materialised from under the bank, right next to where I'd been lying on the sand earlier that day, feeding the exact same fly down to it. Had it been under the bank laughing at me? I suspect so, but it wasn't laughing anymore.

Standing at the tip of the sand spit by this stage, I was thinking the calmer water on the back of the spit might be the best location to wrap things up. The fish mind you, had other ideas entirely. From right in front of me, it launched into a jump like a sprinter exploding from the starting blocks; cavorting through the air directly past my face, it covered at least three or four metres in the process. I don't think I'd ever seen a fish cover so much distance through the air, certainly not right in front of my face. I managed to catch this jump on film too, so if you watch the film, you'll see it. Thankfully, the hook held firm and we continued chasing each other around this tiny stretch of water. It had nowhere to go, and just off the tip of the sand spit, I eventually managed to get a firm grasp on it, removed the hook, and set it free. And where do you think it went? Straight under the undercut bank of course.

This fish wasn't as big as the one I'd secured earlier that day, but at the end of summer, just days from the end of the season, it was a perfectly conditioned wild brown trout, in a clean healthy river, amidst beautiful scenery – it was what fly fishing is all about – the icing on the cake.

But I wasn't finished for the day, not yet. There was one more pool, and one more fish I wanted to settle terms with.

The sun was down and the lack of light becoming an issue by the time I got there, but I still went through the motions. the huge fish I'd seen early that morning had to still be in the same pool, I was sure of it! I went directly to the middle stretch of the pool where it had been sitting, but after a handful of casts, it was a no show. The top part of the pool still remained. In two other pools that day, it was there that I had found success – I'd be lying if I said I wasn't quietly confident.

However, it soon became obvious this fish wasn't about to let me get greedy and it never did reveal itself that night. I suspect it was sitting elsewhere, no doubt with its fins folded, having a laugh at my expense. I was comfortable with that!

By the time I got back to my camp the stars were searching for recognition from behind clouds, and after a quick wash in the river, the rain was coming down. Considering the amount of poor weather I'd had that summer, this had been a three-day window of sunshine that really had delivered, not necessarily a lot of fish, but a few really good ones. With the end of the fishing season just days away, it really had been the icing on the cake.

I wasn't ready to pack it all away just yet, though, I was going to fish to the end, and with rainbow trout possibly starting their spawn-run around that time, there was one last river I wished to fish.

ʳᵎ ▲ ∝

Intermittent rain quickly returned and I spent a few days fishing clearer spells on a willow tree lined creek, waiting for better weather so I might hit the river I was eager to fish.

Why I fished this willow tree lined creek I don't know, it might have been because there was a surprising number of fish it. Why that was the case, I also didn't know. Being a tributary of a larger river, perhaps it was the best of a bad bunch. I definitely wasn't fishing it for its aesthetic qualities. Fishing in an upstream direction saw the watercourse turn into a nitrified, weed-filled, foaming mess, ripped to bits by four-wheel-drives, and seemingly sucked dry by irrigation pumps. Where the water actually came from for the slow flowing, and shallow downstream stretch was beyond me – like a number of New Zealand's rivers – perhaps there was some underground flow managing to escape the irrigation pumps.

Despite the fish having poor selection in which tributary to venture up, there were a decent number of them in that downstream stretch. Late in the day, like flowers blooming in winter mud, there were often quite promising rises. I never did manage to catch one of them.

ʳᵎ ▲ ∝

After two days of rain, a three-day period of decent weather also blossomed like a flower and, beneath blue skies, an icing of snow lay sprinkled across the Southern Alps.

I was back on the didymo-choked river in the Mid-South Island region, hoping for the exceptional rainbow trout fishing I'd experienced, pre didymo, a decade earlier. This was the river I fished for three full days and only managed two brown trout, but despite these poor odds and the fact that I'd battled the didymo for the majority of my first day, I had learnt a valuable lesson – dry flies were my only option!

I arrived full of optimism; confident the rainbow trout would reward me for my efforts.

f, ʌ ∝

Three days passed and the conditions were spectacular, I couldn't have asked for better. The days were warm enough to summon a level of insect activity to make the dry fly a viable option, and I only encountered one other vehicle, which considerately continued upstream, well past mine and we never crossed paths on the water. I suspect we were all happier that way.

However, almost as a direct likeness to the trials and tribulations I'd experienced that summer, it wasn't until late afternoon on my third and final day that I finally hooked a fish, to be sure, a rainbow trout.

Sadly, it almost felt like a fitting end; a fitting end to my New Zealand South Island walkabout, and in my mind at the time, a fitting end to fourteen years of travel where I'd accessed the fishing, either directly, or indirectly, from roads. At the age of thirty-nine, a part of me was fed up with this approach – it wasn't delivering what I wanted . . .

The first seven installments in my Angler Walkabout Series had seen me travelling on land to some incredible corners of the globe: Africa twice, Patagonia, Alaska, Tasmania, Montana, New Zealand, Russia, and elsewhere that didn't make the cut in my 'Best of 2004-2014', book of short stories.

But I was tired of making the effort to reach 'untouched' water, only to discover people paying top-dollar to get there easier, and to be there first. I doubted my plans for the future would enable me to avoid this entirely, but with a little more luck than that which delivered the solitary rainbow trout from three full days of fishing, I hoped it would increase my chances.

It was time for me to sail away, quite literally! It was a dream I'd had all my life, and turning forty a few months after leaving New Zealand, I decided it was time to make it happen.

So, I invite you to join me on my next installment in the Angler Walkabout Series, as I navigate Canada's British Columbia Coastline: sailing, exploring, assessing the environment and fish stocks, considering social aspects of civilisation where it exists, and hopefully catching a few fish, crabs, prawns, (and anything else that I might encounter) along the way. I hope you enjoy it, and I hope we can all work to conserve it.

The scarred brown trout pulled from the base of the cliffs.

The lone tree pool and nymph caught rainbow.

The rainbow that mistook a tiny Adams for a blue dun.

My first large spawn-run brown trout for the summer.

A smaller spawn-run brown that fell to an elk hair caddis.

The plucky little brown that threaded me amongst the weed.

Fighting the rainbow pictured below.

This rainbow and one brown were all I could manage here.

The largest brown trout of my trip.

The brown that got me under the bank beside the sand spit.

AUTHOR'S NOTE

As I finally wrap up the first draft of this book sitting in the cockpit of my 35ft sloop (named Angler Walkabout of course), swinging on anchor in Alaska, I can confirm that I've made it up Canada's British Columbia coast, and I'll be turning to the manuscript of that book and film very shortly.

Fog drifts overhead on a steady nor-westerly, and out across the bay grey whales spout and appear to play. A few powerboats have passed heading north and it seems I haven't escaped people entirely, particularly those paying top dollar to be in the 'wilderness'.

However, please don't get me wrong, I don't wish to escape people entirely. If you've read my previous books you would have seen that I love meeting different people and immersing myself amidst different cultures and ways of life, just as I currently enjoy chatting with folk when I dock at villages for supplies and fuel every month or so, but right now, the fact that I'm writing out here on an exposed north Pacific coastline and haven't spoken to anyone in weeks, well, I'd say my plan is working relatively well thus far.

*

It is for those of us who hope to enjoy such moments of solitude and tranquillity that I have written my New Zealand book in the manner that I have, and all the other books in my Angler Walkabout Series for that matter. I hope you have enjoyed this book, but if you're disappointed that I haven't spelt out exactly where I was fishing beyond stating the regions, then I'm sorry.

I like to think that people can learn from my books: about the environment, history, fish, fishing techniques, etcetera, however, I don't write them to spoon-feed people on how and where to fish. Those books are out there, and believe me, I know they probably sell a lot better than mine. I guess if I adopted that approach I could possibly afford an editor, but it just ain't me I'm afraid.

My simple belief is that there is less and less mystery in the world and, for me, that's a sad and disheartening thing. As they say, the joy should be in the journey, not the destination. Similarly, rather than simple conveyance on an easy journey, I believe there is more joy and reward to be found in discovery. In other words; enjoy finding your hot fishing spot yourself, don't let me direct everyone to the same place – you never know – chances are you might find better fishing than I did.

Added to which, many of these rivers and lakes are resident Kiwis' local waterways, their backyard, or, perhaps even their 'secret spots'; who would I be to reveal them? Already I think I've probably revealed too much with technique, but hey, there's a hell of a lot I don't know.

*

You'll also see that I haven't included a detailed environmental summary in this book.

I didn't do so because if you've got this far in the book, I suspect you've probably had enough of hearing my thoughts on the issues. I'm sorry if it's been an annoyance to you, I can't help but be passionate about it.

In the NZ federal elections of October 2017, well after I departed, I was glad to see that I wasn't alone with this passion. Of the major parties in the mix for that election, it was Jacinda Ardern at the helm of the NZ Labor Party who campaigned with environmental awareness as a key policy distinction. Their win, and their effective governance since, would suggest there are a good number of NZ voters out there who are also passionate about finding some middle ground between agriculture, tourism, and the environment and are happy to have at least one major party that's passionate about conservation and a sustainable future for New Zealand. There's plenty of middle ground out there and it's good to see!

*

In a nutshell, however, I've put together this brief list of activity which I feel there's too much of in New Zealand's South Island. Although I can't comment from personal experience, I'm guessing the North Island isn't much better – with a far larger population, perhaps it's even worse...

• Excessive untaxed (and unmonitored I suspect) natural water usage from rivers, lakes, and aquifers!

• Excessive irrigation, in relatively dry countryside where the 'Dairy Boom' has superseded sheep grazing and crops!

• Excessive nitrogen based fertiliser use, which goes hand-in-hand with dairy farming's demand on water and pasture.

• Too much deforestation! Privately and federally, tree-planting initiatives are required, particularly in combination with other bank stabilisation efforts. I realise it could be happening – but if it isn't – make it happen! Since coming to power in 2017, the NZ Labor government *has* made initiatives to 'make it happen', particularly with their One Billion Trees by 2028 Program. I just hope privately owned property owners help with this; after all, it's through their properties that so many of New Zealand's rivers flow.

• The overdevelopment of tranquil and beautiful parts of New Zealand! The disappearance of once small, quaint villages – much of which is being bought and developed through foreign investment. Keep it wild, keep it quaint, and avoid the USA's Lake Tahoe trend/syndrome, and that of Australia's Gold Coast (and now the Sunshine Coast as well if they're not careful), where councils allow beautiful areas to be covered in high-rise and houses. Please learn from Australia's mistakes, goodness knows Australia's politicians haven't!

*

I might also add that the majority of South Island Kiwis I spoke to agree with me on these issues, retired farmers and a fishing guide included. The only person I can think of who didn't (and quite aggressively), was a business owner whose son was a tradesman and who had another family member that was a helicopter pilot. She took my comment about how hard it has become to get away from people in New Zealand as quite an insult, and was quick to tell me it was better than Australia.

As I have done in this book, I readily agreed. Yes, much of New Zealand *is* less developed and less 'flogged' than my home country of Australia, that's why I love New Zealand so much. But if it's changed so much in ten years, how long will it stay that way? All I suggest to New Zealand is that you learn from my nation's mistakes, look at us in Australia as our small coastal towns still continue to be overdeveloped, and tell yourselves that you won't do the same, don't destroy what makes New Zealand such a great place. Please!

*

Towards the beginning of my trip I chatted with a family member in his eighties who had 'successfully' farmed pigs and beef in Canterbury for the majority of his working life. His farming approach had been far from the norm, in what has primarily been sheep and cropping country, for generations until now.

"Why do they have to milk herds in the thousands, do they really need to make that much money, why can't enough be enough?" I asked him.

He chuckled to himself at my somewhat unenlightened comment.

"Oh, they're not making any money, they only make money when they retire and sell the property."

He was basically saying that a large percentage of the property owners were in debt up to their eyeballs and it was the banks that were making the money.

"Why on earth do they milk such big herds then? I asked.
His reply was short and to the point – one word – "Ego!"

This kind of behaviour is common amongst graziers the world over; at times I wonder if it's their own group-animal persona. Perhaps I shouldn't tar them all with the same brush, however, I'm sure there are responsible graziers out there who put the health of their land and water sources ahead of their perceived social importance, but those who don't are compounding a global problem across this blue planet of ours. I've talked about it in both my African books, and in the Patagonia book. I never thought I would see it in New Zealand, but how naive I was!

The selfish and ignorant misconception amongst many graziers is that the bigger your herd, the bigger man you are. The fact that your stock might be grinding your land into the ground, eroding riverbanks and polluting the water table is often of little concern; particularly when owned by foreigners I suspect. This brought me to my next question.

"How many of the properties are owned by foreigners?"
He said he couldn't really say, but hazarded a guess that close to half
the big stations in New Zealand might well be foreign owned. Taking
into consideration the fact that government agencies only started
recording foreign land purchases in New Zealand from 1998, and the
fact that there's a lot of ambiguity involved in exactly whom is
investing what, while I was there in that summer of 2016/17, Radio
New Zealand reported that of the 1.4 trillion dollars' worth of
housing, land, and financial assets in NZ, foreign owners accounted
for twenty-eight percent of it. The majority of their figures came
from Doctor Bill Rosenberg for the Campaign Against Foreign
Control of Aotearoa (New Zealand). His figures also revealed that in
the two months prior to March 2017, some 1.3 billion dollars in
profits and investment income had left the country. It was, and
perhaps always will be, difficult to get exact statistics on just how
much of the rural land in New Zealand is foreign owned, however, if
the New Zealand Herald reported in 2014 that an estimated forty
percent of wine produced in New Zealand is basically foreign owned,
then three years later in 2017, my family member's estimate of close
to half the larger stations being owned by foreigners, is quite possibly
not far off the mark.

I'd only been in the country for a matter of weeks when this conversation took place, but it had already become quite obvious that many of New Zealand's politicians were quite happily allowing the slow but sure death of the goose that laid the golden egg — the land itself.

Sadly, one might argue, where in the world isn't this happening? But surely we can learn, surely we can learn from the overpopulated unsustainable parts of the world, the nationalities that visit Australia and New Zealand and think that our undeveloped open spaces are 'beautiful'. Should we not be having our say, at least for our children's sake, for our children's children?

I'm sorry if you grew tired of my ranting in this book. I removed this section from the beginning in an attempt to avoid that, but on this occasion, the issue truly is close to home.

I feel that the un-greedy amongst us, those with a conscience, should be standing up for what's right. We should be standing up for a fair balance, for longevity, for sustainability, for nature not concrete, and dare I say it, for bloody conservation. It's not something to be scared of, it simply means conserving what we are currently lucky enough to have, today, and limiting our negative impact on it — surely that can't be bad?

Progress and development is great, as is foreign interest in a nation, but there are no winners if it destroys what everybody came for in the first place.

THE ANGLER WALKABOUT SERIES
2004 - 2020

Book 1. A CATCH ON AFRICA

Book 2. ALASKA

Book 3. PATAGONIA

Book 4. TASMANIA

Book 5. WEST AFRICA

Book 6. Best Of 2004 - 2014

Book 7. NEW ZEALAND

Photo: © Julian Wicksteed

@Angler Walkabout

@Angler Walkabout

@Julian_Wicksteed

@Angler Walkabout

www.anglerwalkabout.com

Made in the USA
Monee, IL
10 March 2024

54783599R00173